Ginger Baker
HELLRAISER

Ginger Baker
HELLRAISER

The Autobiography of the
World's Greatest Drummer

Ginger Baker with Ginette Baker

JOHN BLAKE

Published by John Blake Publishing Ltd,
3 Bramber Court, 2 Bramber Road,
London W14 9PB, England

www.johnblakepublishing.co.uk

First published in hardback in 2009

ISBN: 978-1-84454-817-0

British Library Cataloguing-in-Publication Data:
A catalogue record for this book is available from the British Library.

Design by www.envydesign.co.uk

Printed in the UK by CPI William Clowes Beccles NR34 7TL

1 3 5 7 9 10 8 6 4 2

Papers used by John Blake Publishing are natural, recyclable products made
from wood grown in sustainable forests. The manufacturing processes conform
to the environmental regulations of the country of origin.

I want to dedicate this book to all those I have lost throughout my life: to my mum, my dad, and to George Streatfield the best stepfather I could have wished for.

To my four great drum heroes that I idolised as a young musician: Phil Seamen, Art Blakey, Max Roach and Elvin Jones, all who became dear friends. I had the wonderful experience of playing drums with each of them and their genuine respect was worth more to me than all the money in the world.

To Graham Bond, Alexis Korner, Cyril Davis, Jimi Hendrix, Miriam Lane and Benny Fisher, Tony Williams, Maurice Salvat, Guy Warren, Fela Anikulapo Kuti, Glenn Hughes, Mike Falana, Dave Pearson, Dudley Moore, Harold McNair, Chris Wood, Ronnie Scott, Rick Grech, Dick Heckstall-Smith, Keith Moon and John Bonham, to name but a few. All were good friends who affected my career and character.

And to Colin Edwards, Tommy Harris, Billy Walsh and Bryan Morrison from the polo world.

Contents

Introduction

In the years immediately following the incredibly successful Cream reunion of 2005, both Jack Bruce and Eric Clapton have had a book of their experiences in print. Myths and legends a plenty seem to have grown up around tales of Cream's formation, the ups and downs within the band and what led to its sudden death. Similarly, rumours abound about problems faced during the brief Blind Faith hiatus. For many years I have wanted to voice my own account.

At last, what I think of as 'My Accursed Book' is finally finished and this is another story on its own! Benny Fisher (Miriam Lane's adopted son) first suggested it back in 1978, as we made plans to set up a polo club on Miriam's estate in Ashton Wold. But after several weeks of work Benny died suddenly from a massive brain haemorrhage at the age of 32.

Two years later I was rehearsing with Hawkwind on a sheep farm in Wales when a large, female journalist arrived. She also wanted to do my book; but all she seemed to be interested in was stories of graphic sex.

When I moved to Italy I sat down and wrote the book myself. I took the manuscript with me to the U.S.A. and in 1988 I sent it to ten publishers. Only one replied, totally unaware of who I was and labouring under the misapprehension that it was fiction!

In 1991 I was approached by a writer named Geoffrey Guiliano. By then I wasn't interested, but Karen, my wife at the time, bought into his stories of 'lots of dollars' and persuaded me. After months of interviews Guiliano 'finished' the book and sent it to the publishers, wrongly telling them that I'd seen and okayed the manuscript. The first I knew of this was when my first wife, Liz, phoned me and told me it was 'rubbish'. I contacted the publishers and their response was to draft in yet another writer, who was, if anything, worse than Giuliano. The end result was that the publishers sued me, in my absence, for the entire advance, including the monies received by Guliano and his agent. After hiring a lawyer, I ended up having to pay back my portion; but the book, thank God, was not published.

I had by now written several articles for *Polo* magazine and through this I met Hunter S Thompson's editor Shelby Sadler. With Shelby I wrote the book all over again. But due to problems I had with the United States Justice Department I moved to South Africa. Shelby arranged to fly out for a couple of weeks in order to finish it. But she never arrived and has since disappeared. Maybe Hunter shot her and buried the remains somewhere in Colorado?

After all this, I had totally given up on the idea of writing my book, until in 2008 I was approached by yet another American writer, who again offered me large financial rewards. But on closer inspection I found that his credentials didn't add up. It was then I decided to enlist the help of my daughter Nettie as she had edited several of my polo articles. Fortunately, some 30,000 words that I had already written came to light and so I sent them to her. After a couple of visits to South Africa and lots of tireless work by Nettie we had the book finished.

So here it is, finally (after some teething troubles), an accurate story of my life to date. I sincerely hope that readers will enjoy it. This is the true story, as it happened.

Ginger Baker

Chapter One

Memories of War

My father was killed in action in WWII and ten years later in 1953, when I was 14, my mother handed me this letter that he had asked her to save for me.

Sunday 4 October 1942

My Dear Son,

I am writing this as if you were now a man. As you will be by the time you read this letter. It's just a little advice & the way I should like you to turn out if I should not return from this 'errand', as you called it when I was last on leave.

Well Peter, I want you to grow up as a man able to hold your own ground, to learn how to use your fists, they are your best pals so often. In this way you will be of great help to your mother & your sister. When you are old enough I want you to take my place at home. I guess I can trust you to make a good job of this by what I have seen in the early stages of your life. Therefore, I'll leave it to you & won't say anymore in this direction.

Now for the advice, don't be a fool the same as I was & work hard for your living, that is if you can get a good living another & better way. The best money is always earned by little work. Therefore sacrifice a few years on small wages & reap the benefit of hard study with low wages when you are older. Try not to take to drinking, by all means have a drink but not too much. Keep off smoking as long as you can, its an expensive habit & does you no good. If or when you smoke have a pipe, its better in all respects. Take mother out now & again, give her a little pleasure, I am sure she is worth it, & you will lose little by it. Try to be a man at all times and face hard times with a smile. Go in for all the sport you can afford to give time for. It helps keep you clean in mind & body. Be as honest as possible & don't be underhanded or selfish.

Well, Peter, this is about all I can advise you to do, I only hope I am there when you reach this age so I can help you & mould you into what I should like you to be. But if not, try and follow out what I have said here. I know it all sounds like a lecture to be forgotten, but it is the only way I can possibly have a say in your upbringing if bad luck puts an end to me in this war.

So I will close now, trusting you to look after mother & your sister if this should happen, hoping also you will turn out the man I think you will.

I Remain your Loving Father

My father, Frederick Louvaine Formidable Baker, was born on 1 January 1915, the day the Kaiser's Germans sank the British battleship *Formidable* and in the wake of the atrocities committed by them in and around the Belgian town of Louvain during World War I.

His father, Frederick Albert Baker, had enlisted as a volunteer at Woolwich on 13 August 1914 as a private in Kitchener's First Army. Serving in the Royal Signals for the East Kent Regiment, he was wounded and then sent back to the Western Front on four successive occasions. He once carried a badly injured mate over his shoulders for three miles, only to find on reaching the safety of the trench that his friend was already dead.

Following his last push over the top, he lay wounded for several days in a muddy shell hole and was forced to watch his dead companions being eaten by hungry rats. When rescue finally came, he was loaded into one of three ambulances to make the dangerous journey back behind the lines. He was travelling in the middle ambulance when those to the front and the rear were shelled, leaving no one alive. He was medically discharged at Hounslow on 12 July 1916, but remained scarred until his death not only by the shrapnel in his body but also by his experiences. His discharge certificate read simply: 'Unfit for duty. Aged 26 and five months. Height – 5ft 8½ inches. Butterfly Tattoo on chest. S Wounds – Chest and left wrist.'

The youngest of 13 children, my grandfather was born on 14 March 1891 in Shotley, Suffolk. In 1913, he had come to London to look for work as a bricklayer and was sleeping rough when he walked into a public house and fell in love with the barmaid. Sarah Louise Soper already had a three-year-old illegitimate daughter named Sue. He and Sarah married in 1914 on his 23rd birthday and Dad (known to all as Ted) was born the following January.

But after my grandfather returned to the family home in Mottingham from the carnage of the trenches with what would now be termed untreated post-traumatic stress disorder, home life became increasingly unbearable for my dad and at 15 he joined the army to escape. He stayed in the infantry for three years, but it wasn't a great success because he found it hard to accept the discipline and spent most of his time in the glasshouse. On one occasion, he even had a row with a sergeant about dishing out spuds, which ended with Dad bashing the guy with the potato ladler. His punishment while locked up was to clean a rusty chain which was then dropped into a bucket of water and the process would begin all over again.

My grandfather, who had his own building business, bought Dad out of the military so he could work as a bricklayer. Then Dad's best mate George Brimicombe invited him to his girlfriend Rose's house, where Dad met her sister Ruby, the girl who was destined to become my mum.

Ruby May Bayldon, born 10 August 1917, was the youngest of five kids belonging to Jessie and Harold Bayldon. The two had met while Harold lodged with Jessie's parents and they had eloped and married. Jessie became a mum and stayed at home, while Harold worked hard as a hod-carrier. Money was in short supply and Mum left school at 14 to go into service as a kitchen maid in a big house in Chislehurst where every morning she cleaned the scullery cupboard of its infestation of black beetles.

When she was 16, Mum got engaged to George Streatfield, a delivery boy who regularly brought groceries to the house. But once she met Dad she broke up with George, though he continued to try to see her. Dad was working on a building site on Green Lane and spotted George going by on his bike, so he confronted the hapless delivery boy and threatened to wallop him if he didn't leave Mum alone. My parents married in September 1937 when Mum was three months pregnant with my sister Pat, who was born in Lewisham on 18 March 1938. I followed on 18 August 1939.

A month later, World War II broke out and the bombing forced us to move from Lewisham to Greenwich and then to my aunt Sue's place. I was about 18 months old when my dad found us a huge flat in the upstairs of a house at 130 Southwood Road in New Eltham. It had a scullery, a kitchen, three bedrooms and a bathroom with a very large bath that had a gas copper to heat the water. Another room was used as an office by the owner of the property, Mr Banks.

Another strange occupant from downstairs was Mr Banks's niece, Miss Lynn. She frequently wandered about in the dark and we would hear her swishing down the stairs – she would put one hand on the banisters, one on the wall and manage to get all the way down without using her short legs. But we loved to go down to Miss Lynn's kitchen where she would feed us jelly fat from the top of the meat.

When we first moved in, Mum cleaned the room we would be using as a lounge and when she had finished she put Pat and I in there. We decided to help out by sweeping the choked chimney grate by hand. We carried the soot in handfuls across the room and threw it out of the window: the room was black, we were black, Mum put us in the bath and the water was black. On another occasion, we 'helped' Mum by cleaning the windows with a scrubbing brush and a pot of jam.

At the outbreak of war, Dad's best mate George, who had married Aunt Rose, had joined the Costal Command at the outbreak of war. In 1941, he was serving on board the *Angolarity* – a ship he never liked. Then when Rose was heavily pregnant she was diagnosed with rheumatoid arthritis, so George squared it with his captain that he could take an extra couple of days' leave to be with her. When he got back to the ship, the captain was away and, not knowing of George's prior arrangement, the person in charge had him locked up for being absent without leave.

The captain reappeared to confirm George's story and he was

sent back to his post on the *Angolarity* which was sent out as convoy escort. On the journey she broke down, became a sitting duck for an enemy torpedo and George went down with her. Aunt Rose gave birth to her son John shortly afterwards and they came to live with us.

As a bricklayer, Dad had a reserved occupation, but he was so upset by his mate's death that he determined to join up without further ado. He tried everything to get in and was finally offered a post in the Royal Signals, like his father before him. At first he was sceptical, as he was already a trained Infantry man, but, once they explained to him that the job was pretty dangerous, he took it. He was very good at it too and became a member of the Long Range Desert Group (LRDG), the forerunners of the SAS, who went off to train in Algeria. His letters home are filled with his skilled drawings of Algerian scenes.

The only clear memories I have of my dad are when he came back on home leave. There was great excitement and when the time came for him to go back we went up to a big railway station in London to see him off. Dad was sitting by the window in a carriage full of khaki-clad soldiers with their forage caps and rifles. The train began to move off and I broke from my mother's grasp and ran down the platform with tears running down my face, almost as if I knew that I'd never see him again.

Early in 1944, I saw Mum's face turn ashen as she clasped a yellow telegram in her shaking hand. She let out one anguished sob and closed her bedroom door.

THE TELEGRAM

Mum and Aunt Rose,
Cooking breakfast in the kitchen
At Southwood Road.
We kids at the table,

A loud knock
On the front door downstairs
Disturbs the happy scene.
'All right, Rose, I'll go.'
We all felt the tension
Aunt Rose was so quiet
I think that she knew.
She had been there before;
Uncle George was killed
Early on in the war.
Mum came in very pale
Her shaking hand
Held a yellow telegram.
'All right, Rube, I'll carry on.'
Mum nodded, grateful
And fled the room.
We heard her sob
As she closed the bedroom door.
We all got the message
This was something real bad,
Breakfast was silent,
We'd just lost our Dad.

Dad had been killed on 15 November 1943, on the Greek Island of Leros. Under the command of Captain Jellicoe, the LRDG had been playing an active role in Churchill's 'folly' of the Leros and Dodecanese campaign. Churchill had opened the door for attack and asked Eisenhower for immediate back-up. Unfortunately, due to the distance they had to travel, it was impossible for the Americans to come to their aid in time. The last message out said simply, 'Situation desperate', and it could well have been Dad that sent it.

Mum and Rose pulled together, and in the autumn they picked all the apples and pears from the orchard behind the house that, along with the mulberry tree in particular, played a big part in our lives. They laid the fruit out carefully on the old office furniture that remained in Mr Banks's large room. Then Pat, John and I went in quietly, took a bite out of each one and carefully replaced them all bite-side down, in the vain hope that our naughtiness might go undetected.

MR BANKS

I lay alone upon my bed
Anger and sadness, turmoil in my head
A man's voice calls my name, it floats in the air
I look out of the window, no one is there.
The road below is sunset and still
Perplexed and puzzled I quickly decide
To leave my bedroom's strange eerie chill
Down to the back garden, get back outside
Where my sister and cousin play with my mum.
I open the door and dash down the hall
By the banister rail almost at the top stair
I stop short and turn alarmed and aware
A tall man in a night shirt
With a bobbled night cap
Sings a hymn at Mr Banks' open office door.
The tables and desks behind him I see
Covered with bright red ripe apples
That Mum will soon bottle and store.
He holds one in his hand
Smiles and beckons at me
And I turn and I run
Downstairs three at a time

Out into the warmth of the sun.
Mum's face pales 'neath the mulberry tree
I describe Mr Banks
She knows this can't be
For he was a man I had never seen
He had died nearly two years before.

Inevitably, the war intruded upon our lives. I can remember the sirens going off and being huddled tightly in an air-raid shelter with my mum, Aunt Rose, Pat and my cousin John. After what seemed like hours of ground-shaking explosions and crashes, the all-clear sounded. Outside the shelter fires blazed, smoke was swirling and broken glass and pieces of shrapnel littered the ground, while the clanging bells of fire engines and ambulances filled the air.

The bombing frightened our pet rabbit so much that he ended up being eaten for Christmas dinner. My pet newt also died and I held a funeral for it in the orchard. Mum said a few words and told me that God would take it up to heaven. A few weeks later, they found me crying uncontrollably because I had discovered that my newt was still in situ and had deduced that God didn't want him after all.

I caught scarlet fever and, as I lay recovering in Shooters Hill Hospital one evening, bombs fell close by, causing the hospital to shake violently. Then there was silence and I continued to lie in bed fascinated by the huge flames that were reflected on the white wall opposite. Woolwich dockyard was ablaze a mile or so away.

As a kid, I have to say I loved the war. Opposite the pub in Green Lane was a 16-foot naval gun emplacement. I don't think it ever got anything but they fired it from time to time just to keep people happy. Whenever it went off, our windows fell out. After the war, when the gun was removed, we all spent ages playing in the gun pit with its grease and deep metal stairs.

One night on returning to the kitchen after the all-clear, I looked through the window and noticed that the night horizon was glowing red like a shimmering sunset. Woolwich again; with its docks and the Royal Arsenal, it was a prime target. Scenes of destruction were common, yet as adventurous boys John and I continued to enjoy it all. Whenever there was a loud explosion, I would pipe up, 'Is that the English, Mum?'

Then the Doodlebugs (V1 rockets) began to appear in the skies, often four in a day, always in daylight, puttering along at low altitude. Then the noise would stop somewhere overhead and we'd watch the bug glide downwards, then boom! Another house was gone. One day, I went out on a tricycle with John standing on the back and holding on to my shoulders. Our mission was spotting Doodlebugs and we returned feeling very excited because we'd seen three!

In the summer of 1944, Dad's parents acquired a pub called the Mason's Arms down in Knowstone in Devon. We were evacuated down to them, but they weren't that great with us. The old man would get drunk and beat us with his belt and the old lady often got us into trouble. We only lasted about three months there before Mum and Rose came down and brought us home. Old Fred stayed down there after the war and continued buying land and building cottages which he did up himself.

Many years later, in 1968, I took my family down to Tiverton in my new Jensen FF to see my grandparents for the first time in many years. Old Fred was very impressed with the car and as we drove around he showed me all the cottages he'd built. He got very annoyed when he saw one that had had the thatch replaced with corrugated tin. Then we went to the pub and he turned out to be shit-hot at darts. I liked him then and we got on fine.

Back in Eltham, on 18 February 1945, we celebrated cousin John's fourth birthday. At 8.30pm, just after us children had gone to bed, there was a strange whoosh, then the whole house shook and there were shards of glass all over the room. A V2 rocket had hit a block of flats just a hundred yards from our house. Our windows had been blown in, but all three of us had ducked under our bedclothes and avoided getting cut. We heard yells as Aunt Rose, who had been on the toilet, desperately struggled to open the door to John's bedroom.

Miraculously we were all unharmed but the four-storey block of flats over the shops on Sidcup Road was gone, as was half one side of Montbelle Road. Consequently, there were no lessons at Montbelle Road Primary for ten days. We spent the time watching the firemen digging for bodies as a huge crane lifted out steel girders that had been bent into fantastic shapes by the blast. When we did go back to school, several desks were empty.

After that a young merchant seaman named Gordon stayed at our place when he was on leave because his own house and his parents had been blown to bits. He often looked after us and we grew fond of him.

When the war ended, there was great jubilation, flags were flying everywhere and there was dancing in the street. I suppose this experience gave me a lasting hatred of war, but at no time was I afraid. I loved the explosions.

Chapter Two

Schooldays and Cycling

Mum and Aunt Rose had always managed to get out and about enjoying themselves, and during the war they attended quite a few firemen's dances, at which they were known as The Merry Widows. Rose met up with a really nice fireman called Arthur, who was a carpenter, which was another reserved occupation, and worked building sets at the film studios. They got married and moved just down the road to Forest Way in Sidcup, so my cousin John and I continued to be inseparable mates.

One day Mum met her old fiancé George Streatfield on the top deck of the bus to New Eltham. She later told me he turned to her and said, 'I'd marry you tomorrow if you'd have me.'

It transpired that, although George had also married, he'd returned from the war to discover that his wife had given birth to three children by different American servicemen. Through this chance meeting, Mum and George got together again and they married on 27 December 1947.

We called our new stepfather Pop. He brought his dog Rex with him and he very soon became my constant companion. As children we were enthralled by Pop's amazing war stories. He had been in transport with Monty in the 50th Division of the Eighth Army in the desert at El Alamein and Tripoli. He was also at the liberation of Belsen concentration camp. From his numerous tales we gathered that he was lucky to have survived and he hated the Yanks and the Germans with equal fervour.

One day I told Mum I wanted to sing in the church choir. She had had a big row with the church about the money they'd requested for my dad's name to be included on the stalls among the other local men who'd fallen. Mum thought that this was out of order and I'd often heard her say that the church had quite enough money without demanding cash from the poor. I wasn't very religious either, but the way I saw it I was getting paid sixpence every Sunday. As I sat in the stalls listening to the parson preaching his endless sermons, I began to agree with Mum even more. It was so boring that I acquired a game of chess on a little pocket-sized board, which I played with the boy next to me throughout the proceedings.

At the end of the first three months, we received our pay in sixpenny pieces and my chess partner showed me how to spend my earnings. Outside the newsagents was a vending machine that distributed two Players cigarettes and two red-tipped, strike-anywhere Swan Vesta matches. We piled our tanners into the machine and, with our pockets bulging with cigarettes, we retired to the vestry gardens and lit up. Although I felt a bit dizzy after smoking two cigarettes, we felt very cool and grown up.

I got to sing solo on 'For the Wings of a Dove' in the choir and the parson agreed that I was a wonderful addition – until he looked down one day and saw us playing chess. I was out, so I got a paper round and after an early finish I was off on a milk round as well. At the weekends I also went on a baker's round for a few more shillings. In his younger days, Pop had been a keen cyclist, so he built me a bike out of various bits and pieces and with that Rex and I could do my rounds quicker.

I attended Pope Street School where I enjoyed being in the football team and was considered to be one of the better players. I was also considered to be a troublemaker and a bit of a dumbo, but before the 11-plus exam they gave a general knowledge examination and to everyone's amazement I came top of the class. But when it came to the actual 11-plus, the headmistress still told my mum not to expect anything more than a place at a secondary modern. Again everyone was surprised when I passed and was offered the choice of local grammars. My friend Dave Dormer was a year older than me and attended Shooters Hill Grammar so I got a place there.

I got into a lot of trouble for disobedience. One thing I was well known for was drumming on the desks. At this time I was listening to big band music, Jack Parnell and Ted Heath, and we used to go to the local trad jazz clubs where I would focus on the drummer. If the teacher went out of the class I'd drum on the desk and the other kids would all start dancing. I'd get so into it that I'd never notice the teacher come back in. Everyone would down and I'd still be drumming. I got the cane several times and a prefect set me an essay to be written about prefects, so I described how their desks were always filled with empty beer cans and cigarette packs. I was made to read it to the headmaster and received six of the best.

In our first year we had scripture lessons. I put my hand up and said, 'Sir? Is it true that Christ was a Jewish bastard?'

The whole class erupted with laughter, the teacher went purple and I was taken off to the headmaster's study. Again I had to repeat my contribution.

'Where do you get this rubbish from?' he shouted.

'From my mum,' I replied.

She verified this and I was excused scripture lessons for the rest of my time at the school. This was pretty cool and I used to go and smoke cigarettes out in the playground, while everyone else did scripture. I also gave up French and Latin to concentrate on German, which I was good at.

Shooters Hill was into rugby rather than football. They decided I should be a scrum half, but when you pass the ball you get jumped on by two wing forwards who are twice as big and heavy as you. This was OK when it was wet and muddy but not when it was hard and dry, so I wasn't very keen on rugby. I was useless at cricket, too: I couldn't hit the ball.

My ambition at this time was to go to RAF Cranwell and become a pilot, but the school was affiliated with the Navy and they were all sea cadets. I joined Squadron 56 of the Air Training Corps (based at Woolwich) instead and stayed with them for two or three years. I really enjoyed the whole experience, especially being brought into the band and going on parades through the High Street. I wanted to play a drum, but they gave me a trumpet instead; it had no valves and you had to lip all the notes. I got to play well and would often add in little jazz licks as we went along, which sent them mad; but they could never figure out who was doing it. When the sergeant major did find out, he was furious!

Drummer Geoff Downs and I used to get all the drums out, set them up and have drum-ups. We also camped out on an airbase at Thornton, down near Portsmouth, where I had my first flying experience in an Avro Ansen. I loved it.

All this came to an end when I was 14 and got involved with the school gang. Although Shooters Hill was renowned for producing a high number of university graduates, it was also known for the number of criminals who passed through its portals. The ringleaders of this gang were Paul Edwards, Don Emanuel and Mick Grayley. These were the school heroes, so to speak, all good at sports. I got involved with the gang because of my ability to climb anything. I was light and skinny, so my gig was to get into the local golf club by going through a skylight and then opening the door. They'd nick all the booze and cigarettes, which would then be sold to the prefects.

On the way home from school, we'd visit the record shop in Eltham. I'd go in and listen to records while the rest of the gang stuffed records under their coats and walked out. We did this quite successfully for several weeks. We were all jazz fans and to date I'd been listening to Gerry Mulligan. Then one day I picked out *Quintet of the Year* with Charlie Parker, Dizzy Gillespie, Max Roach, Bud Powell and Charlie Mingus. It blew me away – I just had to have it, so I put it under my raincoat. I'd never stolen anything before but when the gang saw that I'd got a record as well I was accepted as a full member.

Then we moved on to record tokens and over a period of a week or so we must have stolen hundreds; we'd all got stashes of them. One Saturday, the gang called round to see if I was going out on a 'Saturday loon' with them, but I couldn't because my aunt was visiting. The original plan was to hold on to them for at least six months for the heat to die down, then go a long way away to change them. But what did they do? They went to Sidcup, where the record shop is two doors away from the police station. While the guys were trying to cash up the tokens, one of the shop assistants nipped over to the police station.

This was a huge scandal and my mum went super-crazy. It all came to a head when we were in art class at school. Edwards was called out first and then me. I passed Edwards coming out of the head's study and his face was white as a sheet. There were record tokens all over the headmaster's desk. 'Do you know what these are, Baker?'

I said, 'Yeah, record tokens.'

'How do you know that?'

'Well, it's written on 'em.'

End of headmaster's interrogation! A plain-clothes officer took over and came to the conclusion that I hadn't been involved because I hadn't been there when they'd all been caught. I still had some record tokens at home, but I couldn't remember where I'd hidden them.

A few days later on Saturday morning, I heard Mum's voice shout, 'Peter!' When she said 'Peter' and not 'Pete', I knew I was in trouble. She'd found the record tokens hidden under a paper drawer lining and she went totally crazy. I told her that I'd been keeping them for the others. But her face was white with anger and she told me she would call the police herself if I didn't leave the gang.

The result of this was that I got beaten up several times. One day they caught me on my bike down at New Eltham station, but luckily some guy parking his car saw it and came and rescued me. On another occasion at the end of school, they got me in the classroom. This time they were armed with a taped razor blade with which they carved my arms and face into all sorts of patterns. Now this was at the same time that I'd been given my dad's letter and I remembered the advice he'd given me about learning to use my fists. Up to this point, whenever I'd been beaten up I would cry and couldn't understand why people had hit me.

But this time, when I was on my way home, I met one of these same kids, whose name was Irwin, standing at the bus stop. He started taking the piss and I just went for him. I was going to kill him and I was bashing his head on the pavement when a copper came along and stopped it.

When I got home, Mum was aghast at the state I was in. 'What on earth happened to you?' she gasped.

I told her I'd fallen off my bike into a rose bush.

'Oh yeah! You get straight-line cuts like that from falling into a bush,' she replied.

So I changed the story and said that some Teddy Boys had got me in Woolwich. Mum called the police who checked out my story and then came over.

'It didn't happen in Woolwich,' the copper said. 'It happened in school, didn't it?'

'No,' I lied.

But they'd interviewed loads of kids at school, many of whom had been on the periphery of the attack, and the copper who'd pulled the fight apart at the bus stop had reported that I was already cut. So the truth came to light, not through me, but through the other kids. Edwards, Grayley and Emanuel were caned in front of the whole school and expelled. I kept my head down for a couple of weeks after this and stayed over at my aunt Sue's. When I did go back to school, I wasn't exactly a very popular kid, so I got into cycling.

My mum lent me the deposit to get a racing bike and I found that I could easily burn off all the kids who already thought they could ride. Outside the school was a steep hill called Red Lion Lane leading up to the top of Shooters Hill. We'd race up this hill and I'd always leave them all behind. One day when we were out riding, we went up River Hill outside Tonbridge and I had to wait about half an hour at the top before they arrived.

When I was 15 and about to take my O level exams, I joined the local club The Cambrian Wheelers. Things still weren't good at school because I got the blame for getting the other three expelled, even though it hadn't been my fault. But I did get on well with one teacher, a Welshman named Prothero. At one point, he told me in front of the whole class that I hadn't got a 'snowball's chance' of passing the English exam. But, a week or so after this, he wrote on one of my essays, 'Write another essay like this and you'll pass without a problem.' This was the only exam that I did pass.

I left school before the results came out and got a job doing price signs at a ticket-writing firm. I cycled into central London every day from New Eltham and I could do it a lot quicker than the cars could. I met a guy called Danny Talbot, who rode in the Tour de France for the Hercules team, and he got me some Weinmann rim racing wheels with BH hubs. I didn't have a 'double clanger' (two chain wheels); I only had one big chain, 52 wheel, so I was at a great disadvantage because all the other guys had ten gears. I only had five but I compensated with my choice of Avery large 24 (low gear) down to a 13 high gear.

I was training every weekend, doing time trials and massed starts. A massed start is like the Tour de France and is covered by the British League of Racing Cyclists (BLRC). Time-trial riders start at one-minute intervals and ride against the clock, according to the Road Time Trial Council (RTTC). To take part in a massed start you had to be a member of the BLRC and to ride time trials you had to be in the RTTC. I took part in many massed-start races on the roads of England – you had to be good enough, otherwise you couldn't do it.

We used to have massed-start circuit races at Brands Hatch on Thursday nights. One of these nights was 13 August; I was number 13 and the Cambrian teams were taking the piss out of number 13. I needed some new 'tubs' (tubular tyres) and the prize for whoever was first across the finishing line of lap 13, a prime (pronounced 'preem') lap, was a pair of tubs. I thought I'd got it made, but, just as I came flying through the front of the bunch, I somehow got my handlebars entangled with those of a guy called Ginger Booker from the Woolwich Team. I went *bam*! and brought down half the bunch.

I turned up at work that Friday morning (after having got the train) with my arm in a sling and road burns on my shoulder and face. Obviously, with one arm in a sling I couldn't do any work and the art director said, 'Either stop cycling or leave the job.'

And I said, 'Goodbye, I've left the job.' This is the kind of support you got in Britain when you're trying to excel at sports.

I sent some of my drawings in to the Robert Freeman Advertising Company and on the strength of them I got a job as a trainee layout artist. I hadn't done well at art in school; in fact, I thought it was a load of bollocks. I wasn't interested because I didn't like the art teacher. But at home I got ideas for my drawings from the great pen and ink sketches my dad had done and I copied several of them. I would also draw pictures of models in magazines and it was a collection of these that I sent to Robert Freeman. I was surprised I got the job. But I've always liked art; Constable was an early favourite, then Matisse, Modigliani, Van Gogh, Picasso, and Jackson Pollock, but I was basically self-taught.

I was some three months into the job when, one very wet and dismal evening, I was riding down the cobbles of Duke Street St James and a taxi went past, the passenger door facing the opposite way to an ordinary car door. It went into my cape and all of a sudden I was attached to a taxi! I managed to extricate myself but my bike went under. The taxi crushed the frame, wheels, everything – it was totally wrecked. I borrowed a bike for the last 50-mile time trial but now I didn't have a bike to go training with.

One of the few friends I'd kept at school was a guy called John Finch. He had auburn hair and glasses and came from quite a well-off family. One day he invited me to a party in his house where a band was playing. There were also a lot of kids from school there who well remembered my drumming on the desks and they began urging, 'Go on! Get on the drums!'

I'd never sat on a kit before in my life, but they all seemed to think that I could play. I'd been watching drummers for years, so I sat down and just played. Two of the horn players turned to each other and said, 'Bloody hell, we've got a drummer!'

A light went on in my head and I thought, Wow! I'm a drummer! And that was the end and beginning of everything.

Eruption thunders over a cold calm sea
Ecliptic symbols beckon to me
Emphatically stating behind the band
Effective cymbals, sticks in hand.
Evolving with music, flying feet on the ground
Effigurate fill-ins complementing sound.
Edificial manoeuvres 'neath a wailing horn,
Egregious in time, a drummer is born.

Chapter Three

Drums

When I got home, I started looking for a drum kit straight away. As luck would have it, a friend over the road called John Evelyn knew of one going for 12 quid. This comprised of a bass drum, snare drum, hi-hat and one cymbal.

I told Mum I wanted to buy a drum kit and she said, 'You haven't finished paying for your bloody bike yet!' She didn't agree at all that this was a good idea; it was something quite insane to her.

However, I was pretty determined and I managed to get hold of a toy drum kit for three quid. It had only one head on the bass drum, so I cut up my tent to make another one and painted a design on it. The tom-tom was very thin, so I got a biscuit tin and made it deeper so it sounded a bit better. The tighteners were just on the top head with wing nuts, but I had a kit of sorts.

We formed a little band, with my cousin John playing banjo very badly, John Evelyn on trumpet, John Finch on trombone and a guy called Dave Tomlin (who ended up marrying *Melody Maker* journalist Chris Welch's sister) on clarinet. We actually did a gig at

Bungy's Coffee House, near Robert Freemans where I worked, and we earned something like four quid.

I saw an advert in the *Melody Maker* for a 'trad' band. Trad jazz was the thing then, though I was listening to modern jazz drummers like Phil Seaman and Max Roach. All the jazz clubs were playing traditional jazz, Ken Colyer, Chris Barber and the like. So, in answer to the advert, I went all the way over to Leytonstone for an audition with this band The Storyville Jazzmen. I turned up there with my toy kit and I'd only been playing a few weeks! I told them that my real kit was busted and that I was having it fixed. I got the gig though, just like that.

Mum was impressed that I'd got a job in music so she lent me 50 quid to get a drum kit. A regular gig we played was at a place near Wembley called Gladstone Park and one night I became aware of this beautiful dark-haired chick in front of the stage who could really dance. I'd often see her on the station going from Wembley to Neasden, but I was too shy to talk to her, so I got the bass player to chat her up for me. Her name was Liz, she was 17, five months my senior and the only child of Ann and Evelyn Finch, a secretary and train driver respectively, of 10 Elm Way, Neasden.

She dances moving her body in time to the beat of the drum
A smile of abandon,
Enticing, exciting,
Long legs and long raven hair.

Arrows of instant attraction
Hit home like a sweet neat rum
A flame of passion
Desiring, inspiring
Love and a lifetime as one.

With warmth in the cold chill of winter
Cool sense in the heat of the sun.
She would stand by her man
Beguiling, still smiling
Suffering pain and despair.

At that time, the band leader of The Storyville Jazzmen was banjo player Hugh Rainey. The clarinet player Les Wood gave me a whole pile of 78s by Baby Dodds and said, 'This is what we want you to play like.'

This was a total revelation to me as now I realised where Max Roach had come from and it had a permanent effect on me. Baby Dodds was the first jazz drummer and best of the early jazz drummers. Trumpet player Bob Wallis had a good reputation and he joined about a week after me.

Now this was quite a band and we regularly played at the Ken Colyer Club and became very popular. One week I actually earned ten quid, which was astounding. Bob believed in the idea of a 'professional musician' who had no day job and, after earning ten quid, I thought, Yeah, and so I left mine.

I told Jimmy Hillman the art director that I wanted to be a musician and he was dumbfounded. 'You've got to be absolutely crazy!' he said. 'You've got a fantastic career ahead of you here as a graphic artist and we're really pleased with what you're doing. But, if it doesn't work out, you can always come back.'

I got home that evening and told Mum, Pop and Pat that I was leaving home and giving up my job the next day. They were stunned.

A cyclist friend of trombone player Johnny Mortimer had recently lost his mother and was living alone in his flat in Lancaster Gate just off Ladbroke Grove, so I got a room there for ten shillings a week. This was the start of my life as a professional musician and it didn't really work out too well. Most of the time I was skint and at times was reduced to going through the landlord's pockets when he'd gone to work to find a couple of bob. I lived on Weetabix for about three months. I finally visited home and Mum was horrified because I looked like a skeleton, so I moved back.

I had started going out with Liz and she came along to gigs and helped me with the kit. I had no transport then and I had to struggle half a mile down Southwood Road to the station. I rigged up some wheels for the bass drum and it wasn't so bad going down the hill but it was a bugger getting back up again. Sometimes the milkman from my old milk-round days would take pity on me and give me a lift up the road on his float.

One day, Liz invited me over for a meal at her parents' place, which, in the light of the financial situation, was always welcome. I turned up at Elm Way wearing old green cords and suede shoes with the soles split. I was taken aback when her father Evelyn opened the door with his face all scratched. Apparently, he'd said to Liz, 'We're not feeding him,' and she'd attacked him. That's when I first realised how violent Liz could be.

I got offered a gig with the Terry Lightfoot Jazzmen, which was one of the more popular trad jazz bands around. This was the big time – £16 a week and a band suit, blue, white shirt and tie and a bandwagon! I got Vic O'Brien to make me up an all-white matching drum kit to replace my previous one, which had been made up of bits and pieces. Terry wanted me to play a constant four to a bar on the bass drum, but I was listening to Big Sid Catlett at the time. I'd put in off-beat bass drum explosions occasionally, whereupon Terry would nearly swallow his clarinet. One night I did this at a big gig in town when all the women were there, and Terry turned to me and shouted, 'You're not fucking practising on my gigs!'

So I yelled back, 'You can stuff your band up your fucking arse!'

At 18, I was among the last to be called up for National Service. The other musicians said I should go for the Guards and get in a band, but I just wanted to be getting on with my career musically and decided to fail the medical. My future father-in-law reckoned that in his experience I would never fool the army medical board.

In those days, you could buy an inhaler called Nasaltone filled with a folded piece of blotting-type paper, about three inches by one-and-a-half, which was covered with Benzedrine crystals. Some bright spark had discovered that, if you tore off small strips and swallowed them, you could get high and each strip would give you three hits. I thought this was a good scheme and so I bought two tubes of Nasaltone.

I had to go into central London for the x-ray first and then get a bus to Wimbledon for the medical examination. I decided not to take the Benzedrine before the x-rays, but, as I waited for the bus to Wimbledon, I swallowed the contents of both which was a massive overdose. Well, the bus got to the end of its run and I was still on it. This happened again going back the other way. I asked the conductor to get me off at the correct stop, and when I finally arrived at my destination I was so late that the Ws were going in!

Firstly I had to sit a written exam to which I gave very strange answers. I wrote long and complex answers to every question. The medical examination proceeded with my objecting to them shining lights into my ears and it took eight of them to hold me down. It really was most extraordinary! It ended up with them giving me a D4 and saying, 'We're sorry, but we can't take you.' It was great. As I went out, I heard one of them say, 'Poor boy.'

Outside there were loads of blokes looking really happy asking me, 'Did you pass?'

'Of course I didn't,' I replied. They seemed surprised that I wasn't disappointed.

When I finally got back to Liz's parents, I went to bed for two days feeling really ill, all the while praying, 'Please God don't let me die!' He heard me.

All the trad musicians hung out at the Star Cafe (now long gone) on Old Compton Street, Soho. This is where I met up with guitarist Big Pete Deuchar, who asked me to join a band he was taking to Germany. The guitar player in this outfit happened to be John McLaughlin, and I took the job. However, a couple of days before we were about to leave for Germany, I banged into Bob Wallis at the Star. He'd got a job with a much better band. It was led by guitarist Dis Disley and included trombone player Johnny Mumford and Dave Tomlinson, the clarinet player. They convinced me to take the gig. So, on the train going to Germany, I told Big Pete that I was giving him two weeks' notice and I'd already arranged to go on from there by train to Copenhagen and meet up with Dis Disley.

In Hamburg, I stayed in the house of a guy who'd been a submarine captain during the war. My German was actually quite good, so I could converse with him and he was a nice bloke. The band was playing in a place next to a strip club and we all behaved like typical English people abroad. The strippers used to come in and watch us and were all showing out to the band, so we thought we were on to a good thing here. Then, on a Monday night, when we got some time off, we all went into the strip club, where we were informed that the only woman in the show was the announcer! All the rest were transvestites. They had tits and everything: it was all quite extraordinary for 1958, but six hard-ons disappeared immediately.

Now I had to make the trip on my own with my drums to Copenhagen for the new gig. It was a 28-hour train journey, but I really enjoyed it, watching the countryside go by and imagining that I was a spy.

Hugh Rainey had told me in the Star that Bob Wallis had a blood condition called thrombophlebitis and I had to make sure he didn't drink. Of course, the first thing that happened when we got there was that we went out to a nightclub, got horrendously drunk and ended up staggering back to our digs through the snowy streets.

We got thrown out of loads of places in Copenhagen, doing things like playing hide-and-seek in the middle of the night in a guest house and ending up in the servants' quarters of this big hotel, up on the fourth or fifth floor.

I wasn't getting on very well with the rest of the band by now, as trying to stop Bob drinking had become impossible. One of them set fire to a pair of old socks in a waste bin and threw them into my room, so I opened the door and chucked them out into the hall. The next thing I knew there were fire engines everywhere. I'd set the hotel on fire. Not surprisingly, we got thrown out and ended up in a seamen's hostel, where we very nearly got assassinated for playing silly drunken games at three o'clock in the morning. All of a sudden, the doors opened and we were confronted by several large tattooed guys who looked ready to kill us.

But it was good band and the gigs went down well. In the middle of it, we did a whole tour of Scandinavia with the gospel singer Sister Rosetta Tharpe. She was a great lady and really took to me when we first met. She had bright-red hair like me and said, 'Oh, baby, your hair's so cool. What do you use to make it that colour?'

'Nothing,' I said. 'It's natural.' To which she threatened to pull down my trousers to check if I was telling the truth.

She was a laugh. She was hugely popular and the big showstopper we played with her was 'Didn't It Rain?' This had a helluva riff and we used to rock like hell.

While I was abroad, I bought an engagement ring for Liz and sent it to her for her birthday on 8 March. I also sent postcards to my future in-laws. On 19 March, I sent them one of the lobby of a smart hotel. I wrote:

I'm now on tour in Denmark. This is the sort of hotel we're staying in, not bad, eh? On Thursday we go to Sweden and on Saturday to Norway. We're having quite an enjoyable trip. Last night was our fifth concert with Sister and it didn't go too badly considering we've only had one rehearsal. We've got another today before the concert. What a drag…

Another, dated 23 March, shows the North Bridge and Royal Guard in Stockholm:

We had 11-and-a-half-hour train journey here yesterday, all in the same train as well! It's 6 degrees below freezing, the pavement is covered with about 4 inches of ice! This hotel is even more luxurious than the others, with radios in all the rooms and dials on the wall which you set to whatever time you want to be awakened. Also marvellous showers. You'd like the food here even more than in Denmark, they certainly know how to eat out…

On our way back to Copenhagen, there were loads of Swedish military guys on our train, downing lagers at a hundred miles per hour. The station at Copenhagen is on a curve: it's a big 'mind the gap' situation, with a foot-wide cavern between the platform and the train. A huge crowd had assembled to greet Sister Rosetta and a little girl was standing in front with a bunch of flowers. Sister came towards the girl to take the flowers and suddenly disappeared down the gap, so the only things visible were her tits and her face! Everybody rushed to help her out, and she graciously accepted the flowers and we all got on our way. I travelled with her in the taxi to the gig from the station and her shins were scraped to hell. She sat down and let on that she'd hurt herself. Until then, she hadn't reacted at all – it was absolutely amazing. She was a great professional.

By the time the tour ended, I'd fallen out with the band in a big way. We had a party on the last night and I had a row with Dis Disley. He referred to me as 'Terry Lightfoot's drummer' so I called him 'Ken Colyer's banjo player' and he punched me on the nose. As I jumped up to retaliate, I was pounced on by promoter Henry Johannson and his girlfriend. By this time I was very drunk and they carried me up to my room.

I vaguely remember that there was a chick in there and, when I got up to leave the next day, I found that I had only five krone left and the rest of my money had gone. Nobody in the band was talking to me, so I had just enough to buy a cheese roll and a cup of coffee before we got on the train and that had to last me until we got to the Hook of Holland. Nobody helped with me my drums either and I had to make three trips with them on to the ship. I vowed then that I would practise like fuck and leave all these guys behind.

Liz met me at the station and we were now engaged. At Southwood Road, the house was virtually empty. Next door on the right was also empty, upstairs and downstairs were vacant and the only occupants apart from us were the people next door on the other side. So I set my drums up and practised all day long. This prompted a family meeting in which Mum, Pop and Pat decreed that I should now 'get a proper job'.

So I went to the Royal Arsenal Co-op Society warehouse in Woolwich, where I got a job packing and loading shoes from seven 'til five, with the option of doing an hour-and-a-half's overtime. This was great 'cos the manager would always clock off at five and we'd end up playing football in the yard and getting paid for it.

Then one weekend in town I met up with a fellow drummer named Dave Pearson, famous among us for having a 26-inch Zildjan cymbal. He told me not to go to work the following Monday but to go with him up to Archer Street in Soho, where all the musicians hung out to get work. So I went up there and Dave helped me to get a few gigs – busking, nightclubs, anything at all. One of these gigs was with Danny La Rue in a Jewish club when he got booed off stage. But I started doing quite well.

I was still living at home then and several times I had to walk the seven miles back from Woolwich Arsenal station in the early hours of the morning. I was walking up Green Lane on one occasion when I became aware that all these cats were running up trees and I could hear this strange noise across the railway bridge between New Eltham and Mottingham stations. On investigation, I found the cause was an amazing number of rats! The road was covered by a huge mass scurrying along beside the railway line. I ran all the way home.

Another time I got back very late and as usual I had forgotten my key, but I had various ways of breaking into the house. Pop had blocked off most of them over the years, but it was a big old house and the front door had a large window next to it that I managed to get open about 12 inches. I was about halfway through with my feet and lower half outside the window when a local bobby shone a light on me. So now I had to get back out (even though I was nearly in) and explain to him that I actually lived there. I could hear Pop swearing as he came storming down the stairs to confirm my story. He had to get up very early for work and after nights like that he would come in to my room and shout, 'You like being up, you bugger? Get up!'

In the end, I moved out into a place in Grosvenor Avenue near Arsenal Football Club in Highbury. This was a musicians' hang-out and Liz spent a few nights with me there until her mother came round and was horrified that we were living in sin.

We got married on 17 February 1959 at Willesden Registry Office. When I arrived, Liz was nowhere to be seen, having a few drinks with her dad, so I asked the female registrar if she'd marry me instead. But Liz turned up eventually and we had the reception at her parents' house in Neasden. As the place was full of musicians, this quickly deteriorated into a comic food fight, though the in-laws had just decorated their dining room. The next-door neighbour, Mrs Spicer, came and threw us all out and we ended up chasing a friend's drunken dog up and down the road. It was a miracle nobody got run over.

Dave Pearson got me an audition with a big band and casually mentioned it was a reading gig. I couldn't read music but Dave had some helpful advice. 'You've got two weeks to learn – use your ears!'

The gig was with Ken Oldham's band at the Galtymore, an Irish club in Cricklewood, and one quarter of the set was ceilidh music. The accordion player was knocked out with the snare-drum stuff I did and I got the gig. The band leader, however, was very concerned because I didn't know what a repeat sign was and kept stopping before everyone else.

The following Monday, I observed Dave Pearson and drummer Danny Craig going through a drum part and suddenly it dawned on me what first-time bar and second-time bar meant. Now I was playing *with* the band and the band leader was very happy. After that I really started getting into reading. The Galtymore caretaker became a fan too and would let me practise in the afternoons while he danced around with his broom.

One of the alto players, Norman Duvall, who played the ceilidh stuff, sat in front of me. It was pretty complicated 6/8 stuff with lots of semi-quavers all over the place and I was playing every note. After the gig, Norman said to me, 'Were you reading the part over my shoulder?'

'Yeah.'

'You read very well,' he said, and told me to get two books out from the library. One was *Basic Harmony*, which outlines all the rules of classical writing, and the other was *The Schillinger Method*, which explains how to break them. This was the guy Glenn Miller studied under and it was how Miller had come up with that unusual sound. I went over these books studiously and soon I could read almost anything. Norman gave me the score of the top line of 'Surrey With a Fringe on Top' and told me to do an arrangement for the band, which I did, transposing and everything. Now you can do it on a computer but I still don't know how to do it that way. The band played my version three or four times a week. It became a standard part for us and I was very proud of it. This was at the time of *West Side Story* and the song 'Somewhere', so then I did an arrangement of that in C sharp. When I took it to the band, the brass and horn players looked at all the sharps and said, 'You've got to be kidding!'

Liz was now working as an usherette at Her Majesty's Theatre in the Haymarket where *West Side Story* was on and she'd come down to the gigs afterwards. My final gig at the Galtymore came about on one of these occasions. The drums were right on the side of the stage and out of the corner of my eye I could see this drunk bloke hassling Liz and trying to slide his hand up her leg and she, being Liz, boshed him big time. As the guy was about to retaliate, I got hold of a big pair of pliers that I used for my drums, leaned over to him and said, 'If you put a fucking hand on her, you're dead!'

The band leader was pretty pissed off with me for threatening the clients and so my time there was up.

Liz and I left Grosvenor Avenue and took a flat in Cricklewood, the other part of which was occupied by Tibor Szakacs, a famous wrestler from Transylvania. Our kitchen was in a little outhouse and, not long after we moved in, I opened the door and Liz turned to me and said in quite an offhand manner, 'Oh, look, there they are again.' The whole floor was covered with cockroaches. I freaked out and ran, but I overcame this by telling myself that this was ridiculous and ended up by getting a bent iron pipe and hitting them with that. We caught some in a jar to show the landlady and ended up having a big row, so we moved into a place in Mowbray Road.

Next I got a gig with the Les Douglas Orchestra. We were scheduled to play two weeks at Green's Playhouse (later the Apollo) in Glasgow, a place famed for its violence – one punter aimed a bottle over the balcony, five floors up and killed a pedestrian on the street below. We stayed at a place called Mrs Lookers, an incredibly damp and dingy doss-house where I met a tenor and flute player named Howard Morgan. He said our digs resembled a casualty ward from the Crimean War. Howard was a 5ft 1in Welshman, but he made up for his lack of height with an enormous dick. We had a very tall and tasty girl singer and, whenever she sang a ballad, Howard would wander up from the reed section with his saxophone and put his head between her tits. The audience loved all this and Howard got more money than us just for his antics on stage. He was hilarious and you just never knew what he was going to do or how he was going to do it. We became very friendly and we both smoked dope. In Glasgow, we picked up something I've never seen before or since called Rangoon Red; it was the most powerful stuff you've ever come across.

I'd had my first smoke sometime before after a Storyville rehearsal when I caught the last train from Charing Cross. I met a guy I knew on the platform and, as we were the only two in the carriage, he produced a joint and we smoked it on the train until he got off at Mottingham. Mine was the next stop and I walked home up Southwood Road feeling very good indeed.

After we'd finished the gig in Glasgow, we were due at an American base in the south of Germany called Sören. To get there, we first had to take a coach to Bovingdon, north of London. Howard and I were sitting in the back of the coach, rolling up this Rangoon Red and got so stoned we didn't notice the exhaust was leaking until we realised we were covered in little black dots. At Bovingdon, we got on a Dakota DC3 for Germany and had to put on parachutes. Les Douglas's wife and the girl singer had a lot of trouble getting these on over their skirts.

The flight was followed by yet another coach trip, so when we got there we were shattered and raided the base kitchen at 3am. The trumpet player was a Yorkshire guy with a very broad accent and we were all drinking coffee when he piped up, "Ee, I've got no bloody spoon!'

'Give it here,' said Howard, who then pulled his dick out and slopped it in the coffee, before giving it back to him. The look on the guy's face was a picture.

The waitress in the Officer's Club where we played was very tasty. She wore Bavarian costume, with a white blouse accentuating her tits, high heels and black stockings. Howard said to me, 'I'm going to have her.' So one night when she was delivering drinks to a nearby table, Howard, still playing his tenor, removed his trousers, showing his little hairy legs, with socks, suspenders and underpants and went up to this girl. She then threw her hands up in horror and ran off with Howard still playing in hot pursuit, rather like a Benny Hill sketch.

After a while, Liz, Howard's wife Moi and their son Alan flew out to join us. The dope had run out by this time and it soon came to the point where Liz and I decided that the money situation was also untenable. We skimped hard and managed to raise enough money for our tickets home; then I told Les Douglas I was off.

This was like a replay of the trip from Copenhagen; another seemingly endless train journey, with just enough money for a couple of rolls and cups of coffee between us. The sea crossing was very rough: the wind was howling and the passengers were soon seasick. I stacked my drums between the seats on deck, but then one of the sailors came up to me and suggested I move them before they went overboard. He found a place right in the middle of the ship and we wedged them in tight. At one point, the ship was rolling so much the stairs were almost horizontal and I flew across the deck, bashing into the supports that stop you falling into the sea.

After we returned to Mowbray Road, Liz fell pregnant, but we both felt we were unable to afford a baby at this time. Hanging out in the jazz clubs like Sandwiches and Ronnie Scott's, I'd met up with an average bass player called Mike Scott and he got hold of some pills for her. However, although she was very ill, this attempt at a home abortion failed miserably – thank God – and she went on with the pregnancy.

It was the spring of 1960 and I was still going up to Archer Street and doing a lot of gigs. I was getting to know loads of jazz players like Pete Townshend's dad, a tenor player named Cliff who I played a couple of gigs with. I used to get the night bus back to Kilburn and walk home from there. One night I met the drummer Dickie Devere, who had taken over from Phil Seamen in Kenny Graham's Afro Cubists and had a good reputation, and we got talking. He complimented me on my playing and invited Liz and I over to his place.

So, on a beautiful day in May, with the blossom on the trees and the sun shining, we walked along Shoot Up Hill, past Kilburn tube station, into Fordbridge Road. Dickie's wife opened the door and ushered us up to their first-floor flat. While we were talking and having tea, Dickie got out some tiny white pills. 'Have you ever tried this before?' he asked.

'What is it?'

'It's smack.'

'What's it like?'

'Well, it's like smoking dope, but better.'

I had already been told that one smoke of marijuana would have you hooked for life and subsequently discovered this to be absolutely untrue, so I tried it. Dickie crushed it up on a glass table, rolled up a one-pound note and I snorted it, then he gave it to Liz and she did the same. I started to feel really cool, but Liz went as white as a sheet, rushed to the toilet and was as sick as a dog. I took her home and she went to bed feeling awful. This was a great thing for her because she never touched the stuff again. Meanwhile, I was successfully finishing the previous and current day's newspaper crosswords, something I'd seldom managed before.

That Thursday, I was working with the Johnny Scott Band and we had a gig in Brighton. As a result of the smack, I was feeling really super good when Johnny came to pick me up. They all said I played fantastically well that night and I thought, I've found the answer here. All the barriers were down and I was just playing. But when Johnny dropped me off, he asked, 'Did you take something tonight?'

'Yeah, I snorted a jack.'

Johnny got really, very seriously angry. 'Leave that stuff alone,' he warned. 'If you use that, you're not working with my band any more.'

I thought he was crazy and I didn't work with his band again. I was still doing plenty of gigs and, as Dickie was a registered addict and could get the stuff without any hassles, it became a regular thing for me to go round to his place and snort a jack before a gig.

I had a gig with Bobby Wellins over at Stratford in East London, but I still had no transport, so my friend Mike Scott picked me up in a brand-new white Ford Zephyr. We crammed the drums into the boot and on the back seat and Liz sat in the middle of them.

After the gig, we went to some clubs but on the way home we ran out of petrol in the West End. Meanwhile, Mike had explained how he had come by the car. He used to work for a car theft group, and he knew of a vehicle-hire place where people who dropped cars off late would put the keys in the letterbox. Mike, equipped with a coat hanger, simply hooked them up. Now we were pushing the thing up Regent Street and the old bill arrived. 'Is this your car, sir?'

'No, it's my dad's car,' answered Mike. 'He told me to put some petrol in it and I forgot.'

The copper helped us push the car to the petrol station but Liz was shitting herself in the back because she thought we were going to get arrested. Mike dropped us off and drove the car up to Manchester where he sold it to somebody for a fiver.

We had another encounter with the police when my cousin John came on leave from the navy. I hadn't seen him for ages so we had a night in town together. I was wearing my brand-new pair of grey suede winkle-picker shoes, of which I was very proud. We'd just got off the night bus and were on top of Shoot Up Hill, when a Jaguar came past. The car stopped and out got two plain clothes and two uniforms. One of them called me a 'two-bit ponce' so John started to get worried and was making a break for it when they attacked him.

'What the fuck are you doing?' I shouted and one of them punched me in the gut and trod all over my grey shoes, scraping them badly.

I went apeshit and explained who we were and what we were doing. They went off, thinking that was it, but it wasn't. I walked to the next phone box, phoned the police and got a sergeant. This wasn't good enough, so I said, 'No. I want to come in and see a guy with pips on his shoulders.' The nearest police station was Willesden, so we walked all the way there. They'd got this grey-haired inspector out of bed and I told him what had happened. He told me the bloke who'd punched me was also called Baker and it was his first day on plain-clothes duty. The inspector didn't think I'd get much joy because as he said, 'They all stick together like shit on a blanket.' But they put this guy back on the beat in uniform. I saw him walking along one day and he gave me the filthiest look you've ever seen. But it shows that in England you can get somewhere with incidents like that.

Meanwhile, Dave Pearson had introduced me to a lot of people. All the drummers were so helpful to me, because they could obviously see that I had something a bit extra. I used to go to Jackie Sharpe's Downbeat Club in Soho, where all the top jazzers would hang out, and in there one night I saw Phil Seamen.

Chapter Four

Phil Seamen

As a kid, I'd listened in awe to Phil playing with the Jack Parnell Orchestra and I always felt that he was without a doubt the most talented drummer ever to come out of Europe. As I moved on to the modern jazz scene in 1959, I was lucky enough to see Phil play many times. He was the only drummer using the 'matched grip' and I shamelessly copied this right away. The things Phil could say with his drums brought tears to my eyes. His drums spoke eloquently and they always told very moving tales. It just flowed out of him, everything tied together and I thought of Phil as the Drum God.

I'd been hanging out with Dave Pearson and one night we went into Jackie Sharpe's. We sat down and at the next table but one to us was Phil, with the saxophonist and bandleader Tubby Hayes and bassist Stan Wasser. The great Phil Seamen was sitting just a yard away from me! I couldn't help but gaze at him in awe. I would never have dreamed of speaking to him because I imagined how it would have gone:

'Hi, Phil, I'm a drummer and a big fan of yours. Got any tips?'

Phil's reply, I'm sure, would have been the same one that I always give, which is: 'Yeah, fuck off!'

But, a few months later, I landed a cool gig as part of the regular rhythm section for the Jazz Session at the Flamingo all-nighters, along with Johnny Burch on piano and Tony Archer on bass. I'd been playing there for some weeks when Tubby Hayes heard me, rushed up to Ronnie Scott's and told Phil to get down there and 'cop the drummer'. I had snorted a jack beforehand and walked off stage at the end of the set to be confronted by the Drum God.

''Ere! I wanna talk to you,' said God and indicated for me to follow him outside.

We emerged from the basement club into a chill and drizzly early morning in London.

'Where the fuck did you come from?' he demanded. 'What's yer name?'

'Um, Ginger Baker,' I replied.

'Ginger?' His voice showed scorn. 'No. What's yer real name?'

'Peter,' I replied.

'OK, Pete. Forget the fucking Ginger bit, your name is Pete. Now listen. You can play the fucking drums – I mean, you can *play*.'

Right away, I felt like I was 50 feet tall! God had said I could play! Phil then produced a battered joint from his raincoat pocket, lit up, took a huge toke and passed it to me.

'What're you doin' right now?' he asked.

'Nothing.'

'OK, let's get a cab to my place. There's some stuff you gotta hear.'

We got a cab to Phil's basement flat in Maida Vale. As soon as we entered, Phil got out a pile of 78s and put them on his gramophone (this *was* 1960!). The unique sound of the Watusi Drummers boomed into the pad.

Then Phil got out some little pill bottles that were just like Dickie Devere's. He put a few jacks into an empty bottle followed by a large dob of glistening white powder. He then fitted a needle on to the end of an eye-dropper with the aid of a strip of cigarette paper, drew some water into the works from a glass on the table, squirted it on to the mixture in the bottle, struck a match and held it under the mixture till it boiled. He then sucked the mixture up into the works and tied a handkerchief tight around his arm. I watched in amazement as he tried to find a vein. His whole arm was a mass of dark-red tracks.

'When I tell yer, pull this,' he said, indicating the end of the handkerchief. This was to release the tourniquet. After quite a while, he exclaimed, 'Now, Pete – quick!'

I pulled the tag and the handkerchief fell off. Phil squirted some of the mixture into the vein then paused and released the rubber so blood reappeared in the works, then squirted in again. He repeated the process several times. This was the first time I witnessed someone have a fix.

'Nah, Pete, I gotta tell you this – this fucking stuff is bad fucking news. Don't you ever, ever try it.'

I didn't dare tell him that I'd snorted a jack just a few hours before. His attention turned to the drumming on the gramophone.

'OK, Pete, where's the beat?'

I listened and tapped 1, 2, 3; 1, 2, 3.

'Nah, nah, nah, it ain't. *Listen.*' Phil then started tapping a slower pulse to the drums 1, 2, 3, 4, 1, 2, 3, 4. I joined in and for the first time I felt the pulse of Africa.

'Yeah, Pete, I knew you'd get it!' said Phil happily. 'I fuckin' knew it when I heard you play. If you only knew the number of drummers I've tried to show that to, you wouldn't believe it!' He looked very pleased, and record after record went on the turntable. A door had opened, a light had gone on, Africa was in my blood and I couldn't wait to play my drums. Then, as we listened, the calendar on the wall suddenly moved downwards about two feet!

'The bastards are there again!' yelled Phil and he grabbed a shovel and ran outside.

I followed him, puzzled. What on earth was going on? By now, it was daylight and the garden was deserted.

'They're spying on me,' Phil declared, without letting on just who 'they' might be.

He then showed me the warning system he had rigged up, which consisted of a fishing line running from the garden gate along an intricate series of hooks and bends to the calendar. If the gate opened, then the calendar moved downwards. I suggested that it was probably a cat, but Phil was having none of this. He remained convinced that he was being spied upon.

By then, the drizzle had cleared and I walked home along Kilburn High Road in the early-morning sunshine with the drums of Africa still thundering in my ears. I was going over 12/8 rhythms to the 4/4 of my footsteps. What a momentous day! When I got in, I made a cup of tea and told Liz about my great night with the Drum God.

I saw a lot of Phil over the next few weeks and he taught me a great deal. We worked together on his practice pads, which consisted of a large book wrapped in a towel. He was a wicked teacher, though, and would whack me across the back of the hand with his stick if I got things wrong. This seemed to work as I didn't make too many blunders.

Then Phil came up with a suggestion. He told me he was moving into the flat of Eddie Taylor (another very good drummer) on Ladbroke Grove and suggested Liz and I move in with him. Liz was heavily pregnant and the landlords at Mowbray Road had told us we would have to move out because they didn't want kids in the place. This appeared to be an ideal solution, so we moved into the roomy basement flat at the end of November 1960. Shortly after, Jackie Maclean, another heavy junkie, also moved in. I was still picking up my daily jack from Dickie but keeping it a secret from Phil.

Life quickly became very chaotic, to put it mildly, because Phil and Liz did not get on. Phil hated women and truly was a confirmed misogynist. He had once been married to a beautiful dancer but she had been screwing other guys while he was on the road and the break-up of his marriage (so he told me) had led to his addiction. Jackie and Phil would also have very loud arguments in the early hours and the flat was, in Liz's words, 'absolutely filthy and unsavoury characters turned up at all hours'.

A junkie friend of Phil's, who was a regular visitor, ran in the front door one day and announced, 'There's a taxi outside and I'm not paying it,' then rushed out of the back door, leaving Liz to placate the driver. Some days later, we read in the paper that a drug addict had murdered a doctor in his surgery and got away in a taxi that he hadn't paid for. It was junkie lunacy so Liz packed her bags and went back to her mum's. I spoke to Liz on the phone daily as the baby was nearly due. I was torn between her, who I loved, and Phil, who I was learning so much from. Then Jackie split as well.

Phil had many hilarious turns of phrase, or 'Philisms' as I came to call them. He called orchestra conductors 'spastic windmills'. He was a member of the 'die trying squad'. A 'khazi dweller' was a junkie, living in a toilet. 'Fred Karno's army' stood for an untogether team or unit; an ''arris' was a bottom (Aristotle: bottle, bottle of rum: bum). 'Dodgy mincers' came from 'mince pies' meaning eyes. 'Golden bollocks' was a lucky man and 'Mustapha Piss' was an Indian prince. Finally, 'The Lord said to Moses, "Come forth," but 'e came fifth and lost 'is beer money.'

Phil played the drums in the orchestra pit for the West End production of *West Side Story*. One evening, at the most dramatic moment when one of the characters is murdered, Phil began to nod off and the tympani player leaned over and whispered, 'Phil! The bell!' Phil woke up, hit the large gong, stood up in the pit and announced loudly, 'Ladies and gentlemen, dinner is served!' The corpse on stage began to shake with laughter, as did the rest of the cast and the audience.

One morning, when Phil was out, I found a couple of jacks on the floor. I picked them up and without much thought I skin-popped them as this was the latest way of taking them that Dickie had got me into. When Phil returned, he took one look at me and just exploded.

'You're fucking stoned!' he shouted.

I couldn't deny it and finally admitted to him that I'd been using for quite some time. He was actually crying and he suddenly looked very old and deeply upset.

'Oh, Pete, you stupid bastard!' he said.

Then the phone rang and it was Liz's mum Ann, saying that the birth was imminent. I rushed out of the flat to the tube and then ran all the way from Neasden station to the house at 10 Elm Way. Dr Wills and the midwife were there, but the baby was not. Dr Wills put me in charge of the gas and air machine and I held the mask to Liz's face. She started giggling, and very soon, with no screaming or yelling, a baby girl was born. I felt as though I was watching a film. Remembering the attempted abortion, I anxiously counted all her fingers and toes, but everything was normal. Ann then rushed in with her cat in her arms.

'Get that bloody cat out of here!' snapped Dr Wills.

Thus chastised, Ann returned minus the cat. It was 20 December 1960 and we named the baby Ginette Karen. However, Liz and I didn't get much sleep that night because little 'Nettie' proved to have powerful lungs and wailed continuously. At about 3am, I took the squalling little girl in my arms and walked over to the window.

'If you don't stop howling, you little sod, you'll go out of this bloody window!'

Nettie proved to be pretty bright, because she stopped crying and I gave her to Liz who took her in her arms and finally we all slept cuddled together.

I was 21 and a father. Phil's words were still ringing in my ears and he was in such a dreadful state himself that Liz had named him 'The Awful Warning'. I decided – no more smack. I took to drinking spirits to carry me through and by Christmas I was feeling fine.

Through an old school friend, Liz found us a maisonette in Neasden close to her parents. We moved into 154 Braemar Avenue, a ground-floor place with one bedroom, a sitting room, kitchen and bathroom. The rent was £14 a week.

At the next all-nighter, I met up with one of my biggest fans, a very jovial character called Ron Chambers, who always sat in the front row at gigs. He had confided in me that he carried a gun and was a hit man for the Kray brothers. He gave me a fiver for the baby. He also gave us tins of powdered baby milk on a regular basis when we were very skint.

I was now earning just over £20 a week working virtually every night, but we were still only just managing to get by. I couldn't even afford a pound to spend on a jack and that helped me to stay straight for a good couple of months. But unfortunately the die of addiction was cast and I often found myself wishing that I could do a jack before a gig.

One night, I met Dickie in Sandwiches and he asked why he hadn't seen me for a while. I told him about the baby and the rent.

''Ere! Come with me,' he said and led me to the khazi where I skin-popped a jack.

I returned to the jam with the wonderful blinds coming down behind my eyes and played the best set I'd played for months.

Afterwards, Dickie gave me a small package of silver paper containing three jacks. 'There's a little present for ya!' he said.

I snorted one before the gig at Ronnie Scott's the next night, but, although it felt good, a little voice in my head was telling me that I needed a works. Phil came into the club the next night and I asked him if he could get me one.

'Listen, Pete, I ain't giving you one,' he replied angrily. But after a time he relented and put his arm around my shoulder. 'If you're going to do this,' he said resignedly, 'you might as well do it right!' He told me to come back to his place and said he would take me to see a doctor first thing in the morning. Back at his flat, he lent me a works and I skin-popped another jack. There was a female junkie there who Phil introduced as Rutter.

'So, you're getting registered tomorrow?' she said conversationally, as Phil was making the tea. 'Tell her you're using more than you are. That way you can sell what you don't use.' Then she asked me how much I was using.

'About six jacks a day,' I lied – it sounded good!

'Ask the doctor for three of each,' she instructed. 'Three grains of heroin and three of cocaine.' I had never used cocaine, but she told me not to mention this to Phil and arranged to meet me at a cafe on Baker Street at ten-thirty the next day.

Chapter Five

The Road to Graham Bond

Next morning, Phil and I took the tube to Baker Street and
Lady Frankau's consulting rooms at 32 Wimpole Street. The
ornate door was opened by a very severe-looking woman, who
nevertheless smiled as she let us in. I followed Phil up the carpeted
stairs into a waiting room beautifully furnished with antiques and
expensive paintings. Copies of *The Field* and *Country Life* were laid
out on the tables. The two other occupants of the room barely
acknowledged our presence and continued leafing through their
magazines. Phil went in first and came out. Then it was my turn.

A grey-haired lady sat behind a large desk and looked at me
sternly over the top of her glasses. 'Mr Seamen tells me you are a
very talented musician.' She was very well spoken. 'How much are
you using?'

As instructed, I told her three grains of each.

Without any comment, she wrote out a prescription. 'This is for
three days,' she said. 'Come and see me on Thursday morning.'
The consulting fee was £5.

When I came out, Phil was waiting for me and we walked round to John Bell & Croyden, a large chemist on Wigmore Street. Following Phil's lead, I ordered three eye droppers and half-a-dozen hypodermic needles which came with a thin wire through the needle. My script came to £11 and I was now penniless.

Phil and I walked to a gymnasium and went into the shower room. Phil went into a cubicle and locked the door. I did the same and made up a fix of two jacks and a dob of the white crystalline powder which I injected into my thigh. Phil was taking a very long time and the effect of this mixture hit me as I waited. This was a very different sensation. The relaxing blinds came down as usual but with no drowsiness. Instead, I felt super alert and became aware of perspiration upon my forehead. I didn't feel hot though, I felt very cool. Finally, Phil appeared and we went back to Baker Street station, where I said goodbye to him and then passed the time by walking around and looking in all the shop windows. I felt wonderful.

Rutter was waiting in the café with a black American. He was a deserter from the US Air Force and his girlfriend was a French prostitute, hence his nickname, Frenchy. They both had habits but could not be legally registered in the UK. We sauntered to a nearby park where I counted out 36 jacks and measured some white powder into the silver paper from a cigarette pack. Frenchy gave me £50, Rutter took a tenner and I had made a profit of £24. I had entered the junkie world.

I saw a lot of Frenchy and his girlfriend over the next few months. I'd call round at their flat after picking up my script from John Bell's. I discovered that the cocaine counteracted the downer action of the smack and as a result of this I was using increasing amounts and therefore had less to sell on. By the end of my first week as a registered addict, I was already using one grain (six jacks) a day. I felt as though I had become part of an elite group and I was hanging out with fellow junkies for most of the time.

This went hand in hand with the knowledge that my playing was improving by leaps and bounds and that I was streets ahead of most of the other drummers. I started mainlining within a very short time and I found that my veins were incredibly easy to hit. I could inject myself absolutely painlessly and greatly enjoyed the immediate effects that this gave as well as the way the perspiration ran down my forehead.

Poor Phil really had tried to help me, but I quickly fell under the influence of junkies like Rutter. I was picking up far too much stuff and was personally responsible for two of my friends obtaining habits simply by giving them a turn-on. One of these was Mike Scott and the other was a terrible drummer called Davy Smallman. Davy was always bugging everyone to sit in at jams and was so persistent that he always got a play. He had a very bad stutter and we'd get, 'L l l let's 'ave a p p p play man!' over and over again.

He came from a very well-to-do Jewish background and, although he was eschewed by a lot of the other musicians, Mike and I hung out with him on a regular basis. He always had a vehicle, was never short of money, had a great sense of humour and loved bacon sandwiches. Unfortunately, he came to a very unpleasant end. He was cut to ribbons in an alley behind Madame Tussauds in Baker Street, and many of us believed that it had been perpetrated by another junkie who was after his script.

I was still gigging at Ronnie Scott's and after I'd finished my set we'd all hang out in the club. Late one night, the junkie contingent got a chance to show their mettle when a guy who looked like he'd come straight out of a gangster movie, complete with long dark overcoat and trilby hat, walked past Chick the doorman, through the bar and into the office. Mike, Davy and I all remarked that this looked weird.

Then Ronnie rushed out of the office as white as a sheet, shouting, 'He's got a gun!' with the gangster, firearm in hand, in hot pursuit. All the other musicians followed Ronnie's retreating figure but the junkie contingent acted as one by running straight at the gangster and flooring him. The gun flew out of his hand as we hit him and we soon had him under control. Liz was sitting nearby as the gun fell to the floor and the bullets rolled under her chair. She kept them for years until they were stolen in a burglary. I had the gangster in a neck lock, Davy had his arm up his back and Mike took care of his legs.

'The bastard's got a shiv!' yelled Mike and pulled a long, wicked-looking knife from the guy's sock.

''Ere let us go!' begged the man. 'I just got out of nick!'

'Fuck you!' was our unanimous reply and we tightened our hold. The police arrived to take him away and we were the heroes of the night.

As junkies, we would never wait in line at John Bell & Croyden when picking up our scripts. We'd walk straight up to the counter to hand them in and no one ever challenged us. Except that one morning somebody did! 'Hey, I'm in front of you!' barked an irate Scottish voice and I turned to encounter the tall and imposing figure of Sean Connery, who was adamant that I wait my turn. James Bond got his way, but he was the only person to do so. Junkies were treated with the utmost deference by all as most ordinary folks feared us.

Lady Frankau was very fussy about who she would take on as a patient. Most of her junkies were extremely intelligent, particularly Gerry Clancy. He was the son of a brigadier and his mother was a devout Catholic. He had been given a choice of the military or the priesthood and chose the latter. For many years, he had studied as Brother Ignatius until he got into heroin and cocaine, which shocked his family considerably. We would often talk about philosophy and theology and he admired the writings of the Russian philosopher and mystic Peter Ouspensky. We shared the same views on religion, became very good friends and he was the only junkie that Liz ever liked. He often came to Braemar Avenue and sometimes he would babysit as he was one of the few I could trust.

Another interesting fellow was an actor who had acquired his habit during the war. He had been terrified, but found that taking a couple of Omnopon (morphine) dispelled his fear and made him a good soldier. Indeed, the good Lady had been the chief medical officer for the Royal Air Force during the Battle of Britain and it was she who had kept the boys flying around the clock.

I would often meet Phil at Lady Frankau's and we'd pick up our scripts and head for a suitable khazi. So as not to draw attention to our activities, we alternated between the gymnasium, a public toilet in a park and the toilets at Leicester Square where we'd bung the attendant a few bob. After that, we'd head off to Drum City on nearby Shaftesbury Avenue, where Dave Pearson was working and play drum duets for a couple of hours on kits in the basement. Some very heavy drums indeed could be heard upon these occasions.

One morning, as we went down the stairs, we encountered a tall, grey-haired old man who was sitting in a chair in his underpants mending his trousers. Dave Pearson introduced us to Bill Ludwig I – founder of the Ludwig Drum Company! He explained to us that he'd caught his trousers on the stair rail and that, as his wife always made him carry an emergency supply of needle and cotton, he was pleased to have finally had the opportunity to use it. He finished his repairs and then listened spellbound as Phil and I wailed upon the two kits. I don't think that he'd heard anything like it in his life. 'Wow! You guys sure can play,' he drawled as he shook our hands. I was very impressed by the great man.

After a Monday night jam at Ronnie's, Graham Bond came with me and Mike Scott to visit Gerry Skelton, a tenor player friend of Mike who'd just moved from Manchester. We sat around and smoked a couple of joints, then Graham began to talk, talk, talk and talk some more. Mike, Gerry and I just looked at each other with raised eyebrows and, when Graham finally left, Mike turned to me and said, 'Jesus! How can someone who plays that good talk such a lot of crap?' Bond had 'verbal diarrhoea', as Phil succinctly put it.

I had first met Graham at one of these same Monday jams. On that occasion, Harold McNair was playing, but there was a period in the evening when other musos got up to play. One of these was Graham, who was very large in a blue suit and looked like a white version of Cannonball Adderley. But he got on stage and wailed the blues like a good 'un. Most of the jazzers didn't like this as he ignored all the intricate changes on a 12-bar blues by just playing over the three basic chords, but he swung like a demon.

Gerry and I started to play together in an unusual quartet formed by trumpet player Stu Hammer, featuring trumpet, tenor, bass (Tony Archer) and drums. No piano. Stu played a tuned-up Dizzy Gillespie-style trumpet. The music was very 'far out' and we only played a few gigs. Gerry was yet another musician headed for the junkie road.

By now, I was continually high and completely unaware that a huge change in my personality had come about. Lady Frankau was very fond of me and would lecture me on getting well. Yet I didn't feel at all guilty that I was abusing all her good intentions and lying to her, such was the effect of those insidious narcotics. It was only a few months before I was using the full three grains of each.

I knew that I was playing amazing drums, but the gigs started to decrease. Ronnie's manager Pete King came up to me one night and told me in no uncertain terms that he didn't want me 'nodding off' in his club. It was true and I now realise that he was concerned for me, but I was stoned – just a few months ago, I'd been the hero that tackled the gunman, hadn't I?

A huge row then developed in which Pete accused me of selling smack in the club (this was untrue) and we very nearly came to blows. As a result of this, I lost my prestigious gig, which should have been a devastating blow. 'This ain't the only fucking club in the world!' I sneered to Pete and Ronnie as I stormed out, entirely forgetting that both of these guys had been very good to me over the past year.

A blind behind my eyes descends
Slowly a warm blanket enshrouds mentation
By vein to brain the mixture blends
Calm cool control and elation.

Seduced by sister morphine's sister
And her crystalline lady friend
My sultry seductresses whisper
'Have no fear, we are here dear friend.'

That the freezing of stark reality
Isn't there, 'We're together,' they lie
The subtle sinker hook and line
Reside inside resistance died
Diamorphine hydrochloride.

A cold clammy hand clasps my heart
Sneezing silent violent screams
Icy pain tears my inside apart
I wake aching alone from my dreams.

I got an audition for the Johnny Dankworth Orchestra, as Kenny Clare was leaving and I'd been highly recommended as his replacement. Kenny and indeed the whole band was delighted with the way that I played. Alan Branscombe, the piano player, beamed at me throughout the rehearsal and told me that he was sure I'd get the gig.

The following Monday, Ronnie Ross, the baritone sax-player in the Dankworth Band, came up to me in the pub up Archer Street. 'Congrats,' he said. 'You've got the gig!' I was knocked out.

Three days later, however, it was announced that Ronnie Stephenson was joining Dankworth as his drummer. I was dumbfounded and just couldn't believe it. When I next saw Alan, he told me that I didn't get the gig because somebody had informed John that I was a junkie; he very apologetic and sad about it. 'We all wanted you in the band,' he said. A rumour went round that bass player Spike Heatley had been the informant.

Nevertheless, I was still getting quite a few gigs down Archer Street and was earning a whole £4 for the two gigs at the all-nighter. But paying rent and buying food was becoming a struggle and I still had to find the money for my weekly visits to Lady Frankau and for my script. Now was the time that my training with the school gang came in handy. I had become friendly with Chris Thompson, a fine West Indian bass player, with whom I was playing a lot of gigs. Chris was also registered with Lady Frankau and together we devised a great scheme to get the money for our scripts.

Wearing Raglan raincoats, we'd walk into Foyle's bookshop on Charing Cross Road and browse through the art books. The biggest and most expensive books we could find would disappear into our raincoats. Then we'd walk out of the shop, take the tube to St John's Wood, where Chris knew a dodgy bookshop owner, and sell the books to him for about a third of their value. Such is the courage and ingenuity of junkies that, once when I noticed a policeman standing in the doorway as we walked out of Foyle's with a huge book stuffed inside each raincoat, I went straight up to him.

'Excuse me, have you got the time on you?' I asked.

He produced a pocket watch. 'It's twenty past ten.'

'Thanks a lot,' I replied, and we walked off to the tube with our booty.

Elsewhere in London, things were happening. It was 1961 and events held at St Pancras Town Hall heralded the birth of the Swinging Sixties. An exciting and innovative feeling prevailed everywhere, with everyone working together to create great things. The Town Hall was the venue for a wonderful event known as Jazz and Poetry. Poets Mike Horowitz, Pete Brown and Spike Hawkins and two jazz groups would get together on the stage and the jazz players would improvise under the readings. Laurie Morgan played the drums with one jazz group and me, Maurice Salvat (bass) and Bobby Wellins (tenor) made up the other one. The Town Hall was full to bursting with enthusiastic fans at every event and some remarkable things took place. Imagine the musicians' response to Pete Brown's poem 'Eat Well, Eat Walls and Shit Bricks'! ('Eat Well, Eat Walls' had been a slogan for Wall's Sausages!) Another notable piece was Spike Hawkins's 'In Love with the Ice Cream Dragon'.

Back at our little ground-floor maisonette, life seemed normal and happy. I bought a load of timber and constructed bookshelves and cupboards. We had a small back garden where I grew lettuce, carrots, radishes and large cannabis plants among the runner beans. Liz was aware of my habit but had accepted it and to all intents and purposes we were a happy couple with a beautiful young daughter.

We managed to get by and I was playing gigs of all types. Some were one-offs and there were factions that didn't like junkies, but there were also band leaders who turned a blind eye as long as you played well. Liz used to cut my hair, and both our families were very supportive, knitting jumpers and helping with clothes for Nettie. It was a pleasant domestic scene and at Christmas we'd spend the day with Liz's parents, then on Boxing Day we'd travel down to New Eltham on the Green Line bus to see my mum and Pop.

The couple in the maisonette upstairs to us had kids and were moving to a larger flat at the same time as Maurice Salvat was getting married and looking for a place to live. Maurice and I played a lot of gigs together and were very good friends, though he was not into drugs at all. After Liz had a word with the landlady, Maurice and his beautiful young Anglo-Indian wife Gill moved in upstairs. Liz and Gill soon became great friends and they were good company for each other while Maurice and I were working.

We shared many fun times. One day Maurice and Gill had had a big row and Maurice popped down to us for some sympathy. Then Gill came racing down the stairs with a bowl full of dirty washing-up water that she intended to throw over him. Unfortunately, Maurice saw it coming and ducked, leaving me to get the full force of the water. I was soaked and the row dissolved into helpless laughter. The walls were so thin they could hear our arguments and we could hear theirs. Gill was very noisy during sex and one day we heard a crash as their bed broke, followed once again by the sound of hysterical giggling.

The Bert Courtley Sextet was still in existence and we'd play the odd gig. Saxophonist Dick Heckstall-Smith had won the Jazz Musician of the Year award at Cambridge University and always got the May Ball gig. The first time I met Dick was at a Bert Courtley Sextet gig in a jazz club in Germany. The cloakroom attendant refused to take Dick's coat as it was so filthy. We said it resembled a 'child rapist's raincoat' and, as he also looked like the mass-murderer Christie who had lived in Rillington Place, we named him Rillington. He had remained a close friend of mine and he was aware I was a junkie, although he never even smoked grass. What he did like, though, was Teacher's Whisky.

The May Ball took place in June and the Sextet was on the 1962 bill along with several other bands. We were due to play two sets with the same line-up that we'd had in Germany and the band was still crazy. Our set in the Great Hall was followed by a rock'n'roll band. Pianist Colin Purbrook, glass in hand, was observed dancing across the stage while the rock singer had descended into the crowd. Then the singer leaped back on to the stage and chased Colin off, threatening to kill him, while the audience were in fits of laughter.

The set in the Jazz Marquee was really cooking when we became aware of a scruffy young man standing right beside the stage.

'Eh! Let's 'ave a play, man,' he demanded in a Scottish accent.

Oh shit! Shades of Davy Smallman, I thought. This was a gig, not a jam session at Sandwiches! This guy turned out to be the bass player with Jim McHarg's Scottsville Jazzmen, one of the many bands at the Ball. Just like Davy, we could not put him off, the only difference being the Scot's accent and the lack of a stutter. It was obvious that he wasn't going to go away and so it was decided to let him sit in. We chose the most complicated ballad that we could find, with chord changes all over the place, with the intention of making a fool of him. But much to our surprise he made every change and could play really well. The attitude changed: we launched into a 12-bar and he could swing like mad! The band was jumping!

Poor old Maurice looked a bit crestfallen when he returned to his bass at the end. I think he knew he'd lost his gig. Jack Bruce had arrived.

Maurice was a classically trained musician who never played a wrong note, but Jack had a spark that Maurice hadn't. He talked enthusiastically with Rillo and I after the gig and Rillo told him to come to London. He moved into the house on Grosvenor Avenue where Liz and I had first lived and which was still being run by

Johnny Parker. Jack, Rillo and I would get together whenever possible and jam. We had found the bass player. The freedom of the tenor, bass and drums line-up produced some incredible music, notably on Rillo's tune 'The Tube'.

Johnny Burch got an octet together and we'd play every Tuesday night at the Plough in Ilford with Johnny Huckridge (trumpet), Johnny Mumford (trombone), Graham Bond (alto), Dick Heckstall-Smith (tenor) and Glen Hughes (baritone), with Johnny on piano, Jack on bass and me on drums. Later on, Johnny Huckridge got a gig with the Ted Heath Orchestra and his replacement was a brilliant Nigerian trumpet player called Mike Falana. Then Glen Hughes got so busy with Georgie Fame and the Blue Flames that his seat was taken by Miff Mole.

All the writing was done by the rhythm section: Johnny, Jack and myself. Johnny was taking a lot of stuff from the US jazz scene, whereas Jack and I were penning completely original scores and experimenting with time signatures and horn voicing. Ours was probably the most progressive jazz group of its time in Europe. There was an incredible feeling with the Johnny Burch Octet and everyone would turn up early in the afternoon so that we could rehearse before the gig, which was always jam-packed. Among the crowd was a young Ian Dury, who later told me he came down to see us on a regular basis.

I was playing the best drums in town, but because the heroin was making me short-tempered, I had become such a difficult person to work with that gigs were few and far between. The Octet and the all-nighters were soon my only work. To supplement my meagre earnings, I signed on for dole money in Willesden, though I really hated having to do it.

One day, Rillo arrived at an Octet gig and announced that he and Jack had joined Alexis Korner's Blues Incorporated. They were raving about the band but confided in me that they were not too happy with the drummer. I felt somewhat betrayed by them – until the following week when they told me that the drummer in question, one Charlie Watts, had offered to leave the band so that I could join.

I could hardly believe this! I turned up at the Marquee club (then on Oxford Street) the next Thursday afternoon for a rehearsal and Charlie was there: he even helped me set up my kit. I was very impressed by what a nice fellow he was. He told me he was a big jazz fan and had been an admirer of mine for many years. As we were setting up, the rest of the band arrived: Cyril Davies, harp and vocals, my old friend Johnny Parker, piano, Ronnie Jones, a tall black American singer, Rillo and Jack. Alexis himself had yet to arrive.

Cyril didn't speak to me – instead, he took his harp from his pocket and began playing into a mike. Johnny Parker and Jack joined him and I was last, having just finished setting up. Cyril was a revelation, blowing raw blues like I'd never heard before. The number started rocking like mad and soon Cyril was beaming over at me. Then he started shouting blues into the mike and we played on, me listening to Cyril and improvising. When the number finally finished, Cyril came up to me and shook my hand.

'I gotta tell ya,' he said, straight as a die, 'when I 'eard you were coming, I didn't want you in the band at all. But you just blew me away, mate, and I'm fucking glad yer 'ere. Welcome!'

Meanwhile, Alexis had arrived and he too came over to me. 'Hello, Ginger,' he said. 'Very nice of you to come.'

Alexis and Cyril were like chalk and cheese. Cyril was a scruffily dressed, chubby-faced, no-nonsense, working-class Londoner while Alexis was immaculately attired, extremely polite and well spoken, with a large well-trimmed moustache. Neither of them looked the least bit like a musician.

Blues Incorporated really was a most extraordinary mix. Rillo,

Jack and I were modern jazz players, while Cyril, Alexis, Ronnie Jones and Johnny Parker were steeped in the traditional blues. The effect that we all had upon each other was amazing. Our gig that night in the Marquee was like no other I had ever played before. There were so many people crammed in that the very walls seemed to be bulging – I had never seen such a crowd at a gig. They created an electric atmosphere that was totally conducive to good music.

Ronnie sang Ray Charles's 'Night Time is the Right Time' as the finale and I was so moved by the music that tears rolled down my face. Ronnie looked back and saw me crying: 'I caught you!' he said, grinning.

I had a regular gig and it was the best I'd ever had. I left my drums at the Marquee and caught the tube home. Charlie, whose mum happened to be a friend of Liz's aunt Pamela, got off at the stop after mine for Kingsbury. I expressed my gratitude to him for his selfless action and he told me that he didn't really want to be a professional musician as there was no security in it.

The following Saturday, there was a big polo ball on Lord Rothschild's estate in Sussex and we all crowded on to a large bus driven by Alexis. Eventually, I became vaguely aware of an extra body tagging along with the band. He was a young, slightly effeminate-looking kid and he appeared to be a friend of Alexis. We arrived at the huge house and got organised for the first of two sets. I was already pretty stoned as we commenced in front of a crowd consisting of men immaculately attired in black tie and women in an extraordinary array of evening dresses and glittering jewellery.

Although the band was playing incredible music, nobody seemed to be taking much notice. The din of laughter and animated conversation drowned us out and we got virtually no applause; I was used to jazz audiences who listened to the music and applauded every solo. Among the distinguished guests, I noticed the Duke of Edinburgh dancing with a pretty girl and the moustachioed comedian Jimmy Edwards. I was far from impressed with these people behaving atrociously while a large team of servants ran around attending to their various needs. This lack of response from the audience got me very angry, so the presence of Alexis's young friend sitting on the side of the stage doing nothing angered me even more. 'Eh, Jack! Who is this fucking geezer?' I shouted, pointing at the kid in a lull between numbers. 'What's 'e doin' 'ere?'

Jack just smiled and we kicked into the next number. Everyone was dancing about, but as usual we finished to very little applause. I'd had enough. Jesus, I thought, I need a fix. I wandered up a huge, curved, richly carpeted staircase and along the landing far above the din below. A door was open and I looked into a grand bedroom, beyond which, through another open door, I glimpsed a bathroom. I went in there and cooked up a very large fix. The next thing I remembered was Rillo shaking me awake. I was lying on a giant bed with blue hangings and surrounded by people. 'Come on, Ginger! We're late for the second set. We've been searching for you for ages.'

It was Lord Rothschild's bed. Alexis was busy apologising to his lordship, but he was fine about it. 'Oh, that's all right,' he said. 'The poor chap must've been very tired!'

We launched into our second set, but by now the throng of well-dressed 'hoorays' were extremely drunk and their behaviour got even worse. The dance floor was absolute mayhem. People were falling about, drinks were being spilled and the army of servants scurried hither and thither, cleaning up the accidents as they happened. As I sat behind my drums, I was filled with hatred for these moronic idiots. At one point, Jimmy Edwards leaped on stage while Cyril was playing a blues and started blowing a raucous hunting horn completely out of tune.

'Fuck off, you cunt!' I shouted as Cyril helped him roughly off the stage. The crowd thought that this was hilarious and that was the only applause we received that night.

At the end of the set, the effeminate lad got up and joined Ronnie Jones at the mike. His name was Mick Jagger and his singing was awful.

By the end of the night, the band was as drunk as the audience and Alexis drove us back to London with a bottle of champagne in his hand. Cyril was happily singing 'Whack my dickie with a dead dog's dollop', when a blue flashing light appeared and we got pulled over by the police. Alexis handed me the bottle and I hid it under the seat as he wound down his window.

'Good morning, officer,' said Alexis in his cut-glass accent. He sounded as sober as a judge! 'What seems to be the problem?'

It was four-thirty in the morning and the copper was obviously nonplussed by Alexis's accent and demeanour; so we were soon back on our way and Alexis reclaimed his bottle.

The next Wednesday, we had a recording session at Decca Studios in West Hampstead. We were rehearsing a number as the studio technicians were putting up the mikes. Somebody put one right above my head and as I stood up I received a severe blow from it. Once again I was instantly in a fury. 'What fucking idiot put that there?'

On the way home, Rillo, Alexis and Cyril said that they wanted to talk to me. When we got back to mine and Liz had gone into the kitchen to make the tea, Cyril said, 'Listen!' He was very angry. 'If this was my band, I'd give you the sack right now!'

I was astounded, shocked and mortified, because I really loved the band. What on earth could I have done?

They proceeded to explain to me what an obnoxious little git I had become. This was coming from musicians for whom I had nothing but love and respect and it really hit home. What they were saying was absolutely true and yet, until that moment, I was completely unaware. I was getting too stoned and just not thinking at all. That day in the studio I had effectively blown a potentially lucrative recording contract and it was only their regard for my playing that kept me in the band. They had shown me what I had become and I felt deeply ashamed. They had sown the seeds of getting straight in my brain and after that I took great care to keep my temper under control and be on my best behaviour.

Blues Incorporated continued to flourish and every gig was packed with enthusiastic audiences. On Tuesday nights, I still played in the Johnny Burch Octet over at the Plough in Ilford. Things were going so well that I had a graph on the wall at home on which I would plot the trajectory of my earnings and it was moving upwards week by week.

On Wednesday nights, we had a gig at the Ealing Club, a grotty little place close to Ealing Broadway tube station. Mick Jagger had now got together with Brian Jones and played in the interval. Alexis had talked Jack, Johnny and me into accompanying them; a situation that we were not too happy about as it meant that we didn't get a rest between sets. So Jack and I would have great fun playing complicated time things behind Mick and Brian. Mick was very easy to throw off the beat, and Jack and I would grin at each other as Brian, who was pretty hip, would then set poor Mick back in time by shouting, 'One, two, three, four!' on the beat.

After a couple of weeks, I said to Brian, 'Why don't you get a rhythm section?' And, sure enough, they arrived the next week with their own rhythm section. I was pleased about this as I got up for my interval fix and I returned to the club just in time to hear the last half of a number. Brian came up to me afterwards and asked me what I thought of it. 'Yeah, Brian, it's OK, but the drummer is fucking awful. Why don't you get Charlie Watts?' The following week Charlie was playing the drums.

Brian told me about a gig they'd got at the Cy Laurie Club on Great Windmill Street, so Jack and I went down to see one of the very first gigs of the Rolling Stones. Mick was just standing at the mike singing, while Brian was really doing his showman thing, lying on his back while he played guitar, leaping around the stage and even jumping into the audience. The music was atrocious, yet the raw lack of musicianship appealed to the young audience who were lapping it up. Jack and I could both see that this was going to be a big success.

Soon after that gig came some bad news: Glen Hughes was dead. He was yet another who had got himself heavily into smack and, having nodded off in his flat with a cigarette burning, he'd died in the ensuing fire. He was only in his twenties and a very talented musician. Bad news seemed to come in waves. Alexis called a band meeting and Cyril announced that he was leaving. It was an amicable split but it left us all wondering why, when everything was going so well, he would want to go off and form his own band. Then Alexis told us that Graham Bond was to be Cyril's replacement.

'Blimey! You'd better watch him!' I said jokingly. 'He'll nick half the band!'

And so it was that Graham Bond joined Blues Incorporated playing Hammond organ through a Leslie speaker and doubling up on alto. We all viewed this change with some trepidation. The first rehearsal, however, dispelled our doubts because he really could play that Hammond and the sounds he got through the Leslie blew us all away.

It wasn't long after that we got the news, en route to a gig, that Cyril had died. Alexis said that he had been diagnosed with leukaemia, but had actually died of pleurisy. We strongly suspected that he'd left the band when he'd found out just how ill he was and never told anyone. We and the world had lost a genius. It was a very sad day.

Graham got a trio gig in Manchester and Jack and I drove up there with him in a hired black Dormobile. The club was packed and we were well received – the crowd went mad at Graham's rendition of 'Wade in the Water', which began with a Bach-like fugue. Graham was stoned out of his mind and was raving insanely as he drove back down the M1. 'This is it, guys! It's like we've won the pools. Yeah, this is the way to go; we'll leave Alexis and make it big!'

Jack and I looked at each other. Graham was off again, with the expert patter that he'd used in his years as a salesman for Frigidaire.

'Hang on a minute, Graham,' I cautioned. 'It's only one gig. We can always do the odd gig on our own, but we're doing pretty good with Alexis too.'

Jack agreed and we thought that we'd convinced Graham.

The next day, we had a gig with Alexis at the Flamingo. Alexis had called a rehearsal and I arrived at the club and went straight into the khazi for a fix. When Jack arrived, we walked in to see Graham talking with Alexis up on the stage. Then Graham spotted us and rushed over, ambushing us on our way to the stage.

'Yeah, it's done!' he said, bubbling with enthusiasm. 'We've all left the band! Alexis is really cool about it and I gave him two weeks' notice.'

Jack and I exchanged glances.

'John McLaughlin's playing guitar with us,' continued Graham. 'Man, this is great!'

'What about Dick?' I asked, to be told that Rillo had elected to stay with Alexis.

Graham's joie de vivre was unstoppable and Jack and I could do nothing but stare at each other dumbly. Alexis came up, shook our hands and wished us success with the venture. The Graham Bond Organisation was born.

Chapter Six

The Graham Bond Organisation

*G*raham had been very busy. He'd already hired Don Kingswell as our agent. Don had a guy called Robert Masters working with him and quite a few gigs had been booked. On paper, things certainly looked much as Graham had promised, so I gave Alexis Phil's number and he and Chris Thompson replaced Jack and I.

Graham purchased our bandwagon and drove it round to Braemar Avenue. It was an old grey Daimler ambulance with a fluid flywheel pre-selector gear box and still had the word 'Ambulance' displayed above the cab. I joined Graham for a test drive over to Jack's. *Clonk!* We lurched forward. Graham never could master that gear box. You had to select the gear; then depress the clutch and then the accelerator. This was far too complicated for Graham, who insisted on driving it like a normal stick shift.

Our very first gig was at Klook's Kleek in West Hampstead, where we played a mixture of jazz and R&B. John McLaughlin played great guitar and on some numbers Graham would double up on alto and organ simultaneously. We were very happy musically and well received.

Our next gig was in Coventry for the promoter Harry Flick. He was a big jovial bloke, who got us loads of gigs in the Midlands and was rather fond of a joint. He would take a long, hard toke and say, 'Where's it all gonna end, fellas? Where's it all gonna end?' before he exhaled. He always had some grass with him. John didn't smoke or drink so we were a bit surprised to see him take the proffered joint. We were obviously a bad influence on him. During the set, he was wailing an incredible guitar solo, sitting on a chair as he played and rocking back and forth. The more intense the music became, the more he rocked the chair. Eventually, he rocked both himself and the chair right off the stage, which was a good four feet high. As he lay on his back, he played one last, weird chord that echoed on as we ground to a halt and carried his unconscious form back to the dressing room.

Although we were doing loads of gigs as Graham had promised, my earnings graph dipped alarmingly from over £50 a week with Alexis down to £12! I phoned Graham, who said, 'We're doing better than we were with Alexis.'

'You may be, Graham, but we ain't!' I replied and a stunned silence prevailed.

I spoke with Jack and John, who both agreed that something was amiss and I spent all day filling up four sheets of yellow foolscap detailing our complaints and outlining a solution. As we set off for out next gig, four abreast in the front of the ambulance, I read it out to Graham. His face got steadily paler as I read, but faced with such a unanimous front he had no option but to concur and I took over the running of the band. It was then that we became the Graham Bond Organisation.

Graham got Ronan O'Rahilly to manage us. He ran the pioneering Radio Caroline and we did all the commercials for the pirate station with the singers Madeleine Bell and Doris Troy. It soon became obvious that Ronan was spending all his time and energy keeping the station broadcasting, so one night, at a gig in the 100 Club, Robert Masters introduced me to Robert Stigwood. The three of us had a long discussion and we agreed that Stigwood was a far better manager than Ronan could ever be. Then I spoke to Graham and convinced him, but when Ronan was informed he threatened all sorts of law-suits. So I spoke to my old friend Wally Houser, who was a very good lawyer, and he advised me to keep a record of all breaches of contract by Ronan. When Ronan's lawyers saw this, they dropped the case and Stigwood became the manager of the Graham Bond Organisation. Ronan was very nice about it in the end and shook my hand and wished me well.

Running the band, however, turned out to be an increasingly difficult task because Graham was crazy. He turned up one night at a Marquee gig with a very good-looking young chick, which amazed me because he wasn't much to look at himself. After the gig, when I'd picked up my drums, I went to the office to collect the money. In there, I encountered John Gee (the club manager) and he was extremely irate. It transpired that Graham had already collected the money from John's secretary before the gig and had then gone on to pick the money up again from John after the gig. We didn't get our money and now owed 40 quid as well. It turned out that Graham had told his chick how famous he was, taken her out for a slap-up meal and promised her a recording contract.

Yes, when Graham had a bee in his bonnet, nothing could stop him. One day he boldly walked into EMI and came out with a recording contract for the band. But then he did the same at Decca and repeated the act at Phonogram. That evening, three record company executives met in the pub to discover that all three of them had signed the Graham Bond Organisation. He was indeed a top-class salesman – only our chances of getting a contract had now gone from slim to zero.

In my own personal life, I had my habit fairly under control and would pick up my weekly script and make it last. As long as I stayed on my three grains a day, life was normal – I wasn't really getting high any more and was just using the stuff to function. Monday at 9am was my weekly appointment with Lady Frankau. I would leave Wimpole Street with my script for 21 grains of heroin and 21 grains of cocaine, which I would take round to John Bell & Croyden and cash.

So Monday was 'get stoned' day and Sunday was the day I ran out of stuff. Sunday night became Circle Line night on the underground. You could get a ticket to Baker Street and just carry on circling around. There were several junkies sitting reading their papers, all of them feeling the first pains of sickness and all of them waiting patiently for the time when normality would return.

John McLaughlin and I became very good friends. He was still completely straight, as the episode in Coventry had put him right off drugs. We enjoyed playing sling-shot competitions on the road and John could always manage to throw his stones a good 20 yards further than I could. I then created a super-long sling with a cool leather pouch and, when we returned early one morning from a gig, I challenged John to a contest to see who could throw a large stone right across Welsh Harp reservoir in Neasden. My new sling was working really well and we were both dropping half-brick-sized stones to within yards of the far shore. I then found a near-perfect stone. 'This one's going right over!' I shouted as I swung the sling above my head. Bonk! I saw stars and then through them I saw John's worried face.

'Man, are you OK?'

I struggled to my feet, blood running down my face from a great gash on the side of head. I'd managed to wind the sling around my head. We traipsed back to the maisonette and woke Liz to give me first aid. That was the end of the sling shots.

Despite Graham's bouts of madness, the earnings graph was starting to look very healthy once more. The band was extremely popular and the gigs were pouring in. Soon it was not unusual to be gigging seven days a week. We packed the clubs for £40 a night and the university gigs would earn us £70–100. Now that I was in control of the money, I would diligently split it up and we each earned upwards of £50 a week, which in those days was good money.

One week I'd had a particularly lunatic Monday and as a result I was running low on stuff. The long drives were taking their toll on us all and John started moaning. 'I can't stand much more of this,' he complained as we loaded our gear into the ambulance, which was now using as much oil as petrol due to Graham's abuse of the flywheel system.

I was in a very bad mood because it was Saturday and I only had about six jacks left and no more cocaine. 'Why don't you just fuck off then?' I snarled.

So he did. We lost a great guitar player and I lost a good friend. Dick Heckstall-Smith joined the band and he told us the problems that poor Alexis was experiencing with Phil and Chris. One junkie was a problem, but two hardened big-time ones was a disaster. The band wasn't the same and Rillo was happy to be playing with us again. Our gigs continued to pour in as our popularity grew and just about everything that we played was original. Going commercial as we had done created a whole new music. It wasn't jazz, but it was something that we thought people would like and they did. The Graham Bond Organisation was happening!

At one point, we had a 16-day tour booked, starting in the Midlands and working our way up to Scotland and back. On the Monday before it started, I was off up to Lady Frankau's as usual. It was a beautiful day and little Nettie was going 'up to

London' with Daddy. She met Lady Frankau, who was very taken by the lovely child and looked at me very severely as she handed me my script.

Nettie and I walked down the steps of 32 Wimpole Street and out on to the sunlit pavement. I looked down at my beautiful child trustingly holding my hand and she smiled up at me. Suddenly, I was hit by a thunderbolt. What the hell are you doing? I thought. I glanced down at the script in my other hand.

'OK, Nettie, let's go home,' I said and set course for Baker Street tube station instead of John Bell & Croyden. That was it, I was coming off! I walked up Braemar Avenue with Nettie holding my hand and the script uncashed in my pocket.

The band's ambulance arrived with the rest of the band and we set off north. I'd had my last fix early that morning and as we got further and further from town an icy hand grabbed at my heart. I told the others that I was coming off and they were full of encouragement. But, by the time we got to the gig at Swadlincote in Derbyshire, I was sneezing and shivering and had goose bumps.

I got drunk to get through the gig and then returned to the ambulance, in which we were sleeping to save money. I was shivering again, got out of the ambulance and was staggering around Swadlincote for ages. In the morning, I remember seeing the miners sitting on their doorsteps reading the papers in their braces. God knows what they thought of this odd-looking guy staggering past.

I don't remember much about the ensuing gigs, but I know that I managed to play by drinking an awful lot of rum and Coke. After about six or seven days, we were in this nice little hotel in Edinburgh and I actually woke up after having slept and thought, I've done it – I'm straight! The sun was shining through the window and I felt great. Through the rest of the tour I had a few drinks, but I was off, I was straight. But when we got back to

London what did I do? I went down to Lady Frankau's at 9am and told her what had happened. She scolded me for being 'a silly boy' and explained to me how we must do it, which was to gradually cut down on the usage over a long period.

'We need to get you off the cocaine first,' she said.

'No, no! The coke's OK – it's the smack that's the problem.'

'No, Ginger,' she said. 'The cocaine is far more dangerous than the heroin. We'll cut you down gradually on that and a bit more severely on the cocaine.' She said it would take a long time and gave me a script. I began adhering very closely to the instructions, cutting down by half a jack a day and then the following week by a whole jack a day, gradually using less and less.

One night we did a gig in Golders Green in North London. I'd been drinking a mixture of rum and Guinness in order to help with my withdrawal. I was playing a drum solo and Jack decided to play bass with the solo. I was phrasing along with him and really enjoying it when all of a sudden Jack turned round and shouted, 'You're playing too fucking loud, man!' In the middle of *my* drum solo! I just launched into a solo of great anger and it was the last number of the night (as always). At the end, as everyone was going out, I said, 'I'm going for a piss, Jack. Don't be here when I come back.'

But, when I came back, there he was, still on the stage. I rushed up, grabbed him and said, 'I told you not to be here!' and threw him off the stage where he was caught by his girlfriend Janet and by Liz. Then the silly bastard got back on to the stage! I just lost it. I went completely into a red haze, intent on killing him.

A lot of the crowd were still there and began singing, 'He loves you, yeah! yeah! yeah!' They were thoroughly enjoying the show!

I gave Jack a right-hander, knocking him on the ground, and then suddenly a pair of strong arms wrapped around me from behind and I was lifted away from my victim. One of the bouncers had come to Jack's rescue. As he bodily carried me backwards, my head cleared and I was calm again. 'OK, it's all over,' I told the bouncer, who put me back on my feet. I thanked him, and Graham and Rillington escorted me back to the dressing room where they sat me down. They looked deadly serious.

'Ginge, I know that what Jack did was wrong, but you can't behave like that,' said Graham.

Rillington, who was a Quaker, was calm but angry. 'That is just not on,' he said with his lips tight and his face rigid. 'Violence does not solve problems.'

By now, I felt terrible. Jesus! What had I done? We sat and talked for ages and they both made me promise that, no matter how provoked, I would never hit Jack again.

The night before Jack's wedding, we had a gig in Shepherds Bush. It was the first time we had played this particular club, and unusually the crowd were not very receptive to our music. During the interval, we adjourned to the bar for some drinks. Since the incident at Golders Green, I had changed my drink to Bacardi and Coke, because in my mind I'd blamed the Guinness for the red mist. I was still struggling along on Frankau's programme and the alcohol was certainly a great help.

As I approached the dressing room alongside the stage, I saw five tough-looking guys with braces over their T-shirts walk through the dressing-room door. What's their game? I wondered. The public khazi was located at the other end of the club and I suspected they were on the nick – stealing. As I reached the door and opened it, the five toughies came out. Rillington was sitting in the dressing room cutting his reed.

'Don't tell the guv'nor we was 'ere,' said one of the men as they passed.

'I thought they were on the nick,' I said to Rillo.

As I turned round to shut the door, *bam*! One of the toughies landed a bull's eye straight on my nose. I reeled a few paces backwards on impact and stood beside my open 'traps case'.

Lying in the case was the axe handle that I used to bang in my drum spurs. Suddenly, it was in my hand and I returned to the door where the five blokes still stood laughing. I lifted the axe handle high and brought it down on the head of one of my assailants. Just before impact, a voice in my head said, 'Steady, Ginger!' And so I didn't follow through fully with the blow or for sure it would've killed him. As it was, the big 'toughie' fell to the floor with his head split wide open.

'Who's next?' I shouted.

The other four stood transfixed and staring at me in total disbelief. A huge bouncer appeared, rushed at me and shoved me back into the dressing room. He looked like he was about to have a go at me. "Ere, hold up!' I said to him. 'They started it – look at my hooter!'

The bouncer calmed down and actually soaked a towel and placed it over my smashed nose. An ambulance arrived to cart the heavy off to hospital where he received umpteen stitches and we had to have a large bouncer escort from the club. My reputation as a 'hard nut' was developing.

Early the next morning, we set off for another long drive north, my nose still very painful with gauze over it, held in place by sunglasses. Tours were a great test of will power to keep to my programme. I would leave town with a lot of stuff that had to last me until I got back again. As I cut down further, this became increasingly difficult, but so far I was succeeding. The last day was always the worst and I got back from the tour pretty sick.

First thing in the morning, I was in Lady Frankau's, snivelling and sneezing. After I'd picked up my script and put myself out of my misery, I went over to Charing Cross Hospital to get my nose checked out. They took some x-rays and I was confronted by a rather irate doctor.

'Why didn't you report to hospital when this happened?' he demanded.

I explained that I had had to leave in order to go on tour. He then explained that there wasn't a lot he could do now because the bones had set and, unless I wanted to go through a lengthy procedure, such as having the whole thing re-broken, I would just have to live with it. I chose the latter, which was a decision I was later to regret.

After Robert Stigwood took over our management, we saw immediate and positive results. Within weeks, we were in the Decca studios at West Hampstead and the album *The Sound of 65* was recorded in less than a week. I did the artwork one night after the sessions. Then a really big tour came up – Stigwood brought Chuck Berry over from the States. We were to be second on the bill; playing alongside the Moody Blues and two singers Stigwood was trying to push, Simon Scott and Winston G.

The tour started with a matinee performance in town, attended mainly by mums and their kids. The compere was a very funny character named Mike Patto and the atmosphere was completely insane with the Moody Blues, Mike Patto and ourselves all getting very stoned on alcohol and marijuana before the show. When Mike walked on stage, we hid behind the curtain, prodding his rear with drum sticks whenever he came in range. He totally forgot his routine and launched into some extremely salacious jokes that we all found to be highly amusing. The audience, however, were appalled and our tour manager John Taylor was apoplectic, jumping up and down and shouting, 'Get him off! Get him off!'

When Mike finally lurched off stage, leaving a stunned and silent audience, John Taylor fired him on the spot. His dismissal had a sobering effect on us all. We thought a lot of Mike and we'd got him fired; so we cornered John Taylor and persuaded him to give

Patto another chance. Then we set about straightening him out by forcibly holding him under a cold shower and plying him with strong coffee. However, we didn't seem to be making much progress this way and so we resorted to whacking him with cold wet towels instead. This seemed to do the trick and the evening show was fine. Mike kept his gig.

The next day, we left in a huge tour coach and the insanity mushroomed. On that first journey, we invented a mad game to pass the time, which began when Graham and the Moody Blues keyboard player Mike Pinder were sitting together. We were all avid fans of wrestling and had noticed that professional wrestlers would often think up evil little things in order to antagonise their opponents and so the game of 'snape' was born.

The rules were simple: two contestants would be facing each other and the toss of a coin decided who was to go first. Then you took it in turns to inflict pain upon your adversary in as inventive a way as possible, but no move could be repeated in the five-minute match. The eyebrow tweak (which entailed grabbing the opponent's eyebrow between the knuckles of your middle finger and twisting it 180 degrees) was a popular first move. If your opponent refused to take further punishment, he would forfeit the game. Drawing blood would result in disqualification.

We had two teams: The Moody Blues versus The Graham Bond Organisation and we had enlisted Patto as our fifth member. Some extraordinary new moves were invented, such as the dreaded double-inside-leg tweak (involving the inner flesh of both thighs) and the ankle bite, where one would bite the Achilles tendon as hard as possible. We played this game on all the long journeys and the rest of the party, Chuck Berry included, had to endure the screams of pain that came from the happy snapers at the back of the coach. Rillington was our champion – no matter how evil the move, no one could ever raise a sound from his narrow lips.

Halfway through the tour, the Moody Blues' 'Go Now', sung by Denny Laine, shot to No 1. We all found this highly amusing because we were above them on the bill and getting £45 per gig, while they were only getting £40. Of course, this had the effect of making the daily snape contest more evil still!

The climax of the tour was in Cardiff, where the Welsh crowd had a reputation for wild behaviour. Stigwood's protégé Simon Scott was booed and jeered mercilessly and all kinds of objects were hurled at the stage. Winston G then had his act cut short when he was hit on the head with a metal staple fired from a large elastic-powered catapult. Bleeding and weeping, he exited stage left.

The Moody Blues managed to turn the crowd's mood and the GBO was then really well received. The whole place was jumping, my drum solo brought the house down and by the time Chuck Berry took to the stage the crowd was on its feet. Only in Wales would you get an atmosphere like this, and halfway through Chuck's set another wonderful game began. We stood stage right, assisting crazed fans up on to the stage where they would dance madly across to the other side where the Moodies would be waiting to knock them into the crowd. Some of these maniacs made three or four such excursions and were somewhat bloodstained, but still cheerful and having a wonderful time. This was one of the maddest gigs I have ever experienced and certainly took my mind off other things for a while.

I had used my last heroin (the cocaine had long gone), which was one-and-a-half jacks, just before the gig and by the end of the night I felt the dreaded signs of sickness approaching. I discovered that Stigwood and our tour manager John Taylor were returning to London by train that night, so I got them to book me a ticket as well so I could be at Lady Frankau's first thing in the morning. I didn't want to risk going back in the coach with the others and ending up in really bad shape the next day. The first-class carriage was warm and comfortable but I huddled in a corner seat feeling cold and clammy. I noticed Taylor and Stigwood were looking at me strangely and Taylor even remarked that I looked 'interesting', but by now I was feeling too sick to pay him much attention. After the train finally rolled into Paddington at 7am, I got a ticket to Baker Street and rode the Circle Line three times until it was time to be at 32 Wimpole Street. I was there dead on 9am. I explained what a terrible time I was having to the dear Lady and she added a prescription for some Physeptone tablets.

'These will help,' she informed me. 'When we finally get you off, you will be using Physeptone alone for the last two weeks and gradually tapering down.'

By then, I was down to a grain-and-a-half of heroin and half a grain of cocaine daily. I had managed to cut my habit in half and was used to doing without coke. I used it all on my first day, although the prescription was really for three or four days' supply.

Back on the music front, I had now started to drive the Dormobile a little, even though I had no licence. Graham usually acted as my instructor but one day Jack volunteered. After driving around for about half an hour or so, he said he had to get back. We were on the North Circular and I executed a U-turn right across the road. Jack totally freaked out.

'Oh, come on, Jack!' I said, 'There was nothing about.'

I had made certain of this before attempting the manoeuvre and so was unperturbed, but that was the last time that I ever drove with Jack.

One day, while on a visit to my mum, I happened to meet up with one of my mates, Brian Potter from the RACS who lived nearby. He was looking for a job, so I signed him up as our roadie. Brian was newly married and his wife expressed a little concern about his new job, not without reason as it turned out.

The last gig of the tour happened to be in Redcar, a seaside town in the North East. We always stayed at the same hotel and had booked our rooms well in advance, but, when we arrived there after our gig, we discovered the Moody Blues had taken them. We were now relegated to lesser accommodation on the floor above. The Moodies were all very smug and amused at the trick they had pulled on us, which they said paid us back for being billed above them on the Chuck Berry tour. Very droll! A mad party then ensued with us and the Moodies as the only guests. At one point, we called down to the waiter to bring us another round of drinks and, when he entered the lounge, we were all standing on our heads!

After several more rounds and a lot of marijuana, we challenged the Moodies to a game of super-snape. The rules had now changed and a committee would decide what each snape should entail – and it was to be one move only. The roadies were first up and it was decided that theirs should be a shoulder-punching snape. The Moodies' roadie was Phil Robertson and he had been an RAF drill instructor. Brian drew first and punched Phil on the shoulder; Phil returned the blow and Brian's face paled. Brian delivered his next blow and then Phil totally missed and hit Brian in the ribs. We all heard a sickening *crack*! And Phil was disqualified.

One up to the Bondies!

Next in line were the two keyboard players, Graham Bond and Mike Pinder. The committee reconvened and, recalling the Mike Patto in the shower incident, selected a wet bath towel. Graham and Mike took off their shirts and went the full five minutes alternately whacking each other on the back with it, each blow accompanied by a high-pitched crack.

Now it was the drummer's turn. Graham Edge and I squared up. The committee convened again and Denny Laine tied a knot at the end of the wet towel. Everyone bristled with glee at the new knotted-wet-towel-across-the-back snape. I took off my shirt and became slightly alarmed when Denny's practice hit with the new weapon bashed a huge hole in the wall of the hotel lounge.

Edge won the toss and his first blow caught me in the dead centre of my back. As I sagged to my knees, my head hit a bottle on the table, cutting it open. I had no time to recover properly and only managed to hit Edge on the arm. He got me in the back again and I staggered forward. Uh oh – the red mist came down. I was hurt bad and I knew that I couldn't face another blow. I lined up and hit Edge a bull's eye on the base of his skull. He spun round and fell to the floor motionless.

'Christ, he's dead!' someone yelled.

The room fell quiet. Denny poured a jug of iced water over his head and he didn't even stir.

'Somebody call a doctor!'

'Oh, yeah, what do we tell him?'

Phil Robertson knelt beside the fallen drummer and loosened his collar. 'He's still breathing,' he said.

We were all suddenly very sober and crouched around the unconscious Edge. After what seemed an age (but was probably about ten minutes), Graeme groaned and opened his eyes, whereupon his compatriots carried him off to bed. The final game of snape had been played.

The next morning, all the snapers were understandably very sore. Edge had a large bump on the back of his head. Bond and Pinder had backs that were dark blue and black all over, and I had a huge bruise on my back and a cut to the head. Poor old Brian was groaning in pain every time he turned the wheel on the drive back southwards. On his return, his wife took him to hospital where it was discovered that he had two cracked ribs. She was not amused. That was his first and last tour with us and he was replaced by Manfred, a friend of Rillo's wife, Gary. Like her, he was an

Austrian, and he was a very helpful and polite fellow who was destined to stay with us for a long time.

It was after a gig in town that Stigwood invited me back to his office in De Walden Court. I was under the impression that I was there to discuss such plans as a forthcoming album and we sat in the office having a couple of drinks. When I came back from the khazi, I found Stigwood sitting on the couch with his member in his hand and a silly grin on his face.

'Oh, come on, Robert!' I said. 'We stopped playing cock shows at primary school.'

With that he sheepishly readjusted his apparel. I went home and the incident was never mentioned again. He was proving to be a good manager and his private life was no concern of mine.

The GBO's second album, *There's a Bond Between Us*, was soon in the can. We were all involved in the writing of the tunes and, as I had inflicted my left-wing politics upon the band, every song was credited to John Group and the publishing was split equally. I produced artwork for the cover and got a credit, though what appeared in the end was not mine.

The album title, however, proved to be unfortunate because soon after its release the 'bond' began to unravel. We played a gig in Ipswich at which Jack's alter ego, Mr Hyde, made an appearance. He completely lost his temper on stage and started shouting, 'NO, NO, NO!' in the middle of a number. At a post-gig discussion in the dressing room, we informed Jack in a calm manner that this would just not do, because he was upsetting us all. It had shades of the talking-to that I had received from Cyril Davis, Alexis Korner and Rillington. Jack's response was to storm out of the dressing room and sit in the driver's seat of the Dormobile. We loaded up while Jack sat silently but then he refused to let Manfred drive. As soon as we were all in the bus, Jack drove off at high speed with no lights on. He mounted a kerb and

Top: My dad and me in 1940.

Middle: Rex the dog.

Bottom left: Dad and a friend in Algeria.

Bottom right: Dad's grave on Leros.

Above: Getting on my bike.

Below left: Me, Ruby and Pat.

Below right: At the boating lake in Eastbourne.

Above: At the pub in Devon – Rose in the stripes on the left, Granddad with the cigarette, Grandma far right, children; me, John and Pat.

Below: Pat, Pop, Mum and me.

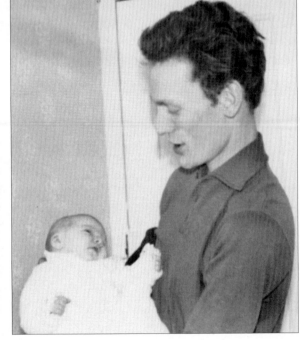

Above: I married Liz on 17 February 1959.

Below left: The wedding reception in Elm Way, Neasden.

Below right: Ginette – Nettie – was born on 20 December 1960.

Above: The Gordon Beck Quartet – Gus Galbraith on trumpet, Tony Archer on bass and Beck on piano.

Below: The Graham Bond Organisation.

Above: Cream by the ponds on Hampstead Heath in London.

Below: In the white Jensen FF outside my house in Harrow, 1969.

Above: The family in 1969: Nettie, me, Leda, Kofi and Liz in Harrow.

Below: Blind Faith behind the scenes – Steve Winwood, Eric Clapton, an unknown person, me and Ric Grech (in shadow)… some time in 1969.

In January 1970, soon after the formation of Airforce, at home with drums that were a gift from Guy Warren.

© *Val Wilmer*

missed a lamp-post on my side by the width of a fag-paper. He skidded to a halt outside Graham's place in Romford and Graham motioned for me to get out with him.

'Ginge,' said Graham, his face white with anger. 'He has got to go! I am not putting up with that.'

I got back in and Jack continued to drive like a lunatic until he reached his flat in West Hampstead, where he jumped out of the cab, slammed the door furiously and stomped off. Manfred then took the wheel to get Rillo and me home at a more sedate pace and I told Rillo what Graham had said. We both agreed that Jack had gone too far, but I said that I would talk to Graham about it. But by the morning he had not changed his mind. He was adamant that Jack must go, but asked, 'Will you do it, Ginge?'

I called Rillo to tell him what had happened and after that I phoned Jack with the news that he had got the sack. Graham, Rillo and I then had a meeting. Graham wanted to play bass on his organ pedals, and we unanimously agreed we would ask the young Nigerian trumpeter Mike Falana to join the band. The Graham Bond Organisation Mk III came into being.

Mike was a great asset for the band and Graham's bass lines on the pedals were amazing. He was playing alto with one hand, organ with the other and bass with his feet – and made a remarkably good job of it! His whole character seemed to be undergoing some enormous changes at this time. He had grown his hair long, sported a droopy moustache and wore extraordinarily colourful cloaks over glittering shirts. He had left his wife and was now always accompanied by his young girlfriend Diane. He had begun to look like a 'pop star' and was taking acid with his grass, but nevertheless continued to play his arse off!

When we got to Manchester at the start of another tour, I received some bad news. Before our bass player neighbour Maurice Salvat married Gill, he'd been diagnosed with testicular cancer and one ball had been removed. Ever since, we had frequently heard him being sick in the mornings. On one particular day, after I had departed for Manchester, Maurice and Gill had had a blazing row and Gill had stormed out to her mother in Kingsbury. After she'd left, Liz heard Maurice being violently sick and thought it sounded much worse than usual.

He came downstairs and she thought his face looked very grey. He was feeling terrible and asked her to call the doctor. Gill phoned and told him to stop being so silly, but Liz managed to convince her of the severity of the situation and she headed home. Dr Wills arrived at Braemar Avenue and called an ambulance. Gill arrived in time to go with him but Maurice was dead on arrival at the hospital from a massive brain haemorrhage. I was still on tour so I missed the funeral, but this tragedy drew the three of us closer together and Gill was always with us whenever I was at home.

Graham now turned up with a Mellotron. Not content with playing alto, organ and bass, he was all set to become an orchestra on his own. At the push of a button, he had a string section at his fingertips, a brass ensemble with trombones, flutes – anything. I asked how much it was, because I was somewhat concerned about our budget. Graham assured me that it was absolutely free and that the manufacturers were letting him use it for promotional purposes.

The Mellotron was little bigger than the Hammond, but it took four people to carry it. After a gig in Sheffield that entailed hauling the monster up three flights of steel stairway, I began to seriously dislike the bloody thing. Yes, it added some great sounds but by Christ it was heavy. Then we had the additional problem of getting it aboard the Dormobile, so we traded that in for a big, dark-green Bedford with a six-cylinder engine. We all immediately took to this new machine. It could do very close to 100mph on the motorways and was comfortable and roomy: a very impressive bandwagon.

One day, Liz, Gill and I were sitting in the living room, drinking tea while little Nettie played around our feet. The phone rang and it was Manfred Mann.

'Hey, Manfred, how're you doing?' I asked, somewhat surprised by the call.

'Well,' he answered, 'I want to ask you what you think about Jack.'

'Oh! I'd say for sure that he's the best bass player around.'

'No, that's not what I meant. I mean, like, how is he to work with?'

I got the picture. 'Oh, Jack's fine. He's a great bloke. Really cool,' I lied. Shit! I still really liked Jack and I wasn't going to screw it up for him.

'Thanks, Ginge,' said Manfred. 'We were going to ask him to join the band, only I wanted to check with you first.'

'No, Manfred, Jack's no problem. You're getting a great bass player.'

He thanked me and hung up.

'Jack's joining Manfred Mann,' I told the girls. 'I only hope he behaves himself!'

Acid – LSD – was becoming increasingly popular and both Liz and Gill had expressed an interest in trying some. So I got three little squares of blotting paper from Graham in return for a couple of jacks. Graham had started to mess about with smack, which caused me some concern. I was getting off it as he was getting on and he would beg me to shoot up for him, which was not an easy task as Graham's arms were very large and his veins so small and deep that he was unable to hit one himself.

After we had put little Nettie to bed, Liz, Gill and I swallowed our little squares with a cup of tea. We sat together arm in arm and awaited the result with some excitement. Soon incredible light shows commenced in our heads and we felt a sense of wonderment. We looked at each other with new eyes, seeing things that we had never noticed before. Our three bodies became as one as a deep sense of love engulfed us. Liz expressed a desire to paint and went off to the kitchen. Gill gazed at me and her dark eyes glowed magically. We exchanged a kiss of ecstatic passion, the like of which I had never experienced before. I had had many affairs with the chicks on the road, but now I felt something enormous and amazing. I realised that I was deeply in love with Gill. She was a goddess in my eyes.

Liz returned and we embraced. I was in love with two women, more in love than I would ever be again. We spent the whole night kissing so tenderly that sex was not a part of it. Finally we slept, our bodies entwined as one. I awoke as sunlight came streaming through the window and a happy little Nettie was in the room. I looked at the two beautiful women in wonder, but my mind was in such turmoil that I just had to go into the bathroom and have a fix. I used twice my normal dose to calm the disturbance in my head. The relaxing blinds came down and dulled my overwhelming feelings of passion. I was detached and could face life again. As we drank our morning tea, I realised that I now had a good reason to get straight: Liz and Gill. 'Take it slow,' I told myself.

Just before Christmas 1965, the band set off on a tour of the north. I had picked up my ever-dwindling script that included five Physeptone tablets and we headed off in the big green Bedford for Carlisle, just south of the Scottish border. As we edged northwards, it began to snow and, by the time we reached the M6, a full-scale blizzard had engulfed us.

We pulled into a garage to fill up with petrol and learned the M6 was impassable and huge trucks were stranded across the carriageways. As we drank our tea, I got the maps out. 'Not to worry, chaps!' I said with confidence. 'We can circumnavigate the M6 by taking Kirkstone Pass.' This was a little-used scenic route through the Lake District and would bring us out at Carlisle. Manfred was an extremely good driver, well used to dealing with snowy conditions and we successfully navigated our way through the winter wonderland of the snowbound pass. We arrived at the gig to be greeted by a very surprised yet happy promoter. 'Wow!' he exclaimed. 'I was sure that you wouldn't make it!'

After we set up, Graham, accompanied as usual by his girlfriend Diane, came up to me in the dressing room with a small dark bottle of clear liquid – concentrated LSD. Just one drop was a big turn-on and he proposed swapping one for a jack. I attempted to explain I was cutting down and that every jack was precious. But Graham could be very persuasive and I capitulated, still somewhat against my will. I prepared his fix and added a drop of the acid. It took an age to find a vein despite the tight tourniquet. Then I had a fix of one-and-a-half jacks, a dob of precious cocaine and a drop of acid. It was the freakiest cocktail of all time and the gig that night was sensational.

Meanwhile, it continued to snow and we got a phone call from Robert Masters informing us that the other two gigs in Sheffield and Leeds had been cancelled as the Pennines were impassable. There was nothing to do but drive home. Graham conned me out of another jack and we repeated the performance of the previous night. I was convinced that I would be home the next day so I was not unduly concerned. Then Graham told us that he and Diane were going back by train, leaving the rest of us to cope with the road. Rillo immediately expressed his concern that we weren't going to make it.

'Oh, come on, Rillo,' I said, brimming with confidence and flying on my cocktail. 'We made it here OK, didn't we? Where's your spirit of adventure?'

It was late afternoon when we finally set off and as we approached Kirkstone Pass, the snow-covered mountains glowed ominously crimson in the setting sun. As darkness descended and we began our ascent of the pass, it began to snow again, but this time the snow was drifting alarmingly. Manfred had his foot down hard as we twisted and turned our way upwards in the darkness, but then we rounded a curve, ploughed into a huge snowdrift and stopped. 'Not to worry!' I said, grabbing a shovel and intent on digging us out.

I opened the door and jumped out of the warmth of the Bedford into a howling, freezing blizzard. An icy blast of wind hit me at more than 80mph and I couldn't breathe. My confidence evaporated in an instant. 'You'll have to back it out!' I shouted to Manfred, but soon the Bedford's rear end was wedged against a dry stone wall. We were well and truly stuck at the top of the pass. Below us in the distance we could just make out the lights of a small village that we had passed miles back. There was nothing for it but to leave the bus and hike back down to get help. Rillo was very worried about Mike because this was the first time that he had ever seen snow or experienced very cold weather. We set off down the winding pass with Manfred in the lead, me following and Dick and Mike bringing up the rear.

Visibility was practically zero and soon Manfred disappeared from view. I looked back and could see no sign of Rillo and Mike. I was alone in this freezing blizzard and, for the first time in my life, I panicked. I literally wet myself in fear and, as a terrible feeling of dread filled my being, I started crying. It took all my will power to pull myself together and continue in the teeth of that terrible blizzard. I cursed the acid, knowing it was a major contributor to my panic and resolved that from now on I would treat it with more respect.

It was an arduous task. The urine froze in my trousers and my face and hair were encrusted with ice. Just putting one foot in front of the other was difficult, but somehow I kept going. After what seemed an age, I reached the little village of stone cottages. Manfred was standing in the doorway of the village pub, seemingly the only habitation with lights glowing. I urgently banged on the door and an attractive young woman came into the hall and peered out. She didn't look too pleased to see us.

'I'm sorry, but we're closed.'

'No, no, you don't understand – we're in trouble!' I blurted out.

As the woman reluctantly opened the door, I could see a beautiful fire glowing in the large fireplace in the bar and I rushed towards it. Then an ice-covered Mike and Rillo straggled in and we congregated round the fire, thankful for the warmth. The woman got on the phone and within half an hour a large snowplough arrived, manned by two sturdy locals covered in yellow weatherproof clothing, their faces only just visible underneath their hoods. We all clambered on to the back but the blizzard had increased in intensity and we hadn't got more than halfway up the pass when the snowplough got stuck. The locals then suggested we hike up to the bus to get our bags while they turned the snowplough round, because we were in for a stay in Cumbria.

Manfred, Rillo and I struggled back up the pass, assuming Mike had stayed with the locals. We reached the bus, which by now was just a white mound, entirely covered in snow. We heaved the door open with some difficulty, retrieved our bags and set off back to the snowplough. If it was hard work before, it was even worse with the weight of our suitcases. I was at the rear of the party and once again I lost sight of the others in the howling blizzard.

As I rounded a bend, a mighty gust of wind knocked me off my feet, depositing me into a deep snowdrift. Suddenly, all was quiet – no more moaning wind and snow, just total silence. Peace! I lay there for a while just thankful to be out of hell, but then my brain started working. Wait a minute – this is how people die! I began digging frantically, dragged myself out of the drift with my suitcase and staggered on down towards the pass. I bumped into something and I noticed a pair of feet facing me in the snow.

'Art thou knackered, lad?' enquired one of the locals cheerfully.

Mike Falana was now sitting in the cab of the snowplough. The locals had heard a moan from the back of the vehicle and found poor Mike frozen stiff and unable to move. His shining black face was now blue with cold.

We returned to the pub to thaw out. It was one of the worst blizzards in history and all the phone lines were down. The landlady had been alone in the pub and now had to cope with four uninvited guests. She was very good about it, gave us nice clean rooms and opened the bar. We spent the rest of the evening drinking and playing darts with our rescue team. One of them turned out to be the local bobby. I was amazed at how much beer he could put away and still seem perfectly sober.

We spent the next two days in that pleasant little place, surrounded by the snow-covered peaks and breathtaking scenery of the Lake District. I was now regretting having shared my stuff with Graham, because after two days the rest was gone and I was left only with my Physeptone pills.

Finally, the weather cleared sufficiently for the snowplough to make it up to our bus and dig it out. The phone lines were restored and I was able to tell a frantic Liz that we were OK. The bus was retrieved, we were ready to drive home and our policeman friend explained that the only navigable route back involved driving round the coast road, which would add a lot of extra miles to our journey. We thanked our dear landlady for her hospitality and insisted on paying her, leaving her surprised and grateful.

We set off happily for home believing that our troubles were over. I was down to my last four Physeptones and felt confident and very relieved that I'd make it. We were finally back on good roads and had just a few miles to go before we hit the M1. Manfred had now been driving for many hours and was totally exhausted. As I was the only other member of our crew that could actually drive at all, I volunteered to take over for a while so that he could have a rest. Manfred and Mike were asleep in the back and Rillington sat beside me in the passenger seat, as the powerful bus roared down the old A5. We were doing 70mph as we rounded a bend to be confronted by a huge truck coming the other way, attempting to overtake a little Austin van on a double white line.

'Christ!' said Rillo under his breath.

I had to react very quickly and the two inside wheels went on to the verge to avoid the van. *Bonk*! We hit a large obstruction that turned out to be a concrete drain duct, lifting the two wheels clear off the ground so were travelling at an angle of 45 degrees. I struggled desperately to keep the bus upright but we went over, slid along the verge and came to a surprisingly gentle halt. Rillington was lying on top of me and Mike was running around inside unable to fathom out where the door was! Rillo slid the door open above his head and we all clambered out. Thankfully, the only injury was to Rillo, who had cut his nose on the steering wheel.

'You'd better say you were driving,' I told Manfred.

The police arrived with a large crane which lifted the Bedford back on to its wheels. It had sustained only a few scratches down one side and within the hour we were back on the road. I was able to get to Lady Frankau and obtain a prescription on Christmas Eve.

Manfred then informed us that he wanted to go back to Austria and our first gig after Christmas was in High Wycombe. The Bedford got stuck in the mud afterwards and a large happy-looking fellow helped us to push it out. We got talking and he told me that he was looking for a job, so I asked him if he fancied being a roadie. He looked at me as if he didn't believe I was serious. When I assured him that I was, he informed me that he'd been 'in nick' for GBH. I appreciated his honesty.

'OK. We'll give it a go,' I said. 'But stay out of trouble, all right?'

And so Mick Turner joined our crew. He showed up on time for the next gig in Southend and proved to be helpful, strong and willing. Humping our gear was right up his street.

Midway through this gig we were to witness the sorry end of the Mellotron. It had been working fine the previous night, but it would seem that the accident with the van had wrought some damage to this incredibly delicate instrument. The bass was wailing, but then vibrated strangely. It got progressively slower and slower before dying completely. We opened the cabinet and its insides gushed all over the stage, a huge pile of tangled tapes spreading forlornly around the dead instrument. The Mellotron had had a brief yet glorious career, but it came as no surprise to discover that Graham's tale of getting it for free was not the truth. He, or rather we, owed Mellotron several thousand pounds.

Hammersmith was the first gig that we had played anywhere near Shepherd's Bush since the debacle that led to my broken nose. We were in the middle of our set when two heavies mysteriously appeared out of the dressing room behind the stage and ran towards us. One ran straight up to Graham and punched him in the face.

'He hit me! He hit me!' shouted a startled Bond.

But these heavies had made a serious blunder, because Mick had brought an assistant along for the evening. Pursued closely by Mick and his friend Pete Joliffe, the heavies disappeared. We didn't see them again, but back in the dressing room there was a lot of claret about. They had broken in through the window and had obviously departed by the same route after Mick and Pete had 'taken care' of them, as Mick put it with a wicked grin. Our roadies bore no obvious sign of injury, so we assumed that the blood had other origins.

In the spring of 1966, we played a big university gig. We shared the bill with the Yardbirds and the Long John Baldry Band. Also working with 'Ada' Baldry was a young Rod Stewart, who used to hang out with us a bit. We were always pulling his leg about singing with Ada and kidding him that he must be a 'poofdah'. One day we were standing outside the hall smoking some grass when a very young-looking guy happened along.

He smiled at me and said, 'I *know* you, Baker! You ain't really a hard nut at all.'

I liked him immediately and he hung around with us for a while.

Shortly after this, we were doing a gig at the Flamingo when this same young fellow turned up with a guitar and asked if he could sit in. Shit! This guy could really play and his name was Eric Clapton.

By now, Graham's personality was getting into the realms of very weird indeed. Before every gig, he would sit cross-legged on the floor in the back of the Bedford with Diane, both robed in the most flamboyant garments, with incense burning and a pack of tarot cards laid out before them. Gone now was the happy musician – he had been replaced by a strange, unsmiling mystic. I had been running the band's affairs for three years, but I had always talked things over with the others, particularly Graham. Yet whenever I approached him now he'd say, 'Oh, you handle it, Ginge,' almost as if he had no interest in the matter.

I was very nearly straight again by this time, having got down to just half a grain of smack a day, but Graham was getting increasingly into it and taking acid. I stopped giving him smack or helping him shoot him up as we were quite clearly travelling in opposite directions. He was still playing great music but we were no longer friends; whereas Rillo, Mike and I would hang out together, Graham was never with us now, except on stage. Back at home, I'd been sharing my concerns with Liz and Gill and I wondered if perhaps I ought now to try to get my own thing together. They both agreed that this was a wonderful idea.

I got a phone call from Stigwood, who asked me to meet him at the office as he had something important that he wanted to discuss.

He told me that The Who had a problem and needed a new B-side for their latest single. He thought that a song I had written for *There's a Bond Between Us* that hadn't been used would be ideal and that if I let them have it I would be paid £1,500. As this was an absolute fortune to me, I agreed with alacrity. Stigwood would be taking his ten per cent commission and I ended up with £1,350. Wow! I was knocked out!

The Who were friendly rivals and our paths had often crossed at university gigs. To me, Pete Townshend was a proper musician rather than just a pop person and I had a lot of respect for him. I also had a lot of time for Moonie, he was one of the funniest people you could hope to meet.

They took the song, which was retitled 'Waltz for a Pig', and I went out and took my driving test. I had taken only one lesson the day before, yet I passed easily. Armed with my new driving licence, I repaired to the dealership of Charles Follett in Berkeley Square and bought a brand-new grey Rover 2000. I drove it home and parked it proudly outside the maisonette in Braemar Avenue for Liz and Gill to admire. I would be off heroin within a month, I had the prospect of forming a new band to look forward to and I felt I was on the brink of a new and successful life supported by the two women that I loved. I was a very happy camper.

Chapter Seven

Cream

I was totally unaware that Eric was already well known. All I knew was that I liked his playing. I phoned John Mayall's manager, John Gunnell, to find out where they were on. He told me they were doing a gig in Oxford, so Liz and I drove down there in the new Rover. As we walked into the gig, we saw Eric sitting on stage looking as bored as hell and it wasn't really happening at all.

In the interval, I went backstage to see him and he said, 'Oh, man, you must come and play.'

So I sat in for a number and it completely exploded; the whole thing was really together and the audience were dancing and jumping about.

After the gig I said to Eric, 'I'm getting a band together, would you be interested?' And he said, 'Yes,' immediately.

Now we come to some discrepancies that occur in Eric's book. I don't recall giving him a lift home, but he was very keen to do it and as far as I'm concerned we had this discussion in the dressing room.

We started talking about a bass player and Eric mentioned Jack.

I thought, Oh, Jesus, no! But I said that I'd 'think about it'. On reflection, I should've said 'no' straight away, but I didn't and Liz and I discussed the situation on the way home. Liz really liked Jack (she still does) and so I agreed that I would give him another chance. I said to her that I hoped he'd learned his lesson after what had happened with Graham.

The next day, I drove over to Jack's flat and his wife Janet was very surprised to see me when she opened the door. According to Jack, I went there to eat 'humble pie', which is absolute crap. We sat down, had a cup of tea together and I said, 'I'm getting a band together with Eric, let's let bygones be bygones and try again,' and Jack immediately agreed to do it.

When I got home, I phoned Eric and told him that Jack was on board. Then I told Chris Welch of the *Melody Maker* what I'd done and he published it in the next issue.

It was only a short article, but the day it came out I got a phone call from Jack giving me loads of abuse. This was because he hadn't even told Manfred Mann that he was leaving the band. He was unaware of the phone conversation I'd had with Manfred prior to Jack joining him: he didn't know that I could have blown his gig but didn't. Jack was shouting away at me and I just thought, Oh my God, here we go again. He obviously hadn't cottoned on and hasn't to this day. He believes that Eric had insisted that he be in the band, which is completely untrue.

When the three of us got together for our first rehearsal at Braemar Avenue, we played some stuff that was totally magic musically. It was so great it was unbelievable! After a few numbers, we became aware there were a whole load of kids from over the Welsh Harp reservoir, standing up on the bank, dancing and really enjoying the music. And that's where the name Cream came from. Eric said simply, 'Yeah, man, we're the cream,' and we felt very close. Two days later, I came home from a shopping trip to find Eric sitting on my doorstep!

My last gig with the GBO was in Bradford. I was still on Physeptone and had decided to take my smart new car up there. I wanted to get straight back afterwards and I remembered hearing some guy say that the car was so good it could drive itself home. On the way, I almost stopped at the Watford Gap services but, as it was only another 30 miles, I decided to carry on. Two miles after that, though, I became aware that my car was bouncing along rather alarmingly. I had dozed off and was now on the central reservation on two wheels and doing 100mph. I noticed a large triangular roadwork sign, which I swerved to avoid. But it was muddy and wet, so I hit it and that knocked the window out. I banged my head against the side of the car and found I was heading straight towards an old Rover 90 travelling in the same direction.

If the driver had been aware of me, he could have moved, but he wasn't and I hit the front of his car, the wheels locked and I did a U-turn right across the motorway in between two trucks coming the other way. Eventually, I came to rest on the grass verge facing north and got out. Amazingly, I only had a small cut on my little finger but the car was wrecked. 'How the hell did you get out of that?' said one of the lorry drivers.

The Rover 90 had gone off the road and into a ditch and all four passengers were injured. I was taken to the police station and owned up to falling asleep at the wheel. I phoned Liz and she went mad. But I got another car on the insurance, exactly the same model, only in white this time.

The first proper Cream rehearsal was at St Ann's Church Hall, Brondesbury, and *Melody Maker* journalist Chris Welch was there to witness it. I spoke to Robert Masters and we agreed to take over all the gigs I'd been doing with Graham. I told him that we should ask for £45 now instead of £40. 'Oh no, man,' he said. 'Nobody will go for it.'

'Just do it,' I replied and all the promoters agreed, except for the Black Prince in Bexley, so we never played there.

Stigwood was supportive, but he had absolutely no idea what he'd got. For some reason known only to him, he was expending most of his energy trying to launch his pet project, the Bee Gees, with a media blitz that included a full-page advert in the *Melody Maker*. So there he was, sinking all his money into the Brothers Gibb, who weren't doing that well in 1966, when with minimal publicity he suddenly had a major happening on his hands with Cream.

We had months of work booked up and every gig was incredible. We'd filled all these places with the GBO, but now there were more people outside than there were inside! It took off like a fucking rocket. At a gig at Ewell Technical College, all the girls were sitting on their boyfriends' shoulders and the grounds outside were overflowing with people still trying to gain entrance.

One show up in Hawick got a bit hairy when the enormous throng appeared to divide into two warring factions, intent on a re-run of the Battle of Culloden Moor as we played. A glass shattered on Jack's mike, cutting his face, so I lobbed one straight back and it exploded on the far wall.

We did a gig in Crawley for a guy I'd known in the GBO days called Bob Potter. It went really well and he asked us to do another set, so I said, 'OK, but for another £45.' He refused, so I got Mick to pack up my drums and off I went.

However, unbeknown to me, Jack had convinced Eric to do another set with just the two of them. He also convinced Eric that they should get rid of me because I wouldn't do another set. Eric changed his mind and we had another meeting in which Jack insisted that the band be co-operative. Everything I'd done had always been co-operative anyway, so I said, 'Yeah, that's fine, but that means everything's co-operative including the writing, because we're all working on the material together.'

'No, no, the writing can't be co-operative,' said Jack.

Stigwood wanted us to make our first single but it turned out to be the worst record Cream ever made. I'd known Pete Brown for years, since the poetry and jazz gigs at St Pancras Town Hall, and I'd really enjoyed some of his stuff. I invited him to come and write some songs with us, 'us' being the operative word! We were at a studio in Haverstock Hill and, although Pete had never met Jack or Eric before, they went off together and wrote 'Wrapping Paper'. It was the most awful song and had absolutely nothing to do with what Cream was doing, but it got released. When it was, I was amazed to see that the songwriting was credited to Bruce and Brown – no mention of Eric or me. There was a big row, but I *had* promised I would never hit Jack again, though I often had to resort to drinking loads of alcohol instead in order to finish the session.

Eric and I became close friends. We went on a shopping spree in the Portobello Road and found a clothing emporium called I Was Lord Kitchener's Valet, where we purchased military coats decorated with frogging. Decked out in our 19th-century garb, 'the Colonel and the Captain' went on the tube and thoroughly enjoyed the stares we got from the rush-hour commuters. We went to many 'funny' shops then and this is when I found the old fur SS hat from the Russian Front complete with skull and crossbones that I wore on the cover of our first album, *Fresh Cream*.

Eric was then living in a spartan flat in Ladbroke Grove with a bed in one corner, a few wooden tea chests and a couple of gas rings. One morning, I turned up there to find him standing over the gas rings making French toast while the Beach Boys blasted out from his record player. Our talk turned to heroin and I advised him never to get involved with it.

We went to a studio in South Molton Street to finish recording *Fresh Cream* and Eric brought a lot of old blues records with him. A happy, mad and Goons-type atmosphere prevailed. On one occasion, we tipped a box of cornflakes over Stigwood's head, then Eric got hold of some scissors and cut his tie off. There was great humour within the band and they were happy times.

During these early days of Cream's phenomenal success, Stigwood brought financial wizard David Shaw into the company. He was the epitome of a London finance whiz; smartly dressed in a dark-grey suit with tie and shiny shoes, dark wavy hair and a very upper-class accent. I don't remember exactly when the following occurred, but it transpired that the Robert Stigwood Organisation was in serious financial difficulties (having spent too much money trying to make the Bee Gees a big hit and failing miserably). I was summoned to Stigwood's office and David Shaw was present. He asked me if they could borrow £40,000 of Cream money to avert imminent disaster, promising that they would pay it back very soon. I agreed, although at the time neither Eric nor Jack was aware of this. Stigwood escaped going bankrupt and the money was eventually paid back.

We were invited to the Cromwellian Club when it opened. I turned up with a tasty chick on each arm and a large bouncer stopped me from entering (but he let the chicks in). I told the thug who I was and that I'd been invited, but after standing about in the entrance for ten minutes I got rather cross. 'Tell you what,' I said to the bouncer. 'You can stick your club up your arse,' and I turned to walk out.

I was immediately set upon by the bouncer and two of his cronies.

Just as I went backwards down the entrance step, David Shaw arrived. 'Ginger! They were hitting you!' he exclaimed.

Eric was already inside enjoying a drink, and when someone told him, 'Ginger's got a big problem at the door,' Eric replied, 'Oh, Ginger's always got problems,' and continued drinking.

Next day, I received a very apologetic phone call from the club owner, who invited me back. I was greeted by the same bouncer who was also very apologetic. They had a drum kit in the club and I played a solo. Now I was everyone's buddy – such is life.

Fresh Cream was released in December 1966 in the US on Ahmet Ertegun's Atlantic Records label and climbed to No 39, remaining in the Top 200 for 92 weeks. In Britain, it came out on Stigwood's Reaction label and got to No 6. One critic tried to pigeonhole our sound as 'Mississippi Delta blues meets heavy-duty British rock'.

Stigwood broached the idea of a US tour, but we still had loads of gigs booked at £45 a time and in my opinion we had no option but to do them. It was getting ludicrous, though. The gigs were coming in so fast we could barely keep up with the demand. Robert Masters booked us nine gigs in a single week and it proved to be one too many. On the Saturday we had two gigs and on the Sunday we were due to play a television pilot, followed by yet another gig in Cheltenham. The TV show, produced by Tony Palmer, overran and we were well behind schedule when we finally left for the gig.

Jack and I were in my new white Rover 2000, and Ben Palmer and Eric followed behind in the Austin Westminster. Not far from Cheltenham there had been an accident and a long queue of cars was backed up along the road, but the police had not yet put up a warning sign. I was speeding along and hit a car totally blocking the road at the foot of a steep hill. I knocked it right out of the way, and then the Westminster came skidding past before coming to a stop 20 yards further down the road. We didn't make the gig and my second Rover went off to the repair shop. I told Masters never to book more than one gig in a day again.

I'd been playing the Vic O Brien kit I'd got when I was first married and over time I'd customised it. This was in the days when I used to lap my own drum heads. I'd decided I wanted a narrow bass drum with an 11-inch shell and I got the idea of using Perspex because it's shiny inside and out. So I bought the Perspex from a shop in Highbury, I bevelled the two edges and heated it up on a little gas ring. After that, I bent it round, then bolted the bevelled bits together and put the hoops over it.

The thing with the double bass drum came about when Moonie and I saw Sam Woodyard playing at a Duke Ellington gig in London. All the drummers who played with Duke had two bass drums. Sam Woodyard did one incredible little fill that I still use today; it's a simple triplet thing, but it sounded amazing and really blew me away. I decided then and there that I'd get a double bass drum kit because I knew I had good feet and I told Moonie. I approached Ludwig and asked them to make me the new kit, which was going to take a while to come through. Meanwhile, Moonie went to Premier, where he bought two kits and put them together. So he was the first person to have one, but he got the idea from me.

I did have a serious falling out with another drummer, Buddy Rich, who was notoriously outspoken. Initially, we liked each other and he had paid me a helluva lot of compliments. When asked if there were any good young drummers around, he answered, 'Yeah, Ginger Baker's the only young drummer I've heard who is any good.'

At the same time, I had got very friendly with Dusty Springfield, who was a very nice girl. Dusty did a show in Las Vegas with the Buddy Rich Band and Buddy was very unkind to her – as only drummers like me, Phil Seamen and Elvin Jones can be – about her singing. She was destroyed, couldn't go back on stage and I got very annoyed with him about it.

Asked about Buddy in an interview, I later said, 'He plays OK, but he's only got one foot,' which was absolutely true. He had incredibly fast hands, but, if he did anything very technical, his left foot would stop going altogether. That was how the feud started, although his daughter was a huge fan of mine. I saw him again many years later and I never went over to speak to him, something

I'm very sorry about now because he died soon afterwards. He was a brilliant drummer for sure, but not in the class of Max Roach, Art Blakey or Elvin Jones who always impressed me. But they were all black – a lot of white drummers just don't understand Africa.

I also faced some criticism myself. The *News of the World* tabloid newspaper had just come up with a mostly fabricated article about the so-called 'drug parties' of the music world, and my picture appeared alongside Mick Jagger. I thought, My mum's going to read this! I really wanted to sue, but Brian Epstein – the Beatles' manager who had joined up with Stigwood in January 1967 – came up to me, and said, 'Listen, Ginge, this is a nine-day wonder. Soon everyone will have forgotten all about it. The best thing to do is talk to your mum obviously, but just ignore it.'

It was good advice. Mick Jagger tried to sue and the paper set him up for the infamous Redlands drugs bust.

Stigwood set up a tour of the States for $3,000 a gig, which wasn't that much money, and sent us over to play the *Murray the K* show at New York's RKO Theatre in March 1967. We were met at the airport by the biggest Cadillac limousine we'd ever clapped eyes on, with both the English and Scottish flags on the bonnet. Our bill included The Who, Wilson Pickett and Simon and Garfunkel. There were four shows a day, each scheduled to run 80 minutes, although the first show, featuring us and The Who, overran by more than an hour. Each band had been asked to play just three numbers, but the instrumentals of both bands stretched far beyond the usual three- or four-minute pop single.

Off stage, the two British bands bantered obscenities and displayed a good-natured rivalry. At one point, Murray came in when I was lying under the table with a bottle of Bacardi. 'How the hell is *he* going to be able to play?' he asked. But I did.

Wilson Pickett's drummer, Buddy Miles, was a rotund, jovial black guy who was always beaming at me from the wings. We got together and he suggested that we repair to a club on 47th Street that he knew. We went down there and jammed together, Buddy and I alternating on drums and Jack and Wilson's bass player swapping bottom lines. It got so intense that I broke a pedal and Buddy went through a snare drum. The uptight club owner demanded we pay for the damage.

The most enjoyable part of the *Murray the K* experience for Eric came on the last night, when we got hold of these 14-pound bags of flour and some eggs to cause havoc on stage. Murray got wind of it and threatened not to pay us if we went ahead with the stunt, so we spread it all round the dressing rooms instead. Pete Townshend's shower overflowed and he ended up swimming fully clothed in a foot of water.

We also met Ahmet Ertegun, who proposed that we go into Atlantic Studios at 1841 Broadway to record our second album before embarking on a tour of the States in August. It would be completely insane but it would also make the band.

Chapter Eight
Disraeli Gears

Staying at New York's Gorham Hotel, Cream began recording at Atlantic Studios on what would be *Disraeli Gears*. It marked the first time we worked with producer Felix Pappalardi, and engineer Tom Dowd, who impressed me immediately with his musical knowledge.

The first thing we laid down was 'Lawdy Mama', one of the old blues numbers that Eric had brought in. We got the track down and Felix asked if he could write some lyrics for it. We agreed to this and the result was 'Strange Brew'. But Jack got pissed off because in one part he was playing a minor chord and Felix's vocal was in a major key. I thought he was insane because it's common to have major and minor together in blues. Then Felix wanted Eric to sing and again Jack wasn't happy about this. He kept turning up with new numbers and Eric and I would say, 'Great, but at the moment we're working on such and such,' and Jack would say, 'No, but I've got this number all finished,' throw a tantrum and get his stuff played.

One day, Jack came in with a riff that seemed pretty fast, so I said, 'Oh, man, that's terrible – let's slow it down.' I put a backwards drum beat on the riff, it immediately went *wow*! and became 'Sunshine of Your Love'. I decided we needed a middle eight and that was Eric's contribution. I had a big row with Jack about getting Eric's name on the writing and I honestly thought that maybe Eric would say, 'Well, you changed the whole thing over,' and that I would get an acknowledgement, but I didn't get anything at all. My reaction to all this stress was to walk out of the studio and go down to the bar.

I wanted to drink as many Bacardi and Cokes as possible until my wanting to kill Jack mood had dissipated. As I drank, I noticed that an anti-Vietnam War demonstration was being broadcast on their TV and the bar was full of pro-war red-necks, who were loudly denigrating the protesters. I just lost it and shouted, 'War? You bastards have never seen war!' before storming out.

I reluctantly returned to the studio and played but I was extremely unhappy about it and I still am to this day. The same thing would happen later with 'White Room'. The whole intro was in 4/4 time and I turned it into a 5/4 bolero, which immediately made the song, but not even a thank you for that. Jack has even said *he* wrote the intro in 5/4, which is absolutely untrue. Many of Cream's arrangements were down to me, including the earlier 'Spoonful'.

What I could see even at that time was that Jack Bruce and Pete Brown were earning more money out of Cream than Eric and I (they still do). Yet I had formed the band and I had wanted Eric. I got Jack in by trying to be nice and all of a sudden he and Pete Brown had taken over the writing. I thought this was incredibly unfair and still do.

And things did not improve. Initially, Jack and I were sharing a suite of rooms at the Gorham and one night I met a very beautiful coloured girl called Jenny Dean and a black girl named Emeretta. No sooner had I got them back to the hotel when Jack turned up and hit on the prettiest one straight away! He dragged her off to his room and I had to lie there with Emeretta and listen to Jack enjoying himself. I wasn't amused.

The next day, our families and partners arrived. Model Charlotte Martin was with Eric, Jack's wife Janet and Liz and Nettie also came.

A couple of days later, Jack knocked on my door looking pale. 'Bloody hell,' he said, 'I've caught a dose!' What with all the rows we'd been having, then him pinching the best-looking chick, I wasn't sorry for him. In fact, I lay down on my bed and laughed – there was a God after all!

To cap it all, Jack made some objectionable comment in the car one night. When we got out, I went up to the plate-glass hotel door and went to kick it open in anger. I was wearing a pair of long, fringed, American Indian moccasin boots and, although I meant to connect with the door bar, I missed and kicked the glass instead. The whole thing disintegrated into a thousand pieces! I walked straight through it and stormed up to my room only partially aware of the stunned silence that greeted my entrance. I was completely unharmed, though I had to pay for the damage, of course.

Eric always got upset when these rows happened because he couldn't understand what was going on. Jack could be very charming and he and Eric were close musically. I felt that Jack thought of me as merely 'the drummer' and not an integral part of the team.

On the plus side of being the drummer, I was invited to the Zildjan factory in Boston to choose some cymbals. I had one of their big K cymbals that I'd been using for years, a very old one that had cracked on the bell. So I picked out a 22-inch riveted cymbal and hi-hat cymbals, all of which I still use today. I didn't pay a penny for them and it was the same thing with Ludwig drums, which was pretty amazing.

We returned to England to finish our gigging commitment and to sort out the album cover. I'd retained an interest in art, having enjoyed my early work on the graphics scene. I dug the abstract work of artists such as Jackson Pollock and produced quite a few canvases. I was also really into sculpture, having started off with wood carving before becoming interested in using fibreglass resin to create unusual designs. I made a few of these, one being a tall wire frame, overlaid with fibreglass resin. In the centre was a vacuum-cleaner motor which revolved and emitted sparks. We also did our own posters. Eric had designed one that on casual viewing looked like an exclamation mark, but was in fact the head of a penis with semen coming out of it. Robert Masters had a silk-screen press, which Liz and I set up in the garden shed in Braemar Avenue and that's where we produced the very first Cream posters, in striking yellow on blue, in 1966.

Psychedelia was very big during 1967 and its influence could be seen everywhere. Martin Sharpe did the cover art for *Disraeli Gears* and he introduced us to The Fool, Simon and Marijke and third member Barry Finch. They were Dutch artists who made far-out furniture and did designs with psychedelic colour patterns. They made me trousers cut especially short to avoid getting entangled with the bass drum pedals and a purple velvet cloak with a rainbow lining. I had several pairs of patterned, multi-coloured leather boots and they also decorated my bass drum with a Cream logo.

I wore the purple cloak for the photo shoot for the *Disraeli Gears* cover, which was done on Ben Nevis in Scotland with the photographer Bob Whittaker. Eric's girlfriend Charlotte and Jack's wife Janet came along, and it was a beautiful day to be driving through the Scottish scenery. Most of us were on acid, then someone remarked that all we needed was to encounter a piper and, as we rounded a bend, there in front of us was a guy in full Highland rig playing the bagpipes. It was a magic moment and the atmosphere continued to feel very special.

On the path up to the summit of Ben Nevis, we were doing silly things for the camera, like jumping across ravines – a picture of me doing that made it on to the album artwork. Jack walked back down with the girls, but Eric, Bob and I decided to race the 4,409 feet down to a snack bar on wheels we'd noticed at the bottom. It was a wild race, ignoring the path and going straight down the side of the mountain – how we didn't get killed I'll never know. We were travelling fast and making huge leaps from rock to rock, rolling with the momentum in our mad rush. I can't remember if it was Eric or I who won with Bob some way behind, but it was totally insane considering we were all on acid and marijuana. The only damage was to the heel of one of Eric's leather boots.

It was in London that the name of the album came up. We were in the back of the Austin Westminster with roadie Mick Turner at the wheel when Eric mentioned he was planning on getting a racing bike. We began to talk technicalities when Mick suddenly turned round and said, 'You mean one of those with Disraeli gears.' (He meant Derailler gears.)

At this, we all collapsed on the floor of the car, rolling about with laughter. 'That's it!' we said. 'That's the name of the album!'

Before our US tour, which was scheduled to begin in August 1967, I found the time to take my family on holiday to Mexico City, but I met a guy at the hotel who had a guest house on a cliff by the sea in Acapulco and so we flew down there for the rest of our stay. We set up our towels and relaxed on the white sands of beautiful Gloria beach, where we admired the towering surf.

Soon a group of Mexicans approached and started discussing football. They were delighted to discover we were English because they didn't think much of the Americans. Then they beckoned me into the bush and offered me a sack full of dope! I purchased a little and we all went back to the beach for a smoke when a Yank appeared across the sand saying that he heard of some dope for sale. In what seemed like no time at all, the Mexicans produced a large glass of orange juice which they proceeded to pass round. Before my turn arrived, one of them caught my eye and privately indicated that I should only take a very small sip ('*polcino*'). The Yank, however, took a massive swig. I soon realised that this juice was heavily laced with acid. The American collapsed and we left him there, but I felt wonderful.

One day, our host invited us to a bullfight and, when Liz refused, I decided I'd go anyway. There were huge queues of cars outside, but the police just waved us through, which I thought was interesting. We took our seats in the arena and in the first fight the bull gored the matador so I stood up and cheered – I wasn't terribly impressed with it. When we left, we were again ushered right through the heavy traffic. That was when I discovered the guy I'd been staying with was the chief of police for Acapulco – and I'd been smoking all that dope in his place!

In August, Cream kicked off the US tour with two weeks at the Fillmore in San Francisco. It has to be said that our attitude was: 'Now we're going to show these Yanks how to play!' and this we promptly did to an alarming degree. Nobody could believe it and the crowd worship was phenomenal. Carlos Santana sat in with us one night and he's been a friend ever since.

One day the notorious Owsley Stanley – a diminutive, bespectacled, professor-like character – turned up at our hotel with a tank of nitrous oxide and loads of different-coloured acid pills that he made himself. Eric had great fun phoning people up and talking in a Donald Duck voice while we laughed uncontrollably. Owsley appeared at every gig with different-shaped and coloured pills that he had manufactured specially to commemorate each occasion in a government-sponsored lab at Berkeley University. Allegedly, the Yanks were experimenting with LSD then, the idea being to distribute it into an enemy water supply. At least, that was Owsley's story!

This was the height of Flower Power and there were hippies everywhere singing in the road and all over the place. Eric had a friend in Sausalito who had a 65-foot yacht and he invited us both for a short trip. Shortly after we got on board, Eric and I climbed up to the top of the mast and sat high above the deck, on either side of the cross piece, rolling joints for most of the jaunt. Everyone seemed to be on acid and weed; it was crazy and the chicks were extraordinary. When we did the Fillmore and stayed at the Sausalito Inn, there were queues of them knocking on the door. One would come in and end up in bed pretty quickly, then she would leave and within literally five minutes there would be another one waiting there. It was quite an experience.

When we were in Boston in September, I got pulled by a gorgeous little chick, but I had some sort of STD at the time, so we only had oral sex. At about five o'clock in the morning, I drove her home to her parents' house. Her dad opened the door; he was a straight-laced American chap and he wasn't very friendly! 'Bloody hell, man, what's your problem?' I asked. 'I got her home safe, didn't I?'

The next time we were in Boston, I met Eric in the lift with a chick and he looked really embarrassed; it took me a while to realise it was the same girl. He thought I'd be upset, but there were so many women.

It *was* a hard tour, but it was a great success and it was a very happy time within the band. *Disraeli Gears* came out and flew up the charts; we were now a 'super group' and earning money – much to Stigwood's total amazement!

One downer, however, was in late August, when we learned of

Brian Epstein's death. With typical British gallows humour, we joked that Stigwood had 'bumped him off'! But, in fact, it was a very sad and unfortunate mixture of downers and alcohol that claimed his life.

We returned to London in November and I took advantage of my new financial status to go back to Charles Follett's car dealership, where he showed me a Jensen FF and explained the Ferguson four-wheel drive formula to me: the prop shaft for the front wheels went in the opposite direction to the one for the back wheels. The set-up was ingenious; it was a pretty cool car, so I bought my first one in silver grey, registration WOY 64G.

Despite our phenomenal success, problems continued to surface. When we were touring (which was most of the time), things began to go very awry with the Marshall speakers. They were incredibly powerful and both Jack and Eric had begun with one or two and then progressed to three or four. This heralded the start of what I now think of as 'the volume period' and was the beginning of the end for my hearing. It got incredibly painful for me and at one time in London Eric had something like ten stacks and ended the show with them all feeding back.

Liz had become pregnant that summer and around the same time my burgeoning romance with Gill came to an abrupt end. Gill and I were on the sofa kissing (which was quite normal), while Liz was making the tea, but when she returned she went totally apeshit. At first, I didn't think she was serious but Gill went back upstairs and Liz said, 'We've got to move.'

I didn't have time to look for a new place then because things were very hectic, with three dates in the States before Christmas as well as a BBC TV show in London. I had actually been straight for nine months, but at that show that I met a friend called Alan Branscombe, a great guy and a brilliant multi-instrumentalist in the BBC band, who looked very straight but was a heavy junkie. I was feeling so down with everything that was going on that I said, 'Alan, can you turn me on?'

'Yeah, sure,' he replied and arranged to meet me in the toilets.

He passed me a syringe under the door. 'This is only a small one, see me again after the gig and I'll give you a good one,' he said.

I got so stoned that you can see it on the film!

After the session, we met in the toilets again as agreed. Alan passed me another syringe-full, said, 'See you,' and was gone. I hit the vein and had only got about a quarter of the stuff in when I experienced an enormous rush. Fucking hell, I thought. But I managed to pull it out and shoot the rest of the stuff down the toilet. I don't remember any more, but apparently Jack and Janet found me on the floor outside the cubicle door and I woke up in hospital.

I was being violently sick but the bloke in the next bed was making a hell of a racket. I called the nurse to complain about this 'fucking guy making all this noise!' only to be informed that in fact these loud and strangled exclamations were his death throes. Anyway, come the morning I discharged myself because I felt OK by then. But if I'd have done that whole syringe it would've been goodbye me. Alan was at that time using so much heroin and cocaine that he was actually under observation by the medical profession, because they couldn't believe that one person could be using that much stuff, but he was!

Chapter Nine
Cream 1968

In February 1968, we flew out to Atlantic Studios to record *Wheels of Fire*. We went on Pan Am and I sat in first class and chatted up the gorgeous-looking Norwegian head stewardess, whose name was Signe. I asked if she fancied coming on the tour we had planned for after we'd done the album and, of course, she said, 'Yes.'

But while we were in the studio recording, photographer Linda Eastman was following me around with her camera, so I invited her to come on the road with us for the gig. On the last day of the recording, Signe called and said, 'I've got six days off and I'd like to take you up on your offer.'

She came round to the hotel, all made up and dressed in a suit and high heels, and we jumped into bed together. Then I took her to the studio and Linda's face was a picture. Signe came on the tour instead of Linda and then went back to Pan Am.

In effect, our tour had lasted for a whole year, with just brief breaks now and then in which we'd get a chance to go home. So I was somewhere in the States on 20 February when Mum rang to say my daughter Leda had been born in the bedroom at Braemar Avenue.

The constant gigging meant our performances weren't always that good, though we'd get on stage to a standing ovation before we'd even played a note. It was also a terrible strain on my hearing. Jack always turned the volume up as loud as he could and then Eric would have to turn up to hear himself and I was sitting in the middle of this. Eric stopped playing once and stood in front of me and then I stopped playing and we both stood there with our arms folded while Jack was in front of these huge speakers, playing away. He was totally unaware for two choruses that we'd stopped.

That was where all that *smash*, *bash* drumming came about. I was hitting my drums that hard because I was trying to hear what I was playing. It was totally insane. I'd get into the hotel after a gig and my ears would be making terrible noises. One night I stood up from my drums and went over to Jack. 'Can you turn down a bit?' I asked, but he shouted over to Eric, 'He asked me to turn down, man!' and made a big thing about it.

After the gig, Eric came up to me and said, 'I've had enough of this.'

And I said, 'I'll tell you what – so have I.'

We decided there and then that it was to be the last tour. Jack was unaware of this because it was Eric's and my decision and we went and told Stigwood (who didn't believe us).

It wasn't just the relentless noise of it all. There had been an article in *Rolling Stone* written by the guy who would one day become Bruce Springsteen's manager. This piece had a terrible effect on Eric, because up until then he had thought that it was the hippest magazine in the world. The article slated Cream from here to China, singling out Eric's 'long, boring, cliché-ridden guitar solos'. Would Cream stand the test of time? the article wondered. The writer thought we wouldn't. Well, we proved them wrong!

It was on this tour I met Janis Joplin. I saw her in the dressing room one night, ran over and simulated sex with her for a joke. We ended up getting on really well. She wasn't attractive but she was a lot of fun. I caught up with her again at a concert in London. I was straight again at this time but Janis called me and asked me to pick up some smack for her. I said, 'Janis, I'm not using at the moment,' but she didn't believe me and got really pissed off; it was a shame.

For some reason, I also had a reputation for being a speed freak, which was totally untrue. The only time I took it was when I was in Detroit once in the khazi and some bloke laid out a line and said, 'Here you are, Ginge,' so I did it, but I'd never really used it before. I was supposed to be driving to the next gig in Chicago, but I went the wrong way and ended up going right round Lake Michigan and only got to the gig just in time to get on stage! It was terrible stuff.

Briefly back in England, I finally got around to moving. I'd got hold of a land shark called Alex Moss, a very old friend, who found us a lovely detached house in Harrow for £10,350. We moved in the summer of 1968 and initiated a crazy 1960s decorating scheme. The walls were different colours, we had Persian carpets and antique furniture and we went all the way down to Somerset to collect a 17th-century dining table and chairs. It was an adventure in itself just to be able to go out and buy things.

I'd picked up an interest in tropical fish from my stepfather, so I decided to have a huge tank running along one wall of the living room. This involved people crawling about under the floor space to jack up the joists in order to take the weight of it. I had loads of varieties of fish and fed them live daphnia and tubifex worms. In the garden, I built a four-foot-deep concrete pond complete with a bridge and stocked it with carp.

Stigwood had also just bought a huge Jacobean mansion, the Old Barn, out in Stanmore, which is close to Harrow, and there he entertained on a lavish scale. In the 70s, we played all-star football there on Sunday afternoons. On one occasion, Stigwood rang me in a panic and I rushed over to find him wearing a fencing helmet, brandishing a tennis racquet and chasing a bat round the house. In the end someone opened a window and it flapped out.

Chapter Ten

Goodbye Cream

By the time we recorded *Goodbye Cream* in the States, our producer Felix Pappalardi had finally woken up to the fact that it wasn't just Jack who wrote songs. Each of us got a track: Jack had 'Doing That Scrapyard Thing', I had 'What a Bringdown' and Eric did 'Badge', which was really great stuff.

One day I was driving back while the others did the 'Badge' vocals when I became aware of a car following me. I turned right, turned left, went round the block and sure enough the suspicious car was still behind me, so I put my foot down and he was on my tail. The band had separate apartments at the Beverly Hills Hotel, and in mine was coke, smack and works (I'd got right back into my heroin and cocaine habit). But I'd forgotten this as I drove up in front of the hotel, stood on the brakes, jumped out of the car, went up to this other car and said, 'What's your fucking game?'

The guy inside calmly pulled down his sun visor, which said 'Police'!

I laughed and said, 'Fuck me! I thought you were a villain or something, 'cos I've got a lot of money on me.' I spoke in my best cockney accent as I explained what I was doing there.

He asked, 'Where's your ID?'

'What's ID?' I replied. So he elucidated and I said, 'It's in my room in the hotel, I'll go and get it for you if you like.'

'You realise you were doing 70 in a 40-limit zone?' he said.

'I was trying to lose you because I thought you were a gangster in your scruffy old car!' I replied and he was quite decent and let it go. But afterwards I thought, Fucking hell, if he'd come to my hotel room, then that would've been the end of that!

We returned to London to do the album cover. What was the photographer's name? He'll never forget mine! We had to wear silver suits, complete with top hats and canes. The cane I'd got just happened to be a sword stick with a big, long blade. The photographer was standing over by the wall and I threw the stick. It flew over his shoulder and embedded itself in the noticeboard behind him! He shit himself. He was unaware that I was well practised at knife throwing because I had a studio in the loft of my new house where I did my woodcarving. I could stick all my chisels into a piece of two-by-four from the other end of the room and I rarely missed.

Just before our farewell gig at the Albert Hall, I went to see my new Harley Street doctor, John Robertson. He was out, but I got another doctor to give me phial of morphine sulphate. (John Robertson became very helpful to me. If I got really down, he would give me a multi-vitamin shot that included a phial of morphine sulphate and this helped me enormously to carry on with life.)

I hated the Albert Hall gig. Although it didn't matter how well or how badly we played, there was always adulation and the crowd going mad, but the Albert Hall gig was pretty awful in my recollection. I didn't enjoy it at all. I just couldn't stand the volume and the last year of Cream damaged my ears permanently.

In March 1969, I did some tracks in the studio with Billy Preston and George Harrison. We were doing 'That's the Way God Planned It' when our roadie Mick Turner popped his head round the door to tell me that my son had just been born in the Avenue Road Clinic in St John's Wood. My friend Guy Warren, the master drummer from Ghana, also known as Kofi Ghanaba, was in town and so I called my son Kofi, meaning 'born on Friday'. I gave him the middle name Streatfield in honour of Pop.

One day, I was walking through Soho with Guy in his African robes, complete with large hat. As we passed a restaurant, I noticed my sister's first boyfriend, Arnold Clark. He had been to Cranwell and was a pilot in the RAF. It was a very odd meeting seeing him with his fellow officers, while I was with (as they would have thought) a crazily dressed African! I spent a lot of time with Guy in London and he gave me a set of drums as a present.

When Reading Festival came up, I asked Eric if he fancied doing it with Phil and I, and he agreed. It was just the two drummers with Eric and it's the best I've ever heard him play. Phil was really on song that night and the crowd went crazy. The film director Tony Palmer happened to be there and he said, 'We've got to get this on to TV.'

I knew right away that Eric wasn't going to go for that because it was a one-off enjoyment thing for him. So we arranged for Phil and I to do a televised drum duet.

I went to pick Phil up early in the morning from his flat in Kentish Town and I just couldn't wake him up. He'd taken a double dose of sleepers and was totally wasted and staggering about so I gave him a fix and then had one myself as well for good measure. We finally got over to the BBC studios at Shepherds Bush and set the drums up.

Halfway through the rehearsal, Phil nodded off and it soon

became apparent that he was not going to be capable of continuing. I ended up having to do the show on my own, and while I was playing I caught the eye of a chick in the audience. Her name was Germaine Greer, though I didn't know who she was. She later mentioned me in *her* book as 'a drummer with a morphine habit'. I think I took her back to designer Martin Sharpe's place in Chelsea and we got down to business.

Philly Joe Jones – who'd been the drummer in the classic Miles Davis quintet with John Coltrane back in the mid-1950s – had also caught the show, having been in town and after some smack. 'You really tell a story with your drums,' he told me, which coming from him was quite amazing.

Chapter Eleven
Blind Faith

When Cream folded, I got back into my drug habit big time, but Dr Robertson helped me get clean again by prescribing Physeptone. It is a good way to come off and I did it 29 times in all over a period of 21 years!

I was in limbo so I was hanging out a lot in the Speakeasy club in Soho or visiting Eric at Hurtwood Edge, his home in Surrey. One day he was on his way out when I arrived. He explained he was going over to Stevie Winwood's cottage, and asked if I wanted to come. We ended up having this incredible drive down country lanes to Stevie's place with Eric driving his Ferrari and me in my white Jensen FF. The lanes around Eric's house are very narrow and all of a sudden we came across one of those grass-verge-cutting machines blocking most of the road. I jammed on the Maxarets (anti-skid brakes) and squeezed past with a fag-paper's width to spare. Then I heard squealing behind me as the Ferrari very nearly piled into both the grass-cutting machine and my Jensen. We just laughed and raced on, ending up in a little lane which opened out into large, ploughed field.

As we got out of our vehicles, an old Land Rover bounced madly across the muddy field with Stevie at the wheel. We piled in and joined some of his friends in a little cottage that couldn't be seen from the road. A drum kit was already set up for a jam session and I really hit it off with Stevie musically. There is a magic with him – he's a jazzer and one of the best keyboard players I've ever worked with.

After that, I started going down to Stevie's quite regularly with Rick Grech, the former bass player with Family – he was pretty good and he could swing. Then Stigwood and Chris Blackmore (Island Records) got together and we decided to make a record at Olympic studios.

Denny Laine turned up in the studio on the first day and we got into a fantastic jam. It was really happening. I waved to Chris in the control room: 'Record this!'

I honestly thought that he'd twigged and we went on for five or ten minutes more.

When we'd finished, Chris's voice came over, 'Yeah, man; that was great, can you do it again so we can record it!'

I exploded! Chris was then removed from the recording of the album and Jimmy Miller came in. The *Blind Faith* album was brilliant, one of the best. For the cover we decided we wanted to feature a young chick holding a winged phallus. Sleeve artist Bob Seiderman found a nubile girl on the tube (we used her younger sister on the cover) and the jeweller Mikko Milligan fashioned a silver aeroplane that he presented to me after the shoot. This cover caused a bit controversy in the States so we had to change it for the American market.

Unfortunately, there was a lot of hype surrounding the band and I became a bit puzzled by Eric's behaviour, especially at the Hyde Park gig in June 1969. On the DVD, you can see that the crowd was huge, but Eric seemed very laidback and strange about it. It turned out that he didn't really want me in the band. It was because I got on so well with Stevie that I was there. Eric says in his book that he was upset because he thought I'd picked up some smack, although at this time I was straight.

The record did extremely well and a tour was booked. It was a strange musical mixture, with other bands on the bill such as Nazareth and Delany and Bonnie, with whom Eric started hanging out almost immediately.

In Detroit, I met up with Signe the air hostess once more and together we picked up a big bag of coke before heading to a party.

We were hurtling down the road in a hired supercar when we passed a state trooper lurking in the bushes. He put his lights on and came tearing out after us. I pulled into a lay-by and Signe shit herself, knowing that there was not only coke in the car but all the usual paraphernalia for smack in my briefcase in the boot. The trooper asked for my ID, so I got my briefcase out and casually left it open as I pulled out my passport and the big *Blind Faith* book that I had in there. He was impressed and waved us on our way, saying that his kids had been to one of the shows.

We arrived at the island on which the party was being held and hooked up with Stevie and Rick, but Eric was nowhere to be seen. He was off with Delaney and Bonnie as usual. At one point on the tour, he said to me, 'Delaney and Bonnie should be the top act,' and I thought, You're fucking crazy! Delaney and Bonnie were a reasonably good white band trying to play black music. I thought they were OK, but Eric was totally enamoured with them and I couldn't understand it. For virtually the whole tour, the only time we saw Eric was when we were on stage.

There was an extraordinary happening when we did a gig in Phoenix. The police gave Eric a hard time when he went outside for a smoke. They had this 'We don't want you fucking long-haired hippies here' attitude. We played on a small, rickety stage and everyone joined us on it for the finale. Bonnie somehow managed to fall over the edge and Delaney jumped off to help her, but he was immediately attacked by the local thug police department in their black jack boots. Afterwards, I phoned the police to complain and was told, 'Oh, I'll tell the sergeant when he comes in.' I wanted a lieutenant but I couldn't get anywhere at all.

At Madison Square Garden, I broke a drum stick. As it rolled to the front of the stage, a kid ran from the front of the audience to grab it and a copper immediately started wading into him. I totally forgot where I was for a moment and with a handful of rings I rushed up and boshed the copper on the head, which caused a complete riot the like of which you've never seen. The whole place erupted and getting off stage was a nightmare. I had the crowd on one side trying to rescue me from the police and the police on the other side trying to pull me away from the crowd. It was horrendous the things that started happening on this tour. The same thing happened again out in the Midwest somewhere. A kid ran up to the stage and a copper started beating him up. I saw all this while I was playing and so I bounced a drum stick off his head! *Bosh*! Only the audience saw it and, by the time he turned round, I'd got another stick. The crowd were delighted with this one.

According to the media, I also managed to 'die' on this tour! One day, I was driving along the coastal 101 route from LA to San Francisco with three tasty chicks in a Shelby Cobra. The radio announcer said, 'We've stopped the music to tell you that Blind Faith drummer Ginger Baker has just been found dead from an overdose of heroin in his hotel room.'

I looked round at the chicks and thought, Fucking hell! I must be in heaven!

Chris Blackwell joined us for part of the tour. He had bought a Pontiac Firebird in which we drove to a gig in Canada. I had all my drugs in my new super-8 camera box and when we went through customs I nonchalantly showed them the box and they didn't even take the camera out. When we got back in the car to drive off, I handed Chris the box and grinned. 'Look what we just brought through customs, Chris!'

'Oh no! Don't show me!' he exclaimed.

I was totally fucked up again by then and at one time I even had a policeman delivering me smack. The guy I was getting my cocaine from in LA was the first person they arrested as a suspect in the Sharon Tate murders because he'd gone up to deliver the coke for her party. He phoned me up as soon as he knew they were after him. 'Fucking hell, man, I've just seen my name on the television!'

'The best thing to do is give yourself up,' was my reply.

'Yeah, but I've got all this coke still. Will you take it off me?' (Very cheap it was too!)

Later, he left a message, calling himself Ben Franklin, and came round to the hotel. Then I went to see Stevie in his hotel and told him all about it. He was amazed. 'Ginger, how *do* you get into these things?' he asked.

I'd taken all the coke off the guy, so I had a pile of it. Then the guy with the smack kept not turning up and so now I had no heroin but a huge amount of cocaine. It was August, it was my birthday and we were flying to a gig in Texas. When we emerged from the hotel to go to the airport, there were plain-clothes police in all the doorways, due to the murders. It was very odd.

I had a fix of coke on the plane and fucked it up. There was claret all over the toilet and red dots everywhere, it was a total nightmare. We got to Texas, did the gig, then the entire audience stood up and sang 'Happy Birthday'. When I got back to the hotel, I realised that, if I kept all this coke, I was going to kill myself and I tipped the lot down the toilet. My family were due to come out soon and so I phoned Liz and asked her to bring me out some Physeptone.

Liz, Gill and the kids flew into Utah and so high was my social standing that the local sheriff drove me down to meet them. We took in all the sights including the amazing Bonneville Salt Flats, where all the land speed record attempts were held.

My family witnessed yet another unsettling incident that occurred at the Fontaine Hotel in LA. I drove into the parking lot underneath, where the smooth concrete surface caused the tyres to squeal as I drove slowly in. I parked the car and we all got out. As we walked to the lift, I was confronted by a guy in Bermuda shorts who flashed his police badge and got his gun out. He berated me for driving too fast and, when I attempted to explain, he shouted, 'You're a fucking loudmouth!' before whacking me on the shoulder with his pistol, ignoring the fact I was holding a baby in a carrycot!

The two women kept close and pulled me out of it and we let the copper go up first. It was very close and if I'd attacked him he would have shot me for sure. Again I made complaints to the police and again I got absolutely nowhere. I remembered that earlier incident with my cousin in London and I thought how different things were between the two countries. At least in England your complaints are listened to.

The last date of the Blind Faith tour was in Honolulu. I was coming off once more and decided to stay on for a family holiday that I documented with the Super-8 camera. We booked into a smart hotel on Waikiki Beach, and then Gill and Nettie decided to commit suicide! We were driving around in a hired shiny, white Ford Convertible when we found a beautiful little beach with a waterfall flowing into the sea beside it.

Liz and I were sitting on the sand because I wasn't feeling too good and Nettie and Gill were swimming. Suddenly, Liz said, 'Oh look! They're waving,' and, sure enough, we could see these two little figures waving at us. We were happily waving back to them, when Liz exclaimed, 'Wait a minute, they're in trouble!' and, throwing her clothes off, she dashed into the sea! Only then did we realise that the waterfall caused a huge out-tow.

Liz got out to them very quickly 'cos she was going with the current. She managed to get Nettie and started back. She was making progress, but I could see she was really struggling; so I ran into the water, but I've never been a good swimmer and I knew if I went too far I could easily drown. I waded out as far as I could and whenever a wave came I jumped up to keep my head clear of the water. Liz was getting nearer and I shouted, 'Come on, come on!' I grabbed hold of her hand. She was exhausted by now, but Gill was still out there so I ran down the beach, where I approached a local guy and pointed to Gill. He swam out immediately but instead of swimming straight back to the shore, he swam parallel to it for a few hundred yards and then came in. The current where we were was deadly, but being local he knew the best place to get in. That was quite an adventure.

I soon realised that there was more heroin on Hawaii than anywhere else in the world! Bodies were coming in from Vietnam packed full of the stuff. Everywhere you looked there it was. This is not the place to be coming off! I thought, so we decided to fly over to Jamaica and checked into an exclusive resort called Tryal near Montego Bay.

Finally, I was coming off and it was an amazing holiday. I had a very good time and got well into scuba diving. The family went out in a glass-bottomed boat and marvelled at the creatures beneath. We had our own chalet with a swimming pool and 18-month-old Leda charged in, disappearing under the water. I rushed in and dragged her out, spluttering but quite unperturbed. 'I fwimmed to the bottom!' she crowed triumphantly.

The car I'd hired wasn't too good so I decided that I would fly my Jensen out for the last week of my stay there. This, of course, was total insanity! It took about a week to arrive and when it did it had no windscreen wipers because the FBI had been all over it. They thought I was importing marijuana into Jamaica, which seems a bit odd as the place was awash with it already. I went with a friend to Kingston to collect it, where I managed to get some tiny Land Rover wipers and we drove back along the undulating roads in the darkness towards Montego Bay. Suddenly from out of the limited vision afforded by my dipped headlights, a huge cow appeared in front of me! I just about managed to stop, but the bonnet went under the cow, which then somersaulted, leaving a gentle dent in the hood. What a disaster!

Nettie was due back at school, so she and Gill flew home to England as I stood and watched the tail lights of the jet disappear into the sky. Liz and I had decided to return by sea with the two smaller children and the car. By now, I had bought a lot of grass and commissioned nine hollowed-out wood carvings into which the dope was carefully packed. The carvings were then sealed up with wood glue and packed, ready to leave with the rest of our stuff.

At Morgan's Harbour, I went to book on to the boat. I got into a row with the dockers when they banged the gate into the car, then I noticed a guy standing nearby holding a briefcase with 'captain' written on it. Another American approached me and began talking about dope. Is this guy a copper? I thought, because he looked like a one. At his invitation, Liz and I went down to his cabin, where he took several little packets of dope from his wardrobe. We lit up a joint. 'I thought you were old bill,' I said.

'No,' he replied with a laugh and pointed to a large yacht moored nearby.

He explained that his movie-location company was really a cover for marijuana smuggling and the whole yacht was packed with dope on its way to the States. His accomplice, 'the captain', was one of his pilots who'd just returned from Cuba, where he'd been forced down for accidentally trespassing in their airspace. They thought he was an American spy but when they found out he'd got dope on board they let him go!

The next day, we boarded the 7,000-ton *Prince Der Nederlands*. The car was safely loaded and we had first-class cabins. A Jamaican policeman arrived with his gun, but he just said, 'I hear you had some trouble earlier and I've come to make sure you come to no harm.' He then presented us with a bottle of Appleton rum and came to our cabin for a chat, which I found to be a very nice little touch.

Shortly after this, we discovered that, although the ship was going to London, it was first bound for Curacao, Aruba and then Paramaribo, where we went for a walk round and I filmed the town and scenery. I bought two drums that exactly matched the Ghanaian ones I'd got from Guy Warren, and then we got some local guy so stoned that he just collapsed. They obviously didn't come across it very often out there.

Next stop was the Azores, where they had to unload the car to get something else on. They came to ask me to move it, but I was drunk as a skunk, absolutely out of my wig. I managed to knock over a huge pile of pallets that were stacked at the side, clipping the bottom one so the whole lot went over behind the car, so I got another dent in it.

What a trip! At one point they thought I'd gone overboard because they couldn't find me after I'd climbed up into the crow's nest and passed out. One day I wore a T-shirt with a swastika on it; this did cause some offence, but I explained, 'Look, we won the war and so we're entitled to wear the flag of the enemy.'

On the last night before we docked at Southampton, we were sitting at the captain's table when he began his speech, 'Ladies and gentlemen... and Mr Baker.'

At Southampton, a customs official remarked that with all the drums and masks we'd bought we'd probably been ripped off, without being aware that several of them were full of Jamaican ganja. Once back home, I chiselled them open, removed the dope then squashed them back together and placed them on a shelf, where they stood for years. I did up a nice little bag and drove down to Stevie's with the present.

I hadn't been in touch with anybody for ten weeks, so that's when I discovered that Blind Faith was no more. Stevie told me that Eric was getting a band together with Delaney and Bonnie (which horrified me) and that he was thinking of getting Traffic back together. So I said I'd like to get a big band together for just a couple of gigs, and Stevie and Chris Wood (Traffic's sax and flute player) agreed to do it.

Chapter Twelve
Air Force

Ginger Baker's Air Force started in 1970 with Jeanette Jacobs on vocals, Denny Laine on guitar and vocals, Rick Grech on bass and violin, Harold McNair on sax and flute, Graham Bond on alto, Chris Wood on sax and flute, Phil Seamen on drums, Steve Winwood on organ and vocals, and Remi Kabaka doing percussion. Harold was very ill at this time, but I didn't know this until some time later. We booked gigs at Birmingham Town Hall and the Albert Hall on 12 and 15 January.

We'd been rehearsing for a long time and the first gig went down well, apart from the police arriving to arrest Graham for non-payment of maintenance. As they were taking him away, Denny picked up a pack of Rothmans and said, 'Here, Graham, some fags for you!' Then we all settled down for a smoke and Denny suddenly went, 'Oh fuck!' He'd given Graham the pack filled with a large block of hash! Luckily, the police had let him take them into the cell with him. He realised the mistake and over the next hour he managed to eat the entire stash.

Graham was still floating along with a lazy smile on his face by the time of the London gig three days later. The gig included some pretty amazing stuff, especially the encore which was recorded, released in France and was No 1 for a few weeks. The success prompted 'the office' (RSO) to appear in the form of Robin Turner, saying, 'Oh, man, you've gotta keep this on, it's really fucking great...' Blah, blah, blah...

I said, 'Look, I only did it for two gigs just to do it. Stevie can't do it, Chris Wood can't do it.' I didn't think Rick could do it. But in the end we got Bud Beadle to replace Chris and brought some other people in; it wasn't the same but we went on a successful and crazy tour. Once we stopped at a shop in the Lake District and got hold of all these pies and eggs. Harold was always very straight and didn't take part in silly antics, but somebody thought it would be a great idea to squash an egg on his head and soon cream cakes and eggs started flying all over the coach. By the time we arrived at our hotel in Edinburgh, we were plastered in the stuff.

I flew to the States to bring over a singer called Eleanor Barooshian for the new line-up. At the address I was given, the door was opened by a naked chick with very obviously silicone tits sticking out a mile. I found Eleanor but she'd taken God knows how many downers, so I had to carry her on to the plane. We flew back and I installed her in my secret flat in Fulham (which was pretty cool and filled with interesting air force books). Now I had both Eleanor and Jeanette – who was Chris's girlfriend – staying there. I got very involved with both girls. Jeanette was very tasty and one night when they were both staying over at Chris's place she phoned to say he was out on the road. Did I fancy coming over? So I did and was right in the middle of this crazy threesome when there was a knock on the door. We took no notice and carried on. When I left the next morning, I found Chris sitting outside in the passage. I felt terrible about this, really very bad.

Chris and Jeanette then got very fucked up and Graham brought his new wife Diane Stewart in as singer. I had a drummer friend called Chris Elkington, to whom I'd given my Perspex kit. He had gone off to Tanzania and left his wife and kids behind and I knew them quite well, so I asked his wife if she'd like to come on our Scandinavian tour. There was no kind of sexual relationship with her at all: I just thought she'd like the trip. But Eleanor got severely pissed off and came on stage completely out of it, falling over backwards with her legs in the air. I was so annoyed that I left her in the hotel and we did the next part of the trip without her.

It was that same year I met the great jazz drummer Elvin Jones. I was a big fan but we'd got into a slanging match in the press when I'd said I preferred his playing with Coltrane and he retorted that I should be fired off on a rocket for my 'delusions of grandeur'! After that, I threw out a challenge that we should have a drum battle and when he accepted it was reported in the *Melody Maker* of October 1970. It was a fantastic event and we became good friends.

Eric and I were still friendly and we had a bet as to who would be the first to screw all the waitresses in the Speakeasy. I won it. The waitresses in the Speakeasy *were* pretty amazing. A girl called Aliki Ashman was the most difficult to pull, so I got her in the band first and after a few weeks I managed to get her to fall in love with me. I was staying at her flat on one of the main roads into town and we happened to walk out on to the street just as Liz drove past in her Mini Cooper S. She spotted me and we ended up having an incredible car chase through the narrow streets, when I nearly ran Liz over. She went seriously apeshit and bad things started happening at home, so I collected the kids from school and took them down to my mum's where I thought they'd be safe. But the next day 12 policemen arrived in police cars to take them back. Why they needed all those police for my mum I fail to understand, but Liz got the kids back.

We did a gig in France, where Phil was in such a terrible state that he couldn't get served because they thought he was already drunk. I had to buy one for him. Later, when we launched into the first number, the PA went off, so we went into a drum thing until it came on again. But the same thing happened about three times and I got really pissed off. I went storming round backstage and kicked out at one of the big speaker stacks in anger, accidentally knocking it over and squashing a guy behind the stage who ended up in hospital. I met him several years later and he said, 'How did you know it was me?' It turned out that he had been unplugging the PA.

The night after one of my regular Sunday football sessions playing for the Robert Stigwood Wanderers, someone backed into my Jensen and knocked the handle into the door. Liz went into forensic mode and discovered some bits of broken back light on the ground fitted the neighbour's car. She knocked on his door and there was much shouting as she threatened to report him for drunk driving.

A few days later, I was leaving for a gig in Germany with Air Force when four policemen turned up in a van. 'Is this where the party is, Ginge?' they asked.

'What party is that?'

'Is this your car?'

'Yeah.'

He reached inside and picked up my football kit bag. 'Is this yours?' he asked. As usual, I'd left a bit of dope in it.

'Oh, for fuck's sake!' I said. The guy over the road had got his own back on the off-chance of me having some gear. 'Jesus Christ, I'm just off to a gig in Germany right now.'

One of the police got in my car and I followed the others to the Wembley cop shop and bailed myself. Then I sped to the airport.

'You're late!' said Colin Heathcote, the pilot.

'I know,' I answered. 'I just got busted!'

The story of my bust got into all the papers and Nettie was asked to leave Heathfields, the private school she attended in Harrow. For such a tiny amount of dope it was ridiculous.

The flight was turbulent and I arrived in pouring rain some distance from the gig on the Isle of Femar. A Merc appeared to pick me up and, as we turned up at the gate, a guy appeared briefly from behind the post then crouched down in fear. It was like a gangster movie, with gunshots and ricochets going on. It transpired that the German Hells Angels had hijacked the gig and taken all the gate money, resulting in a huge running gun battle between them and the security guards. We decided to get out of this pronto and return to the hotel where I met up with Jimi Hendrix (who was also on the bill).

We spoke to the promoter and agreed to play that afternoon instead.

As soon as we came on stage the rain stopped and as soon as we went off it started again, which was really quite amazing. The postscript to this incident is that I think the promoter got killed later when the Hells Angels returned for a rematch.

We travelled on to Düsseldorf, where we did the soundcheck and repaired to the local pub. We were in high spirits and Denny, Graham, his wife Diane, Aliki (from the Speakeasy) and I sang 'Aiko Biaye' from our album, to the annoyance of a bloke sitting nearby who asked us to stop. This we did for a while, but then resumed our singing. Then another guy came over and called Diane a 'black bitch' so it all went off. There followed an enormous brawl in which a bearded guy confronted me and I smashed my litre tankard across his face. Denny was standing on the tables, jumping from one to the other, punching people as he went past. Someone grabbed me from behind and tried to drag me out. I went limp until we got to some steps leading outside, when I grabbed his legs and he went down headfirst. Scrambling to his feet, he punched Aliki in the face. I went crazy, wrapping my arm round his neck and running his head into a car. The next thing I heard was Graham telling everybody that he'd got a black belt in judo and that it had all 'got to stop'!

The police arrived at our hotel later and took us back to the pub, where I've never seen so many damaged Germans in my life. I think we did very well. Only Aliki was slightly injured, with a cut mouth. I said to the policeman, 'Look! They hit my girlfriend. Are we supposed to sit and let that happen?' I explained that we had been defending the women.   That was that, but it *had* been quite enjoyable. It wasn't too long after this, though, that Jimi Hendrix died.

Chapter Thirteen

Hendrix

I first met Jimi Hendrix when Cream played at the London Polytechnic on Regent Street on 1 October 1966. Backstage, Jack said that Chas Chandler had brought along this great Yank guitar player who wanted to sit in with us. I wasn't keen on this idea to say the least – in fact, I was totally against it. Things got a bit heated and we ended up having a row. Eric was our guitarist – what did we want another one for?

Finally (and with great reluctance on my part), it was agreed that we would let him sit in. I was not impressed. Yeah, he could play all right, although for me, Eric was still the best guitar player around. But what really got up my nose was Jimi's onstage cavorting. It was very much like Brian Jones with the Stones and definitely not Cream's thing. Eric just stood there and wailed, while Jimi was getting down on his knees and simulating oral sex on his axe. I was not into it.

Jimi, however, was always very friendly to me and I must say that I liked him a lot as a person. We often met on the club scene and in the Speakeasy, where we were involved in some very cool jamming sessions, in which Jimi played for the guys with no cavorting. I thought he sounded all the better for it. As Cream and the Jimi Hendrix Experience simultaneously rocketed spaceward, our paths were destined to cross many times.

When we played in Chicago, we were approached by two young chicks in the hotel lobby keen to make a business proposition. One was really good-looking and the other, who carried a briefcase, far less so. We sat around a table in the foyer and they asked if they could make plaster casts of our erect penises to manufacture and market 'pop star dildos'! The prettier of the two would give the star a helping hand while the other slapped on the wet plaster before things took a downward turn. I have to say that we were pretty amazed, though later the 'plaster-casters' attained legendary status. Their first samples were of Jimi and Noel Redding. Well, Noel's certainly had us all laughing, because his hard-on hadn't done too well when the cold plaster was applied and an odd, twisted little thing was the end result. Jimi's, on the other hand, had fared much better. I was glad to note that he was very similarly hung to me – not extraordinary at all but rather a good-sized normal.

Jimi's enormous appetite for gorgeous young chicks became very apparent at the Spalding Festival in Lincolnshire. Mitch Mitchell kept appearing with Polaroid snaps (the new hip thing) taken in their dressing room. Jimi was captured balling girls one after the other in a seemingly endless stream.

I was always in the Speakeasy and superstardom meant it was easy to pull, even though my long-held fantasies of a threesome with Liz and Gill were now long passed. One night, I met three stunning young ladies at the club, one a blonde Marilyn Monroe lookalike, another a great-looking coffee-coloured babe who was incredibly slender and the third a beautiful West Indian. They welcomed me to their table and we sat and chatted and laughed through several rounds of drinks.

'OK, so are you girls going to kidnap me?' I joked.

I was stunned beyond belief when they replied that that was indeed their intention. So we all piled into my Jensen FF and drove round to their flat on Brook Street. Two of the girls went off to get some drinks and I was left alone with the Monroe girl who began to kiss me. By the time the other girls returned, we were already making love and they immediately joined in. They took me to another planet and a place that I had never dreamed existed. To this day, it remains the most incredible sexual experience of my life. This was when I fulfilled the dream that I had always desired to share with Liz and Gill, where I felt that relationship could and should have led.

The West Indian girl had a baby to go home to, but the other two continued my education and performed the most wondrous acts upon me which took me to orgasm after orgasm, each one more fantastic than the last. I was truly in heaven. We'd get food in and then go back to making love. This went on for a couple of days, during which I kept hearing the girls talking about 'Jim'. Finally, during a brief lull in proceedings, I asked, 'Who's Jim?'

'Jimi Hendrix,' they replied.

Uh oh, I thought. But it was too late. The appearance of Mitch Mitchell terminated the wonderful tryst and I rather reluctantly drove back to Harrow, my whole body trembling and my heart still pounding from my experience. Not long afterwards, I saw the same girls again in the Speakeasy. The blonde came over to me and told me that Jimi was back.

Oh shit! I thought and my face must have betrayed the same because she said, 'Oh, yes, we told him about you!'

Suddenly, Jimi himself appeared in front of me but instead of punching my head in, as I fully expected him to, he grabbed my hand and smiled at me. 'Now we truly are friends,' his eyes said. I was both amazed and impressed, because here was a man unlike any that I had met before. We sat and drank together and I invited Jimi over to my house for dinner.

Jimi arrived on time with the beautiful blonde. Liz had cooked a sumptuous meal and we sat around our antique farmhouse table. Both Jimi and his girl were charming and intelligent conversation flowed. I felt that there was a real close feeling among us all. It had become clear to me that Jimi was not into smack, because it was common knowledge that I was using and he'd never mentioned it. We talked about getting some music down together, a project we agreed could be awesome.

We retired to the lounge with good French wine and smoked some dope. Nettie, who was then nine, spent hours sitting cosily on Jimi's lap and I got the strong impression that he felt utterly at home in a family setting. It was as if he had everything that I believed I desired and yet I had something that he envied – a family. When we eventually parted late that night, I knew for certain I had made a wonderful friend. Jimi was such a gentleman that to know him was to love him.

Just a few days after the dinner, I met a West Indian cat who had nicked two large Robinson's Marmalade-size jars of cocaine from Charing Cross Hospital. I bought one for £350. Sly and the Family Stone were in town staying at the Airport Inn and I drove round with Liz to say 'hello'. Sly's eyes nearly popped out of his head when he saw the jar of coke. I was also doing smack at this time and I went into the bathroom for a fix. Sly followed me in. He didn't do smack, he just said he wanted to be with me and he snorted a lot of coke. Mitch turned up and also admired the jar, which was still pretty full, although we'd all been at it. I told him about the other jar.

'Oh, man, Jimi'd really go for that,' he declared.

So Liz, Mitch, Sly and I all set off to find Jimi. We looked everywhere. He wasn't at his flat, he wasn't in the Speakeasy, nor was he in the Revolution. At 3am, we abandoned the search and returned home, not thinking any more of it.

The next morning, I awoke to discover that I'd done all my smack, so I repaired to the bathroom and fixed up a very large dob of the coke, somehow thinking this would be OK.

Unfortunately, as soon as I'd emptied the works into my arm, I realised that I'd fucked up and OD'd on coke. Strange noises were going on in my head. Uh-oh, crisis! I rushed out of the bathroom and yelled at Liz to get me down to Harley Street and into Doc Robertson's double quick. She immediately understood the urgency of the situation, so she bunged me unceremoniously into her Mini Cooper and sped off into town.

I was in a terrible state with awful stomach pains, rolling about in the foot well and moaning. As we got on to the A40, Liz realised with horror that the exhaust pipe had come adrift and begun to scrape along the ground. Hoping we wouldn't meet the police, she kept on driving until we reached Harley Street. I rushed into the consulting room and told John Robertson that the best cure was a large shot of morphine. It worked immediately and I was back to normal. Then he dropped the bombshell that Jimi was dead.

He explained that Jimi had been having a few drinks and some downers with a Swedish chick in a hotel. He'd been sick in the bed and she'd left to sleep in the other room, leaving him lying with his head in his own vomit, totally crashed out on the downers. In the morning, she had found Jimi (already long dead), panicked and phoned his manager. It was only then that help was called and, although they tried to unclog his airways, it was way too late. Jimi was cold. As I digested this information, John and Liz went out to the car where they tied the exhaust up with picture wire.

The irony to me is that had we found him first and he'd had that jar of coke he would most certainly not have fallen asleep. Jimi did not die of an overdose, but from inhaling his own vomit after a few downers and drinks – as simple as that. If he had been found in time, he would certainly have survived. The medical team did everything possible. He died because of a silly bird and simple misfortune.

I would just like to reiterate in the strongest possible terms that Jimi was not a junkie at all. Yes, he was getting high like everyone else at that time, but, to my knowledge, he didn't use smack and only did coke and other drugs occasionally. He liked his women too much and whether he would have become a junkie eventually, no one can say, but I don't think so.

Chapter Fourteen

Africa

So Jimi was dead, but I remained impressed with his attitude towards everything. We had a tour booked for Air Force in the States, but it was called off. Liz was behaving very oddly and, looking back now, I suppose I don't really blame her. To get away from it all, I decided to drive my white Jensen down to Ghana to see Guy Warren. I took Aliki with me as far as Marrakesh, where we waited at a hotel for a few days for Robin Turner to fly out with the various visas I needed for the countries I had to pass through to get to Ghana. Robin also decided that I needed a gun for the trip, so I bought a 9mm rifle and several boxes of ammunition. I put the gun under the floor of the boot with the spare wheel.

I left Aliki at the hotel and that was the last I saw of her for many years. I drove off across Morocco and into Algeria, heading south. I had got as far as In Salah when one of the bolts busted on the alternator. I got a local mechanic to fix it, but then a guy in a Land Rover turned up and asked, 'What the hell are you doing with that car down here?' The road was going to run out shortly and there were loads of rocks and ruts that the car was far too low to negotiate. 'You won't make it,' he added.

I had to drive back to Laghoaut anyway to get someone to re-tap the screw on the alternator, so I decided it would be best to drive back and then fly down. The engine was pinking like mad because the petrol was so bad, and I ran out of fuel at about 3am in the middle of nowhere. A battered old truck turned up with some young guys and I went with them with a jerry can to get some petrol. A nearby farmer had his own petrol pump so they got him out of bed. He wasn't that pleased, though, as my name was Baker, a very well-known name in Algeria, I was soon well accepted.

I was back on the road and driving through the Atlas Mountains at high speed by about 9am when I saw a very beautiful chick walking along the side of the road. I think I spent a bit too long looking at her, because all of a sudden I came to this huge S-bend with a massive drop off the side of the mountain. I managed to do a 180-degree turn and park the Jensen on an olive tree about ten feet down the cliff.

I got out and filmed it and, although the place had been deserted, there were suddenly hundreds of people there. The local copper told me that Allah had been looking after me, because if I hadn't got that tree then that would have been the end of everything; it was about 400 feet straight down to the bottom. They towed the car into the garage of the local village Aintemouchant, where I discovered that, due to a combination of incredible luck and incredible skill, I had only broken the wishbone on the front axle.

I booked into the local hotel but I had a very upset stomach and my mood wasn't improved by the water system, which was only working erratically. I complained to the guy at the garage, who was really nice and invited me to stay with his family at his beach house on stilts for the weekend. We rescued a drowning kid while I was there – I had my hair in a bun at this time, all matted and rasta-like (the kids called me 'madame/monsieur'), and the boy's face when I pulled him out of the water was quite a sight.

When the family went back to work on the Monday, my host gave me the keys and said, 'You can stay here until they come to pick your car up.'

I stayed there for about a week. I tried to go scuba diving but the sea was too cold. I did do a bit of cliff climbing, but halfway up I had one of those low blood pressure incidents and I had to stay up until it cleared.

After the warning about the condition of the roads, I decided to fly to Ghana, but the only way I could do this was via Paris. On the plane to France, I got chatting to the guy next to me. He was a Palestinian who began showing me photographs of the house that his family had lived in for generations, a place that was then officially in Israel. His family had been kicked out and he'd just finished a two-year stint in Algeria and had a permit to work two years in France. He was never given permanent status – the Wandering Jew had now been replaced by the Wandering Arab.

When I eventually arrived in Ghana, Guy Warren was there to meet me, dressed in his African robes. A huge crowd of Ghanaians greeted me with great joy and I got so carried away that I didn't follow procedure and go into the office to get my passport stamped. I stayed with Guy for about three weeks and we did a few drum things with the locals. It was very enjoyable and Guy's sister looked after me very well.

During this time, I kept hearing this music that I was really digging. I found out that it was coming out of Nigeria so I decided to go there. I went to the Nigerian Embassy to get a visa and they said, 'Don't you know there's a war going on in Nigeria? There's no way you can get there.'

I moved into a hotel in town and met a nice Ghanaian chick;

then I decided I would just get a plane to Nigeria anyway and I sent a telegram to Fela Kuti.

I'd known Fela for many years, since the Flamingo all-nighters in fact, when he used to play trumpet along with Remi Kebaka. Incidentally, when we'd done the Air Force gig in France, Remi had assured me that everything was 'cool' with his passport when I'd asked him. But when we flew back Remi was arrested at the airport because he'd overstayed his three-month visa in England by about a year-and-a-half. They promptly put him on the next plane back to Nigeria and he was still there so I sent him a telegram as well.

I walked to the airport with this new chick, and the big black guy there looked at me with intense hatred and said, 'What are you doing with my sister?'

'She's just come to see me off,' I replied.

He took my passport and said, 'You're going nowhere. Come with me.' He got his gun out and locked me in a small room.

I sat there thinking, What the fuck's going on? I'm under arrest. But after 20 minutes or so, the door opened and in comes this guy again, only this time with a big smile saying, 'Oh, man! Ginger Baker!' He'd found out who I was and how I'd got in without having my passport stamped. After that, he let his sister come on the little twin-engine prop plane to say goodbye.

It was roughly an hour's flight to Lagos and when I arrived it was pissing down with rain – which I soon discovered is normal for Lagos. They ran the steps up to the plane and I could see a whole line of soldiers, all with rifles on their shoulders and very smartly dressed. At the bottom of the steps was their captain, who said, 'Ginger Baker?' He saluted in slow motion, shook my hand and said, 'Welcome to Nigeria.' I went with him and they took my passport and told me to come back for it in two or three days.

This visit reminded me of being in New York in 1969, when I'd come across a black guy in the street collecting money for the conflict in Nigeria over Biafra and I'd donated everything that I had in my pocket. By the time I arrived in Nigeria, the conflict had mushroomed. Now I was meeting the other side, the Nigerian army, and I subsequently got to know some of their top brass rather well. Colonel Adenkule, known as The Black Scorpion, told me the Biafran leader was secretly being financed by the US and that was where my donation had gone. Exxon wanted oil, but so too did Shell UK and they were apparently covertly backing Nigeria. A photograph of the colonel with British Prime Minister Harold Wilson took pride of place on his mantelpiece. 'Nigeria's future is in your hands, Harold Wilson,' ran the caption. Artillery Major Adenihun told me that on an average day £10,000 worth of shells were fired.

Remi and co were there to meet me and we went straight to the Afro Spot nightclub where it was all happening. In Nigeria, they don't pass the joint around; they just give you one that is made on a cigarette rolling machine. After smoking this and having a drink, I was so out of it that I staggered outside the club and threw up into one of the open sewers that ran by. There were mosquitoes all over me.

Unfortunately, Remi's mother had died that same day and so that night I stayed at his uncle's house. I woke up in the night itching all over and it was terrible. I got out of bed and found that I couldn't open my eyes. When I finally did get one open, I saw this hugely fat person in the mirror; it was me! I shouted, 'Fucking hell!' It was 4am by then. They all panicked and Remi rushed me off to a doctor who gave me an injection of anti-histamines, cortisone and God knows what. The itching stopped immediately, but it took me 24 hours to go down to my normal size; I was a fat man for a day.

I had been invited to travel to Remi's mother's funeral, about a hundred miles inland from Lagos. She must have been an important person because there was a huge parade of army vehicles and her coffin was on a gun carriage. We drove sedately round the town and people lined the streets with their hats off. After the church service, there was a party in a big house and everyone was splendidly dressed in lace *agbada* ceremonial robes. Drummers played all day, doing amazing time changes. Everyone was dancing and I was enthralled. The only drummer who had made me cry before was Phil Seamen, but here I was crying again. I was the only white person there for miles and miles and it was quite an experience.

'What do you drink?' I was asked.

'Bacardi and Coke,' I replied.

'Well, here's your bottle of Bacardi and the Coke's in the fridge.'

Everybody who went to that funeral got a whole bottle of what they drank. You've never seen so much booze in all your life!

After we returned to Lagos, I picked up my passport and found I'd got a three-month visa, plus a return visa for the same again. A member of Remi's family had arranged my entry.

As we had all chatted at the party, Remi mentioned that it would be a great idea to build a recording studio in Nigeria. Another friend called Bayo had a nightclub down by the docks and this was proposed as the site for it. I decided to name it Batakota, after the royal African drum that I'd been presented with at the funeral. I stayed in Lagos for quite a long time after that to get the studio plans under way.

Chapter Fifteen

Holidays

Christmas 1970: I patched things up with Liz and we took the family to the exclusive Frenchman's Cove hotel in Jamaica. I had wanted to go to Montego Bay but it was fully booked and so my travel agent Frank Hepner got me this place instead. We flew out first class and I sat on the plane resplendent in one of my new African shirts.

I soon got right back into diving again. I met up with some guys who had a boat with an outboard engine, so Liz and I took a small plane down to Ocho Rios. There we went out in the boat and would usually take eight tanks of air, a pile of grass and some chillum pipes. If you breathed slowly, you could make a tank last a long time and it was great diving deep and seeing the wonderful fish and marine life. We'd do a tank, come up and have a smoke, then go back down again.

Once back on shore, I needed a piss and was about to go in the sea when my companions said, 'No! You'll get us the sack, because the Americans will all complain.' So I went up to a high-sided, deep-sea fishing boat, brought it to me by pulling its rope and stepped on board. I pissed in the sea off the other boat so the Americans wouldn't see it.

When I got back, Liz was on the quay with the Jamaican guys and I started talking to them as I let go of the ship's rope and jumped. Unfortunately for me, the boat was moving away from the quay, I was in mid-air and just had time to think, Oh, shit! before I fell. The only thing that managed to make dry land was my teeth. My chin hit the quayside with a terrible crack and I fell over backwards into the ocean. I was knocked out for a moment but somehow I managed to grab hold of an anchor chain and my diving companions pulled me clear. They took me to a doctor, who explained that I was too badly smashed to stitch. Instead, he put a pad with a bandage around my head and tied it with a bow on top so I looked like Marley's ghost.

After I'd got bandaged up, we headed to the airport in a taxi. A Mini Minor van overtook on an undulating stretch of road and its two Jamaican occupants laughed merrily at my strange bandage as they passed and failed to notice the car in the dip speeding towards them. *Bang!* The two collided head on and the Mini Minor somersaulted over our taxi as we skidded into the ditch. Liz broke her toe but the guy in the car coming the other way was stone dead on impact. We could see his arm dangling from the window of his old Vauxhall. The occupants of the van got out, one staggering about with his forehead totally cut open. The driver was on his hands and knees, blood gushing out of his mouth, pleading, 'Help me. Help me.' Sadly, both of them died. Not surprisingly we were fairly shaken when we got to the airport and, remembering the old adage that accidents come in threes, we asked the pilot of the light aircraft to 'Fly carefully, please.'

That incident was the beginning of the end for my teeth. I had a bridge put in, which was successful for many years. But I was driving the truck along in Nigeria one day when it fell out. This was when Paul and Linda McCartney were there and she took a photo of me with no teeth for one of her picture books. It was repaired several times until in 2007 it fell out again. As I grind my teeth so badly, the lower set were worn away and a dentist in Denver in the 1990s took them all out, so now I have a denture.

The diving had also caused me huge problems with my sinuses and John Robertson sent me to see a Harley Street specialist who looked after the divers from the Royal Navy. Due to the whack I'd taken on it at that GBO gig in Shepherd's Bush, the bones had been pushed back into my sinus cavities causing a blockage and now they would have to be sawn off. I wasn't too unhappy when I left his surgery though, as he had liberally dosed my nose with cocaine. But shortly after I underwent the excruciating operation in a private clinic and heartily wished I'd let the original doctor reset it when he'd wanted to!

Chapter Sixteen

Ginger Baker in Africa

I needed to get back to Nigeria and decided to drive there in a good car. I bought one of the first Range Rovers ever made, in 1971, and as a trial run I took the family on a holiday to the West Country. I drove off-road whenever I could and managed to get it stuck on a beach in Cornwall and had to dig it out.

When we got back from this latest adventure, I spoke to Tony Palmer, who wanted to do a film of me in Africa. Tony's idea was to film my trip as I drove down to Nigeria. Bob Bolt was to be our cameraman and we were scheduled to meet him in Algiers. With roadie Mick Turner as my co-driver, we loaded up the car, set off down to Marseilles and from there took the boat over to Algiers. The next day Bob Bolt flew out with his camera and we spent a whole day with the Algerian government getting the paperwork in order to verify our permission to film.

Finally, we set off through the Atlas Mountains and we had hidden the gun that I'd bought on the last trip under the back seat – which was not a clever move. As we drove along, we kept noticing all these signs in French and Arabic, but as we couldn't read them we just kept driving, stopping now and then for a bit of target practice. We rolled into Tamanrasset at three in the morning and checked into the only hotel. Much to our surprise, we heard a sudden bash and as the door burst open a Thompson submachine-gun came into the room, followed closely by a soldier from the Algerian army. We were all arrested, our passports were taken and we were told to report to the fort first thing in the morning. When we got there, the captain went crazy and asked us why we hadn't checked into the Gendarmerie at every town as required? (This is a safety measure if you're crossing the desert.) Of course, as we hadn't been able to read the signs, we had failed to do this.

By now, the cameraman was shitting himself and then they said I had to go back to the hotel and bring the car round. I had to do some quick thinking, so I told them that I'd left my keys in my room and an armed guard escorted me back to the hotel. The room was on the first floor and, as we reached the entrance, I ran up the stairs, went into my room, locked the door, jumped out of the window, ran to the car (I had the keys with me all the time), opened the car, took the gun out and stuck it under some rubbish. Then I ran back, climbed up over the balcony, in through the window, opened the door trying not to appear too flustered and said, 'Oh sorry, I couldn't find the key.' Accompanied by the guard, I drove the car back round to the fort, where they took it to pieces and there was stuff all over the place! Of course, they didn't find anything.

Finally, after several days, the cameraman decided to produce his documents from the government which unsurprisingly squared things up pretty quickly. They let us go and we had to load everything up again. Next day, I put the gun back in the car and headed south, but the cameraman kept freaking out and saying, 'I'm not doing any more filming if you keep that gun!' So we had to sling it out in the desert somewhere just to keep him happy.

We went flying down towards the next border post, though it was completely the wrong time of year to cross the Sahara. Huge black clouds arrived and it started pissing with rain. Visibility was bad and it seemed like fog and a sandstorm all at once. We were following tyre tracks and British military signs at every mile down the road. But then we noticed there were no more tyre tracks and the signs had disappeared. We were completely lost. Even in low ratio I couldn't get the car into top gear because it was so sticky that, by the time you got it up to third and then to fourth, you'd slowed down so much that you had to go back to second again.

We were crawling along like this when we found some tyre tracks in the mud and thought they must have come from somewhere or be going somewhere! They led us to a huge weather station right out in the middle of nowhere. We rolled in there, a guy came out and we explained our predicament. We had one tyre that had completely destroyed itself and we had to saw it off, but we soon got the car working properly again; then they killed a deer and we had some dinner.

The next morning, we set off for Agadez, following one of the guys from the weather station in his Land Rover. At the hotel, a bunch of kids appeared and we paid them to watch the car. They sat on it all night making sure that nothing got stolen.

The food in Agadez was absolutely amazing. There is an oasis that runs all the way to Arlit further south, a thin strip that is all green. They grew vegetables and you could jump in a fresh spring-filled tank if you gave them a few bob. I liked Agadez.

When we got to the first town in Nigeria, we were greeted by a huge crowd of people cheering and blowing trumpets. As it was the wrong time to be travelling, we were the first vehicle to appear for many months.

When Tony Palmer arrived, we flew out to the town of Osogbo in a little Italian plane (with its engine facing the wrong way) to see the artist and musician Twins 77. He was the first African guy to braid his hair as women did. When we got there, several drummers had already arrived at the venue and started playing, but then Tony started trying to direct them. This you don't do. He was trying to move them all into various positions and then saying, 'OK, play!' and it was getting hairy. Someone came up to me and said, 'We've got to get Tony out, 'cos if he spends the night here, they're going to kill him.'

So we took him to the airport, where the runway had become grass after the rain. The pilot's VW had already got stuck on it, but he thought they could do it. 'If we take just one person, there's a chance we'll make it,' he said. So Tony Palmer went in the plane with the pilot and the wheels clipped the trees. He only just got it off. Luckily for him, Tony did get some film, but the party didn't really happen until he'd gone. He could've got some fantastic stuff if he'd just had a good time and let them do their thing.

Next, we flew down to film Fela at Calabar in the rain. The jam session was shot at Bayo's dockside club and I'd said to Remi that it would be a good idea to put a roof over it so that people could sit outside when it rained. They agreed and we set off on the journey home, up to Kanu, then to Agadez, which was about a 32-hour trip and I didn't want to stop apart from the odd brew at the roadside.

We arrived in Agadez at about 10am and the usual lot of kids appeared to look after the car. A few people walked past and one of them was the most gorgeous chick. I said, 'Wow, look at that!' and one of these kids went running off after her and brought her back. So I went off with her while Mick checked into the hotel at the other end of town. She took me to her house where there was a big mattress on the floor with curtains all round and I jumped into bed with this gorgeous woman and had a fantastic time. I hadn't slept for the whole drive, so pretty soon afterwards I was out and gone from the world.

The next thing I remember was Mick shaking me and shouting in a panicked voice, 'Ginger! You've got to get out of here, quick!' In the end he said, 'Fuck this, I'm out of it!' and was gone.

I finally awoke to see this huge fucking Tuareg guy standing in the doorway with a bloody great sword – her husband! I thought, Fucking hell, what do I do? I grabbed my wallet from which I pulled a thousand CFA franc note, worth about 100 French francs and a helluva lot of money then. I pulled on my underpants and, with the rest of my clothes over my arm, I held out the note, which the guy took with a smile as I ran past him down the road.

Back at the hotel, I filled Mick in on what had happened and thanked him for leaving me in the house to die… Then we drove up to Marrakesh to meet my family and Mick's wife Elaine. I had three great loaf-size wads of Nigerian grass rolled up in newspaper in the back of the car and on the way up we met a gendarme and gave him a lift to somewhere between Agadez and Tamanrasset. After that, I didn't want to push my luck with all that dope, so we took a strange inland route on a terrible road because the maps showed the border posts were along the more direct way. As we came past a French Foreign Legion fort, we noticed a colonel standing in full uniform with make-up – mascara and lipstick, the most extraordinary sight you've ever seen in your life. He saluted and smiled at us as we went past.

In Marrakesh, we got a couple of sieves, sorted all the twigs and seeds out of the grass and then got some 10x8-inch plastic bags, which we filled to about half an inch with dope. We rolled up the bags, took the inside of the car out and taped them round the whole loom of the car with insulating tape.

I took the car on while Mick flew back with everyone else. Now that I was back on tarmac roads, the tyres that had been good in the desert were useless and the tracking had gone to shit. Between 25 and 50mph, the car was juddering so much it was unbelievable.

I got to the Spanish customs and they started pulling the car to bits, but they couldn't find anything and they had to let me go.

Then I drove up to Calais and on the boat to England I met these two Australian chicks. One of them was a stunning blonde, so I volunteered to give them a lift up to London. We went through customs and a couple of miles up the road I pulled one of the things off the dashboard, got a knife, made a slit in it and rolled a joint. The chicks were very impressed. I dropped them off at a flat in town and ended up in bed with the blonde. Then I went home.

I got all the dope out of the car and gave lots of people presents from Nigeria. I never sold any of it. I just did it for the kick.

Back to work in London, I started working on the edit of the African movie. I'd written some music in 8/8 time and suggested that we do 88 frames a second, recording all the music without struggling. The editor was very impressed and we used the top session guys in town, among them trumpeter Ian Hamer.

I met with Sandy Brown, who was not only a musician but also the top BBC acoustics guy, and persuaded him and his colleague David to get involved with my studio project.

We flew out to Nigeria, where I met Remi at the airport and he took us to see what was happening at the club. He said they'd got the roof up and that it looked fantastic. Well, it might have done at one point, but, when I saw it, it was just a load of corrugated metal and wooden posts spread all over the ground. They hadn't applied for planning permission and Lagos city council had turned up with a truck, put a rope round the supporting beams and pulled them away.

Sandy pointed out that it wouldn't have been structurally sound enough to support a studio anyway, so we went on to plan B. Bayo also had a plot of land in Ikeja, about a quarter of a mile from the main runway of Lagos airport, so we used that.

I flew back home to prepare for the next trip. My plan was to take a truck from the UK to use as a mobile studio, so back in London I bought a four-wheel-drive Bedford RLW from the army. It had a big winch on the back which I thought might come in handy. We also had a former RAF radar room fitted on top of the chassis.

Mick and a guy called Colin (known as 'Little Ginge' and later killed in a helicopter crash) came in the truck for the journey back out and I took tenor and flute player Bud Beadle as my co-driver in the Range Rover. As usual, every time I got back to England, I got fucked up and so every trip I made across the desert was a Physeptone trip. I found that the heat was very helpful to coming off and by the time I got to Nigeria I was straight.

We decided to try a less travelled route this time, but the truck started playing up quite early on. It was only firing on four cylinders and we couldn't work out why. We also had 350 jerry cans of petrol stacked in the back of the truck, some of them were plastic and it was obvious that a few of them were leaking as we could smell petrol. So, when we stopped to brew up, we'd park the truck and go another 400 yards away from it before we lit anything!

We were steaming down through Algeria and I was feeling a bit rough, so I said to Bud, 'OK, you drive for a bit, but just stay on the tracks and whatever you do don't leave them.'

I settled down to rest with my eyes closed and the seat back as far as it would go; then we pulled up to have a cup of tea and the truck arrived.

'You've gone the wrong way!' Mick said.

'What do you mean? Bud, did you stay on the tracks?'

'Yeah, definitely,' said Bud.

'So what do you mean, Mick?' I asked.

'You should've turned right miles back. You went straight on instead.'

Bud once more assured me that he'd stayed on the tracks so we continued on, passing amazing mountains of smooth black stone. All of a sudden, we came into a clearing where we saw hundreds of camels, a big military barrier and all the guns came out. We'd driven into an Algerian military border post, which was a no-go area.

They called the captain who came rushing out and we explained what had happened. It transpired that they changed staff every three months and brought supplies in with them, which explained why the tracks looked so new. Bud had gone the wrong side of a huge mountain range. So the officer let us fill up with water, but he said the only way to our destination was over the mountains and he doubted that our vehicles could make it.

There was nothing for it but to travel about 60 miles back to where we'd gone wrong and drive round. At the next town, we needed fuel because by now we'd used up all the jerry cans. But they wouldn't accept our English travellers cheques – dollars yes, French francs yes, but those, no. We thought we were fucked because we had a long way to go to get to the next place in Nigeria where they would take our money. So we filled up the Range Rover and the plan was for the truck to follow on as far as it could; then I would buy more fuel and come back for it.

After this was done, we stopped by the River Niger. The truck was still playing up, but we finally discovered what the problem was. It was a six-cylinder engine and at the points was a six-sided steel thing that spun round to open the points and it was worn on two sides. So I came up with this great plan to file down all the other four sides to be the same as the ones that were worn and then I thought it would work. I spent all day with emery paper, sanding it down, checking it and sanding it down again.

As night fell, we became aware of these incredible sounds, like that of a bow bass, accompanied by the sound of drums. Bud had a tape recorder which he put on a loop and got out his flute. As he began to play, an ethereal sound floated out which had the amazing effect of making all the drums stop immediately! After that, we were visited throughout the night by several groups of people who were extremely curious to know what was going on. They were very friendly and we discovered that the haunting bass sound we'd heard earlier was the sound of hippos.

I expressed a desire to film them and we found a couple of locals with a boat fashioned from a hollowed trunk. Before dawn, we crept up the river. The boats were leaking merrily away and so we had to bail them out regularly as we went along. We were instructed to keep very quiet and soon enough we came across the hippos, which were like double-decker buses playing in the water. I filmed for a while till our boat was nearly full and we had to go. We paddled gently back, beached our craft and got into another boat full of fish. This took us back downstream, stopping at intervals and delivering the catch to all the small settlements along the river.

We entered Nigeria via the Niger, at a point where there was very little habitation. By the time we arrived at the border post, we were low on petrol but, as before, we couldn't change our travellers cheques. The official very decently lent us some money and gave us his name and address before sending us on our way. Finally, we arrived in Lagos and visited the site in Ikeja where they had started building the studio. We sent the money back to our Good Samaritan and received a nice letter in return before I had to fly back to England once more.

Chapter Seventeen

Drug Bust: 1971

I had planned to do some recording with Fela Ransome-Kuti, and EMI's Nigerian managing director Mike Wells thought it was a great idea. I would do an album with his Africa 70 band and Fela would play on one of mine. An audience of 150 crammed into a large studio at Abbey Road with coloured spotlights dancing about the walls to give it the feel of a proper live gig.

Fela Ransome-Kuti and Africa 70 with Ginger Baker: Live! was recorded in just a few hours and I'm still very proud of it. 'Ye Ye De Smell' was written by Fela and referred to some incidents involving chicks that we had shared. It featured drum solos by Tony Allen and I. We finished up with 'Egbe Mi O (Carry Me)', another Fela classic with Igo Chicpo on tenor. The whole session was truly electric and we were all convinced that Afrobeat was going to be a really big scene. A gig at the Commonwealth Centre was also a huge success and the crowd went wild.

Then we recorded what was to be the 1972 *Stratavarious* album along with Bobby Gass. This wasn't quite as good as the last one, but the song 'Ariwo Biaye', a different version of Air Force's 'Aiko Biaye', really stood out and was sung beautifully by Sandra, one of Fela's girlfriends. Things were looking good and I got together with Robert Masters to organise a three-week tour that would begin with a show on BBC TV. We would be visiting all the big universities and end with another TV show for the independent channel. Fela seemed very excited and I booked my ticket to return to Nigeria on the following Monday.

On the Wednesday before, I got a phone call from Fela. 'Ginge! We got a big problem!' he cried. 'Mike Wells says that EMI won't pay the band's airfares for them to come over for the tour.'

'Listen, Fela, when Mike sees the contracts and everything that we've arranged there'll be no problem,' I reassured him.

Fela continued to gabble. 'I'm sending over a guy called Lewis to sort things out!'

'There's really no need, Fela,' I said. 'I'm coming back to Nigeria on Monday; leave Mike Wells to me.' Convinced that I had now calmed his fears, I hung up.

It was a beautiful Saturday and at around 4.30pm Liz and I sat having a cup of tea in the living room with the kids. Then the phone rang and it was the immigration department at Heathrow. 'Mr Baker,' said the voice. 'We have a man called Mr Lewis here. He has no luggage and is carrying a large drum. He tells us that he is here to do a record with your band.'

'Well, he'll have a hard job,' I retorted, far from pleased, 'because I'm leaving for Nigeria on Monday morning.'

'He has your address,' continued the official. 'And he says he's been sent by Fela Ransome-Kuti. Can you come and pick him up?'

I agreed reluctantly.

'Bloody hell!' I said to Liz. 'Fela wants me to pick up some bloke from the airport! I'll drop him over at JK's.' (This was a friend who had been dealing discreetly in Nigerian grass over here for years. He would always lay super stuff on me very cheaply and he'd never yet been busted.)

'Don't go; it's a set-up!' Liz shouted at my retreating back as I drove off to the airport, feeling well annoyed that my tranquil evening had been shattered.

I arrived at Heathrow and walked into arrivals, where I approached an immigration officer and informed him that I'd come to collect a Mr Lewis as instructed.

'Are you Mr Baker?' he asked. I said I was, and he requested that I accompany him to a small office and indicated that I should take a seat. 'I must warn you that anything you say will be taken down in evidence and used against you.'

I was dumbfounded! 'What the hell is going on?'

His eyes twinkled. 'You don't know?'

'No, I bloody well don't!'

He could see by my reaction that I really didn't have a clue what was happening, so he explained that Mr Lewis, a black American, had arrived in London with a large Ghanaian drum and no other luggage. Apparently, he had been playing the drum in customs. The customs guy soon realised by the standard of his playing that Mr Lewis was no drummer and the drum didn't actually sound too good either. He opened the drum and discovered 35 pounds of pure Nigerian grass inside it. This was a major bust and I was in big trouble.

He showed me the drum and I thought that they had made a pretty pathetic job of it. Inside it, you could clearly see that the head was only six inches round, but outside it was nearly two feet! Fela had panicked and, because he was so desperate to do the tour, he had decided that this would be the best way to raise the airfares.

Then I was grilled by the customs officials, who thankfully seemed to realise that I had indeed been unaware of this plan. But I was instructed to wait around for the head of Customs and Excise to arrive. When he did, I was led into his office. This bloke was quite different from his friendly minions and was very unpleasant indeed. He questioned me extensively, although finally I did manage to convince him that I was innocent of any complicity with Fela's friend.

'Do you smoke marijuana?' he asked me.

'Yes,' I replied, 'but I'm doing extremely well, so I don't need to smuggle it.'

'Have you ever been busted?' came the next question.

'Yes, I was busted last year, for a very small amount,' I admitted. 'It really hurt my daughter; she had to change schools because of the publicity.'

'Have you got any at home now?' he shot at me.

Truthfully, I admitted that, yes, I did have a little.

He looked jubilant. 'Well, now you're going to get busted again.'

What a fucking arsehole, I thought.

It was now late evening and I found myself escorted back to Harrow with no less than six customs men, two of them in the Jensen with me and the other four following in an official car. Once we arrived, they all bowled in with the intention of searching the house.

In the sitting room already, drinking tea with Liz, was Detective Sergeant Darrel of the drug squad. He smiled benignly. 'OK, Ginger, where's the stuff?' he asked in his pleasant Scottish accent.

I went over to the mantelpiece and picked up a beautiful pewter pot that had been a present from my sister. 'It's in here,' I said.

'No, don't give me the pot or I'll have to confiscate that as well,' said Darrel.

I thought that was pretty decent of him and I opened the pot and handed him about a joint's worth of hash.

'Jesus Christ! Have they called me out on a Saturday night for this?' exclaimed the detective. 'I tell you, Ginger, I'd rather sit here and smoke it with you than bust you, but the chief of customs has insisted that I do so and there's nothing I can do about it.'

Meanwhile, the customs men were all over the house, making a terrible mess, looking under the kids' beds and finding nothing. All the while, the three masks that I'd brought back filled with grass from Jamaica were sitting in full view of all above the fish tank. But, just to prove how competent they really were, they came up with the two drums that I had bought in Paramaribo and that perfectly matched the ones that had been given to me by Guy Warren.

They decided that these drums smelled of grass and would prove that I had been importing it by the same method as our friend Mr Lewis. This was, of course, a load of bollocks but they confiscated the drums anyway and I never saw them again. The customs men then departed with their booty and Detective Darrel thanked Liz for the tea (her own special blend made from mixing Earl Gray and Assam with grass seeds and stalks, always served to and enjoyed by the Wembley flying squad whenever they happened to drop by). He at least believed that I was innocent of the smuggling charges and did prove to be a nice fellow. I explained to him the hard time that Nettie had had as a result of the previous year's publicity and, when I appeared in court, he had a quiet word with the judge and the press were excluded from the proceedings. I was fined £100.

Back on the night in question, I phoned JK just as soon as everyone had gone, to discover that he had also been busted. The police had been trying to get something on him for ages and now they were sure that they had their man, but this time for something that he genuinely knew nothing about. Although he'd been living trouble free in London for the past 14 years, JK had two passports just in case. He was now charged with conspiracy to import drugs and his Nigerian passport was confiscated. So JK booked a ticket to Ghana (where his mother came from) and left the country on his Ghanaian passport! When I arrived back in Nigeria, one of the first people I saw was JK, complete with his lovely Irish Setter Jamba, which he'd brought over with him. He wasn't that happy, though, as he'd left his frozen bank account behind.

Neither of us was too pleased with Fela following this incident. All hope of the tour was over, because if Fela were to arrive in the UK he would be immediately arrested. It was a shame. He was the person most harmed by it all, because if Africa 70 had done the tour I feel sure that they would have found great success and they remain far and away the best band that Fela had ever been in.

After this latest excitement, I went back to Nigeria in 1972 and formed the band Salt.

Chapter Eighteen

Salt and the Batakota Studios

I gathered a few English and Nigerian musicians together, and we rehearsed Salt down in Nigeria. My singers were twin chicks Kehinde and Taiwo. I was to get very involved with Taiwo. We began our tour with a date at the Munich Olympic Games Jazz Festival and I drove down in the FF to meet the band. Art Blakey was also on the bill; he'd always been one of my heroes and, although I'd never met him before, the idea came up that we should do a drum battle totally unrehearsed.

It began with me playing something, then Art playing something and he took the piss and went into a 3/4 and I went into a 12/8 African thing. Then, at the very same moment in time, we went into exactly the same pattern on the cymbals and tom-toms. It was total magic! We looked at each other and the beam that came across Art's face was unbelievable. For the rest of the time, we just played together, complementing each other like the African drummers. From that day, Art Blakey became a very good friend of mine.

After this, I drove back to London with Taiwo who had become very ill due to a botched abortion she had undergone in Nigeria (an incident I shall always regret). John Robertson's partner in Harley Street examined her and said, 'We've got to get her into hospital quickly!' She went into the Harley Street Clinic where she received several pints of blood.

Then we went to America on a gig that was billed as the Tour of the Heavyweight Drummers, opposite Buddy Miles. This turned out to be a horrendous situation though, because, while we were playing very subtle Afro stuff, Buddy was playing straight-ahead rock which the Americans preferred, so we didn't go down terribly well and it wasn't a great success. As a result of this, I had a big fall-out with Roger Forrester; I called him outside the hotel and barked, 'OK, Roger, take your glasses off!'

'Why?'

'Because I'm going to smash your fucking face!' I replied.

Roger ran away, but we made it up later.

I was feeling pretty disillusioned by now and so I got myself some smack in Florida. I didn't have a works but necessity is the mother of invention, they say, so I made one out of a biro. I carefully removed the pen part and wrapped some cigarette papers round the ink tube. I managed to get a needle on to the end of it and it actually worked.

On this same tour, I had yet another 'leaving the briefcase open' incident when I was driving a big hire car out near Ventura. It was getting dark and I'd switched the lights on but it took me a while to realise that it was a foot dipper. I had just worked this out when I noticed a police car was requesting that I pull over, obviously because my lights had been on full beam. I explained the situation to them but they still wanted to check everything. Once again, I had all my drugs in my briefcase open on the seat. They searched everything and ignored that!

Meanwhile, the office had arranged the visas for the tour through

Frank Hepner and had omitted any mention of my drug busts. I got the H1 visa from the office and perhaps they assumed that nobody would notice and everything would be all right. We did a gig in Toronto and I was driving back with Bud Beadle and the twins in the car. When we arrived at American immigration, they descended on us like a ton of bricks. They couldn't find anything and so decided to submit us to a strip search which I was well pissed off about. Once I was naked, they noticed all the tracks on my arms (I've still got them).

'Ginger Baker? Weren't you busted?' asked the official.

'Yes, in England.'

'I know, it was in the papers. So where's your waiver?'

'What's a waiver?' I asked.

'You're not going to America. We're not letting you in.'

I had to get hold of Roger Forrester to call in the lawyers who negotiated a deal so I could finish the tour.

At one point, I was in a hotel on one side of the border in Windsor, Ontario, while the band was in Detroit. Finally, it was agreed that I could cross over for the gig but then I had to go straight back out again, which I did for two gigs and after that I was allowed to play the rest of the tour. But the serious implications of this were that I had a cross against me on my passport for fraudulently obtaining a visa. This was even more upsetting when you consider that it wasn't down to me at all, but was the fault of those who obtained the visa for me without declaring the bust.

The tour ended and one thing I was glad about was the fact that my studio was now well under construction. I moved into the airport hotel to be close to the site which consisted of a two-storey building with two flats above it. I had the top equipment guru, Dick Swettenham, designing and building a recording desk for me in London along with our BBC friend Sandy Brown. I also had a local architect who thought I knew all about these things and was forever showing me the drawings. Mike Wells was, as always, very supportive of what I was doing and said he'd been trying to get EMI to do the same thing for years without success.

One day Mike said, 'Let me take you out and show you the peaceful side of Lagos.' (Lagos was hustle and bustle big time.) I'd started living with Taiwo and she came along. The three of us loaded fishing rods and a crate of beer in a little boat with an outboard motor. As we tacked across to the fishing grounds, a light boat appeared in the harbour and all the people on its deck gesticulated wildly at us. We just waved back, 'Hello!' Too late we noticed another boat that displayed a red and white diving flag.

Out of the blue, the sea erupted into a huge mountain about a hundred yards from our boat and we felt the blast go across us, followed by a great fountain of water. The boat rocked madly about and I thought, The war's started again and they're shelling the harbour!

As we came closer to the boat flying the diving flag, we saw a big bearded guy whose face was as red as a beetroot. 'What the hell are you doing?' he shouted.

We discovered that ships sunk in the harbour during the war had become a danger to shipping and needed to be blown up. The divers had laid their explosives and resurfaced as quickly as possible to detonate them before the wires were pulled out by the 14-knot current. They had got as far as pressing the plunger before they saw us: a close call.

Somewhat shaken, we repaired to the yacht club for several heavy drinks.

Not long afterwards, Mike left Lagos. He'd been there for 12 years, working for EMI for ten of them and was very happy with it. But he went on leave and they sent him to work in Argentina.

I got into rallying next. Range Rover had got some big orders as a result of my taking the first vehicle into Nigeria on the film trip. I was now approached by three guys who wanted me to join their team on the Shell 1000-kilometre overnight rally: John Thornton, 'Mad' Jack from Trebor Mints and a guy from Crown Paint who had a Range Rover. I only had to finish in order for them to win the team prize. I agreed and Tony Orlando, a new engineer who'd come out to work on the studio, came as my navigator. I was the last car to start off but I was catching up. We even came second on a mud stage and only didn't win because I eased up as the going was a bit dodgy.

Towards the end, I got right up behind another car and Tony said, 'You're driving too close – you'll get a stone through the windscreen.' This was in the days before laminated windscreens and, sure enough, we finished without the windscreen!

We came third overall and the other Range Rovers came fifth and seventh. We won the team prize easily and were the only group to finish intact. This is where I forged my reputation for being 'Sideways Baker', the man who could 'make a Range Rover dance'. Taiwo wore her best outfit for the awards ceremony and afterwards we drove back to the studio off road. I went through a huge muddy puddle and the water came through the empty windscreen and we got drenched.

In October 1972, I had to go back to the UK after Phil Seamen died from an overdose of sleeping pills. While I was back for the funeral, I met Ian Farrell (who worked at RSO) and asked him to come back to Nigeria and do some work for me. The studio still had no windows or water supply, but I decided to move into the flat so that I was actually on site and Taiwo taught me the trick of bathing in a bucket of water mixed with disinfectant to keep the mosquitoes away.

Ian and I inspected the walls, which hadn't been finished properly, so we spent a sweaty couple of weeks sorting them out. Finally, it was almost complete and three engineers came out from the UK to install the equipment. A 50-kilowatt generator arrived and everything had to be soundproofed, even though the walls were already three feet thick because of the proximity of the airport. The engineers had malaria shots before they came, but two of them were diagnosed with it when they returned to England. They were only out for three weeks, yet I never took anything and didn't get malaria. We got a local carpenter to make up the sound absorbers to Sandy Brown's specifications – one took the bass frequency, another medium and a third for high. They were all mounted in special positions on the walls. People from Decca came along and stood inside the studio clapping their hands to test the acoustics and, as Sandy Brown the top man had done it, it was of course spot on.

The Nigerian architect had decided to super-strengthen the building and he'd erected a huge, two-foot-thick, reinforced-concrete beam that wasn't supposed to be there. Yes, this strengthened it enormously, but the air-conditioning ducts had all been designed to run across the same area. We now had to get the designers on it to reconstruct the ducting in order to get it under this bloody beam.

The result of this was that there was a whole load of ducting lying about that wasn't usable. While they were laying the cement outside, I inserted the aluminium ducting into the concrete, creating a very large sculpture with a solid base. Then I got a rivet gun with which I secured the ducting in an upwards direction to about 40 feet high. This formed a very surreal ARC (Associated Recording Studios), the letter A being the biggest. I was often to be seen up there with my rivet gun, cutting strange shapes and fixing them on to the side.

Things continued to go wrong; one day, I was fitting a plug when the screwdriver melted in my hand because the Nigerian electrician had connected neutral up to earth, an extraordinary trick. The problems took over two years to rectify but finally we made it to the opening ceremony in January 1973 with half the government in attendance.

By then, that included my partner Bayo, who had owned the original nightclub and was now the Minister of Information in the Western State government as a result of his work on the studio. Liz came out for the opening, which caused a bit of a headache, because when the knock came on the door informing me that she was on her way I was still in bed with Taiwo and a farcical panic situation ensued.

Nevertheless, the opening was a great success; it got in all the papers and was a high-profile event.

An American representative for Paul McCartney had a look around and was very impressed. I was knocked out because a booking from Paul would really put us on the map. But, at the same time, without my knowing, EMI had some old eight-track stuff moved into their studio. Through our contacts in the government, we arranged for Paul, Linda, Denny and the rest of Wings to get visas to come to Nigeria, and they were allocated three houses and staff thrown in. Mad Jack from Trebor Mints also lent us two Range Rovers for their trip.

They arrived at the airport at 8pm and my staff picked up their equipment and took it to my studio. I had been recording with Fela until very early in the morning and was in bed when McCartney phoned. 'Oh, Ginge, me old mate, we've got a problem,' he said.

'What's that?'

'Well, we wanted to move our stuff out of your place and into EMI's studios but your partner refused to let it out.'

'But you booked our studio, Paul.'

'Yeah, but I'm an EMI artist and I've got to record some stuff at their studio. We'll come back and record half the album at your studio, but we have to do some at EMI.'

Bayo went mad when I let them go to EMI. He told me I was a lunatic as I tried to explain the situation to him.

The next day, I got another phone call from an EMI guy asking me to come over to their studios because they had yet another problem.

'What do you mean you've got a problem?' I asked.

'Well, Fela's army are all down here and they won't let Paul record.'

Fela and I were very close, so I told him, 'Look, he's coming back to my studio to record half the album, he's an EMI artist, he's Paul McCartney...' I talked Fela into withdrawing his forces and allowing Paul to continue with his recording.

I later discovered that EMI had been unable to obtain the band visas for Nigeria and so they had used me and booked my studio in order to get McCartney into the country. But Paul was as good as his word and came back to record a couple of songs in our studio. We got an ARC Studios credit on the back of *Band on the Run*.

Paul, Linda and Denny were out one day when a large black Merc pulled up beside them containing four Nigerians wanting autographs. For some reason, they thought they were about to be robbed and Linda said, 'Don't hurt him, he's an artist!' then they promptly emptied their pockets, giving all their cash to the surprised autograph hunters.

The McCartneys threw a big farewell party which began in the afternoon with a riverboat trip around the harbour. Denny Laine came up to me and said, 'Ginger, I'm really sorry about what's going on, but you've got to understand that I've got a really good gig here.'

I didn't quite understand what he was talking about because I am very slow to catch on. It sounded ominous but I had no idea what was happening. That same night, EMI hosted a party at a big house in Lagos to say goodbye to Paul.

Above: With Salt in Nigeria 1972.

Below: In Africa in 1971.

Inset: A still taken from my film of when I got saved by a tree after I drove the White Jensen off a cliff in 1971.

Courtesy K Maughan: www.rockstars.co.uk

Above: Building the studio in Africa.

Below: The studio opened in 1973 with Fela Kuti among the launch guests.

Inset: The front of the studio brochure.

Above: The Baker Gurvitz Army in 1974/5.

Below left: With Liz in Spain.

Below right: After the mosquito bite when I stayed at Remi's uncle's, 1971.

Above: Crossing the Sahara in 1974.

Below: Our 1974 holiday in Marbella: me, Liz, Jane Gurvitz, Paul Gurvitz, Nettie and Leda.

With some of my Pollock-influenced art.

Below left: Sculpture in the garden at Neasden.

Below right: *Oscar* sculpture in the garden in Harrow.

Above: 'Sideways Baker' in the Argungu Rally 1974.

Below left: Start of the Argungu Rally, February 1974.

Below right: Behind the wheel.

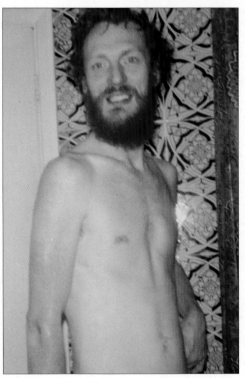

Above: With Liz, Harrow 1975.

Below left: In the bathroom in Harrow in 1974...

Below right: ...have you got a light?

Above: Chukkas at Cowdray Park – I'm in the centre on Nino.

Below: With Chamango at Ham in 1976.

As a forewarning of doom, my accelerator cable broke on the drive down there, but I fixed it temporarily with a piece of wire that I passed up through the dashboard. I was relaxing at the party with a much-needed Bacardi and coke when I was approached by a guy in a pinstripe suit, shirt and tie, grey hair – you know, typical businessman. This was the managing director of EMI overseas.

'Ah, Ginger Baker. We're going to screw you, you know,' he said to me.

'What?'

'We're going to screw you,' he repeated, 'because this is our territory. You can't build a studio here – this is EMI territory and you've got to get that into your head.' And that was when I first realised that there was something going on with EMI. They had 50 per cent or more of the artists in the whole of West Africa signed up to contracts and they wouldn't let any of them record in my studio, even though it was much better. McCartney had to stop recording at their studio because of the noise of the air conditioning, but we'd had all our air-conditioning ducts lined. We had all these modular absorbers running the generator and the generator was mounted on rubber. Worse, EMI and Decca jointly owned a record-pressing plant in Nigeria, called Record Manufacturers Nigeria Limited (RMNL), and they refused to press any of our records. As a result of this, I had to do a deal with Chris Blackwell at Island Records in England. This involved sending the master tapes over there, where they would press the records and ship them back to us. Goodbye profit.

Another enemy was promoter Chief Abioro. He turned up unexpectedly to record when the engineer wasn't there. It was down to me and when I couldn't get the echo to record properly he made it into a big deal. EMI even managed to turn Bayo, my own business partner, against me. We had a meeting at his house one day and he wanted to take over the studio and run it from eight till four and I said, 'No, it doesn't work like that.' This ended with him having me arrested and trying to get me deported. Fortunately, Torch Tairie another partner and big jazz fan came and talked him out of it.

A couple of weeks later, we were recording a couple of bands in the studio when two truckloads of armed police arrived – I wouldn't let them in the studio until the red light went off and friend and musician Raime Ndjoku ate the stash before they got in. Then they were all over my flat searching for heroin, cocaine, arms, you name it. Raime came and told me that he'd seen one of the policemen with a bag of grass in his pocket and thought that he was trying to plant it. After that, they began to threaten him so I called in the chief policeman and went bloody mad at him. I said that if any of my workers was harmed in any way I was going to get on to President Yakubu Gowan straight away. With that, they left.

Meanwhile, Fela's Kalakuta Republic was going from strength to strength. We'd been recording at the studio one day and, as the airport was only a ten-minute walk away, we went over to the all-night restaurant there for a snack and a cup of tea. I was sitting with Taiwo, when we noticed five or six white guys gathered round a table, all very drunk. Obviously, we knew the staff very well and, when one of these guys shouted out, 'Hey, sambo!' to the waiter, I went over and said, 'Look, guys, can you cool it, because I don't find that very amusing.' Then we had a cup of tea and left.

The next afternoon, Taiwo and I went over there for a drink and ended up in a booth next to these same five guys. One of them called Taiwo 'a little nigger bitch' and she threw her drink in his face. He went to go for her and I immediately stood up, so two of them offered me outside and I agreed. It was very crowded out there so they asked if I knew somewhere quiet. I beckoned them down the track that led to the studio and through the little village it was part of, where I was the neighbourhood hero. By then, the guys had taken their belts off and were proclaiming loudly, 'We're going to whip the shit out of you, nigger lover,' without noticing the ever-increasing crowd following behind.

When we reached the side of the studio, I said, 'Thanks for walking me home, guys. You can go back now.'

They looked at me and one of them asked, 'You mean you've led us into a trap?'

'No,' I replied, 'I just let you walk me home.'

Then the villagers set on them. Later that evening, several people, both white and black, congratulated me outside the hotel.

Taiwo phoned Fela because she was afraid of reprisals so he arrived with his army. If you can imagine 40 people on a Land Rover, that's what it was! They took over the hotel and, meanwhile, these guys, who turned out to be from the Canadian Air Force, were sitting in the outside bar. Fela's captain called them out one at a time and they had to stand there and have their faces slapped while everyone looked on. The captain asked me if I wanted to join in but I declined. But the next day it was all in the papers about Ginger Baker and a gang of Fela's thugs taking over the hotel. Not a very complimentary article!

A couple of days later, I was up on top of the sculpture when this huge military aircraft roared as close to the top of the building as it could. They were saying goodbye. I think they thought they were in Texas or something and we had pointed out to them in no uncertain terms that this was Nigeria.

Fela had by now moved to The Shrine with his Kalakuta Republic and formed the political party of the same name. We used to meet in the back of the club and sit round a big table made in the shape of Africa. One night I went in there with Taiwo and as usual I was the only white man in the vicinity. As I went to walk in, I was threatened by an American Black Panther-type idiot who got very heavy and said, 'You can't go in there.' In a flash, he was taken up and brought before Fela who made him get on his knees and apologise to me. 'This is Nigeria, boy,' said Fela. 'Ginger is one of us.'

Chapter Nineteen
The Argungu Rally

I was approached by the same guys as before about entering the Argungu Rally. In the meantime, I'd flown home and met with the Range Rover people who were extremely pleased with everything I'd done. In gratitude, they offered me a blue Range Rover that had appeared in all their promotional adverts. There was less than a thousand miles on the clock and they let me have it for a thousand quid, which was really cheap.

I picked it up and set off back to Nigeria in time for the rally. I took Liz with me on this trip and I was driving with two wheels off the ground for most of the way. We did London to Lagos in seven days. The other Range Rover had now been fully converted to a desert rally car. The back springs went on the front, heavy-duty springs went on the back, heavy-duty shock absorbers on the back and it had big wheels and tyres from the Land Rover One Ton, which made it faster. It was four inches higher than the standard Range Rover and that made it ideal for the desert.

I had left the converted vehicle in Nigeria awaiting further repairs and had given my secretary out there some signed cheques to pay bills while I was away. When I arrived, I went to check on my rally car, only to find that they hadn't done a bloody thing to it and this was because the bill hadn't been paid. The secretary had emptied the bank account with the cheques I'd left her. So I had to chat up one of the guys at BEWAC and he helped me take all the desert stuff off of the old car and put it on the new one. We worked the whole weekend to get it ready for the rally on the Monday morning.

When we got under way, as usual, I was passing people on the first stage. They were all professional rally drivers and two of them got stuck at the bottom of a sand dip. They couldn't help but hear me approaching because my exhaust had been knocked off quite early on. They got back in their cars sharpish as I came flying over the hump, put two wheels on the roof of their car and off I went.

Towards the end of the first day, the engine suddenly stopped and I thought, What the fuck is going on here? I needed to have a look at the pump, but the old mechanical model had been replaced by an electric version. First of all, I couldn't find the pump; then I finally located it down under the passenger door. I was lying down there with the pipes, sucking and blowing and drinking petrol but I just couldn't get the thing working. In the end, I just hit it with a spanner, said, 'Work, you bastard,' and it started!

My new navigator was Alain George, who came from one of the richest families in Nigeria. I was unaware of this at the time and gave him 400 naira for expenses when we started off! I had my toe on the floor to the end of the stage and went sideways past one of the other Range Rovers; he couldn't believe it. I arrived at the stage, leaving braking till the last minute and executed a 180-degree turn so I passed the papers out of the window to the checkpoint instead of the navigator. I was really annoyed but was still in fifth place.

Out of the huge cloud of dust that I'd stirred up, I heard a voice say, 'Bloody hell! The way you drive, you should play polo!'

'You've gotta be kidding!' I replied. I thought of Polo as a 'hooray' thing, but that was how I got to know Colin Edwards. We spent the night chatting at our camp out in the open and got very friendly – he was a really funny guy.

As mine was a privately entered vehicle, we had to buy our own petrol, but I was second on the second day and, as a result of this, Shell gave me tickets to get fuel from their gas stations on the rally stages. I spent most of the rally airborne, flying humps and over rivers without even touching the bridge. Liz cheered us on, waving and shouting, 'You're winning! You're winning!' I'd taken the lead from a Dutch rally driver in a Toyota who'd busted his car and I'd gone 200 points clear.

We pulled into the stop before the last stage, having run out of wheels. Alain went to see if we could borrow a wheel from Range Rover but the main men weren't there and nobody else would authorise his request. Meanwhile, I was at the gas station when a Volkswagen K70 came in and the guy in it said, 'Get off the pump!' He didn't realise that I'd got a ticket. So I was having a big row with one bunch of clowns while Alain was battling over the wheel with another lot. Eventually, we got set for the last stage.

The last part of the rally on the fourth day was just 200 kilometres of tarmac. We were both in a foul mood and I had my foot flat to the floor as we flew along at around 100mph. Alain told me that there was just one 'bad bit' left to navigate up ahead.

'Where's this bad bit, then, Alain?' I asked.

And cool as a cucumber he replied, 'There it is.'

It was a concrete slab across a riverbed but I was way over to the right of it. Somehow I managed to get on to the slab, but we hit the far bank at an angle and flew up into the air.

'That's it,' said Alain. 'We're finished.'

'Don't worry!' I replied as we hit the ground and the front wheel came off, axle included. I'm the only person ever to have broken the front axle on a Range Rover. Ours was now dangling behind on the brake cables with dust and sand everywhere. That was it. Goodbye to winning the equivalent of £10,000.

Alain said there was a back-up Range Rover on its way so we sat in the car with one blanket between us – which Alain, being desert-wise, wrapped himself up in. It got very cold and the backup never arrived. In the morning, a couple of blokes came past on sit-up-and-beg bicycles. Alain flagged them down, we gave them 10 naira each and pedalled 12 kilometres to the nearest town where we squashed on the bus to Kano; I had two fat women either side of me all the way. When we got there, Alain decided that we'd go to the Kano club to check out Colin. He wasn't there but we were instructed to wait for him.

All of a sudden, a Range Rover arrived that was shaped like a cathedral; the roof went up to a point and there wasn't a window in it. Colin had been driving a Citroen DS 21 which had knocked a great big hole in the sump so the car was dead in the desert. He and his navigator had sat and waited for the backup car which they had spotted speeding towards them. But as they watched they saw it fly up into the air and do a 360-degree roll before coming to rest the right way up. Colin rushed over and the rally official – who had caught malaria on the previous year's rally – now had a broken arm and a broken leg. The driver also had several busted bits, so Colin got in their car, which miraculously still worked and took them to hospital.

We got in the wreck with him and he pulled into a petrol station for a coffee and said to the attendant, 'Clean the windows.' There weren't any! When we came out, Colin began talking to this guy in Hausa and the man began sweating. That was when I realised that Colin was more than he appeared to be, because whenever he spoke to any of the black people they all bowed to him.

Then Alain told me Colin's story. Apparently, his father had come to Nigeria to build a factory and a hospital for the Emir of the state of Katsina, one of the richest men in the world. His father had stayed for two years and Colin, the blonde white boy, would play with the Emir's children. When he died, the Emir had over 200 children by 92 wives! The Emir became very fond of Colin and, when his dad was ready to return to England, he suggested that Colin stay with him. Knowing how well off the Emir was, Colin's father had agreed and the boy was brought up from a young age as one of the Emir's children. This is how he learned to speak Hausa with a royal accent and why the ordinary people saw him as royalty. White or not, his accent marked him out as such and he was a very powerful fellow.

They towed my vehicle in, but there were only two right-hand-drive Range Rovers in Nigeria and they were both mine. I would have to fly to Lagos and get the axle off my other car.

I arrived back in Lagos as the sun was rising. I got back to the studio and went up the steps to the door, but my key no longer worked. The lock had been changed.

Sylvester, who was our trainee engineer, opened his door, saw me and shut it again. As I'd built the place, I just went round the back, climbed up on the air-conditioning plant, took three panes of glass out of the kitchen window and I was in. There I was met by Tony, the American engineer, and he went as white as a sheet.

'Did Sylvester see you?' he asked me.

'Yeah.'

'Fuck! He'll call the police; they were all round here yesterday with their guns, looking for you!' He was shitting himself.

I looked out from the first-floor window over the eight-foot-high bush grass that led to the road.

'Look, there they are!' shouted Tony, and sure enough I could see the blue lights.

I ran out, jumped over the balcony and got into the car. A police vehicle was bumping along the single track but I knew the terrain so I just went straight through the grass. I couldn't see where I was going but I knew it ended up at the road.

I heard shots ricocheting around me so I put my foot down. There was a large drainage ditch beside the road which I had to go fast to clear. I sailed over, on to the road, did a big sideways turn between a few cars and flew down to where Colin lived. When I got there, I did another huge 180 and Colin came out, squinting at me through the huge cloud of dust. 'The police, Colin, they're firing guns at me!' I shouted.

The first thing he did was to get on the phone, then he said, 'OK, Baker, come with me.'

He took me to Lagos Polo Club where I met Umoru Shinkafe, one of his polo-playing friends. Umoru was a big black guy, well over six feet tall and he was also Assistant Commissioner of the special branch of the Nigerian police. After I had explained everything to him, he called them off and gave them a severe reprimanding.

I was locked out of my studio now, but my former partner was still around, so Colin asked me if I had anything on him. On my very first trip to Nigeria, I had lent him some money to get some equipment for his firm and he was paying me back £10,000 into my Isle of Man bank account (which in those days, before they changed the rules, was a good place to have one) and I'd give him £9,000 and take £1,000 back on the debt.

I'd done this a couple of times, so Colin advised me to phone up my bank to find out where the cheques were coming from. I discovered they were coming from Blue Circle Cement. Bayo was now minister of trade and he was getting bunged £10,000 now and again for signing cement contracts. There was a huge problem going on in Lagos at this time with the harbour. They had knocked down part of it to build a new superhighway, but, as a result of this, there were now not enough berths for all the ships so about 400 of them ended up in a big queue outside. Consequently, they were all getting paid $1,000 a day and this became a big scam. One ship full of cement sprung a leak and was beached, where it was quickly looted.

Colin instructed me to write a letter to the Inspector General, copied to two of the governors and to the police. This resulted in the firing of Bayo, Brigadier Rotimi, the governor of the Western State and others. I had no more trouble from my former partner and he agreed to the sale of the studio to Phonogram for the giveaway price of 47,000 naira (about the same in pounds sterling). I got 40,000 and Bayo got 7,000. I had invested over £300,000 in this venture and the other two partners Bayo and Torch had sunk £30,000, so we all lost a lot of money. At that time, there was no currency exchange between England and Nigeria, so I had to sort it out illegally and ended up with only about £20,000 by the time I'd paid the transaction fee. I had lost a fortune and my dream was dead.

Chapter Twenty
Polo in Nigeria

I was staying with a friend of Colin's in Apapa, in May 1974, when I came outside to find the words 'Graham Bond ded [sic], ring London' written in the dust on the rear window of the Range Rover. I discovered that Graham had gone under a tube train at Finsbury Park and I went back over for the funeral.

Back in Lagos once more, I started frequenting the polo club, which was cool because the clubhouse had a bar that was open all day. On my third visit, I had imbibed several Bacardi and cokes when Colin said, 'OK, Baker, it's time you got on a horse.' I'd never been on a horse before in my life.

We walked up to Colin's part of the stables by the polo field and there in front of me stood a big Argy mare with a large shiny backside. She was being held on either side by two grooms. Colin got me on board, adjusted my stirrups and put the reins in my left hand English style. 'Right, Baker. Are you comfortable?' he asked.

'Yeah.'

The grooms let go of the reins. Colin produced a whip,

whacked the horse across the backside and we were off at full gallop at 500mph. The exercise track ran around the field and in between the stables. The horse and I went flying down it. She took a left-hand bend between some more stables, where the track narrowed and a groom was casually working a horse at a hand canter. I bumped into him and heard shouting, but I went hurtling on, by the gate, across the road, and finally back up to Colin where the mare stopped. He told me that my sunglasses were round one side of my face and my beard was round the other. But I was still on the horse.

'Right, Baker. How was that?' he asked.

'Great, Colin,' I replied, 'but where are the fucking brakes?'

Colin won a lot of money that day because they'd all been taking bets as to whether I'd stay on or not. But I must have done all right because Colin said, 'OK, Baker, report for duty tomorrow morning at eight o'clock.'

For ten days, he taught me the rudiments of how to turn right and left and to stop and go. On the tenth day, he said, 'You're doing great so I've put you down for four chukkas this afternoon,' and that was it.

They found me a pair of old boots and a battered polo hat, put a stick in my hand and I was on the field. I fell off every chukka and people were saying, 'But he keeps falling off!' and Colin answered, 'No, no, he always jumps off after every chukka and runs round to make sure all the legs are there!'

I was lucky enough to have the pick of several horses and I used to stick and ball all day long. At weekends, I'd play four chukkas and the rest of the time I'd umpire either with Colin or with Captain (now Brigadier) Arthur Douglas Nugent. I got very fond of one particular horse that Colin had called Je Taime. He said she was a 'ballet dancer'. She got very sick but all the grooms were terrified of her and I volunteered to give her the injections twice a day. I walked in, stroked the horse and put the needle in virtually painlessly – I was used to doing it myself. I got very close to this horse and when she recovered I rode her and asked Colin if I could play her.

'You're crazy,' he said, 'even I can't play that horse!'

But he let me do it and she played perfectly for me: it was unbelievable.

When the French team came, a five-goal player who'd seen me on Je Taime asked if he could play her. Colin and I were umpiring at the time and we spotted this French guy coming along at a full gallop, down the side of the field and back to the stables. When he arrived there, the Cocahero bit was upside down in the horse's mouth. 'Fucking hell!' said the Frenchman.

Chapter Twenty-One

The Kalakuta Party

THE GIFT
Lagos one night, in a dark and secret place,
Flickering fireglow lights the witch doctor's face
Chanting. A chicken-white clasped close to his chest,
Shining steel blade held aloft, JuJu gods called to witness.
He weaves dancing around me
I kneel within a circle of friends,
Drums thunder crescendo, sharp blade deftly descends.
Warm blood flows staining white feathers dark red,
Transferred by bloody thumb firmly to my forehead.
Powerful chill, charge like electrical kiss
Flows into my being I receive my gift.

While I was getting into polo, I remained friends with Fela Kuti, whose Kalakuta Party was a major force. They'd had a political rally in the Lagos City Stadium (built in 1973–74 for the All Africa Games), attended by 250,000 party supporters, all smoking dope as Fela had promised to legalise it. He was so popular that he was a threat to the Nigerian government.

Then Fela arranged to marry 27 of his dancing girls and singers in one day. Several of these chicks were under 16 and one of them was the 15-year-old daughter of a high-court judge, who was not impressed by this development. The police arrested all the underage girls at the mass wedding and took them to the police headquarters. We had a meeting round the table with a lawyer called Kubaye and came up with an extraordinary plan. At 3am, all the girls were to creep out to be picked up by Fela's bandwagon. From there, they were driven off to Fela's homeland, Abeokuta, 64 miles north of Lagos. It was one of those places where they grew a lot of grass and, if you went there and they didn't know you, you never came out again. With the girls gone from custody, Fela ended up suing the police for a million naira and actually won the case. He later put the whole story on record.

The Shrine, Fela's HQ and nightclub, was opposite his house on the main road out of Lagos and, before his gigs, Fela's boys would go out and stop the traffic. Fela would take his time and finally be led across the road on a donkey with his saxophone round his neck. This happened every time and there was always a massive traffic jam to the great annoyance of the authorities. This put me in an increasingly difficult situation, because I was now playing polo with most of them.

Fela's drummer Tony Allen fell ill one week and so I did some of the out-of-town gigs. The reaction to a white (*Oyinbo*) drummer playing the Afro music was amazing. I'd always been made to feel extremely welcome in the country – from the start they all called me 'Ja'Baka' – but after that gig I could go anywhere in Nigeria, on my own at any time.

The polo club objected to Taiwo not because she was black, but because she was from a poor family and so I had to let her go. Certain types of people were not welcomed by the authorities. For instance, some chicks from Ghana had come over to stay with Fela.

One of them was a very gorgeous creature called Salome, and so I mentioned in passing that I liked her. That night, I heard a car drive off, there was a knock on my door and there she was. They'd given her to me for the night. But, a couple of days later at the polo club, Umoru Shinkafe asked me if I knew Salome. I said I did and he was already aware that she had stayed at my place. He asked me if I knew that she was an illegal alien.

Fela began to get out of hand. Umoru told me that four black Americans who I'd seen hanging out at the Shrine were pretending to be part of the All Africa Arts Festival, and were suspected of being involved in a coup. They had been arrested and taken to the airport to be deported. The vehicle was waylaid by Fela's army and its two immigration officers were beaten up while the four suspects were taken back to Nigeria and were happily back in the Shrine. Naturally, the police were not too pleased about this.

My own experiences at the hands of the traffic cops inspired one of Fela's songs, 'Zombie'. Whip-wielding members of the army were on duty and they were known for thrashing anyone who infringed regulations. They pulled me over on my way to play polo and one was already saying, 'I'm going to whip the shit out of this *Oyinbo*.' But then they spotted all my polo gear in the back. 'You play polo?' they asked.

'Yeah.'

They knew that Nigeria was practically run from the Lagos Polo Club at that time.

'Oh, sorry, sir!'

The thing was that everybody in Nigeria loved Fela and even a lot of the army were fans. But unfortunately other incidents now took place that further damaged this relationship and caused things to turn out badly for him. Some soldiers chatted up a couple of Fela's chicks who ended up stealing their money. A colonel who happened to be a big fan turned up at the Shrine one night and Fela stopped the band playing and had him thrown out. It was a silly thing to do. From this time on, the army took against Fela and his Kalakuta Republic, defiant as it was, with the fence all around it and a guard on the gate. No, you don't fuck around with the Nigerian army and to prove it they arrived there one night with both a bulldozer and a tank, which they drove straight into the compound. Unfortunately, Fela's mother got thrown off the balcony during the confrontation and died as a result. Many others were severely beaten and Fela ended up in jail. This was all very sad and it happened at the very time when I was planning to leave Nigeria and got involved with the Gurvitz brothers.

Chapter Twenty-Two

The Trans-Sahara Trucking Company and the Baker Gurvitz Army

These two ventures ran roughly parallel throughout 1974 and '75 and coincided with the end of my time in Nigeria. It was hard for businesses to get their goods around the country and I'd met several contractors in the north of the country who were desperate for equipment to continue with a huge irrigation plan. The harbour in Lagos was jammed with boats and vital gear was rusting in the holds in the punishing climate and just not getting through. Because of this problem, companies all over the north had to wait up to a year for their goods. Colin had a scheme whereby we would form a trucking company to bring the stuff across Europe in about 14 days and therefore solve the problem of the blocked harbour.

Back in England, Liz introduced me to Norman Sopp and his partner Keith, who expressed an interest in the venture. Norman was involved in drag racing and I was invited along there one wintry day to have a go in a super-fast American 1000cc machine powered by a mixture of nitrobenzene and methanol. I got in the car, but we couldn't get it started with the generator spinning the wheels. Suddenly, Keith indicated for me to switch off, which I did, but the whole thing exploded, drenching me in fuel which miraculously failed to ignite. I got out quick and that was the end of my drag-racing experience!

Keith agreed to drive to Nigeria with me to check out the route, and before long the press got hold of the story and added their own touch by saying we were to be broaching 'the last frontier' with armed guards on every convoy, which was utter rubbish. But I didn't realise at the time that this would be my last desert trip.

Morocco and Algeria were at war so we had to go via Marseilles to Algiers and straight on down to Tam. On the track between El Golea in Algiers and Tamanrasset, we came across various bits of trucks and two 50-gallon drums of fuel squashed into odd shapes in a pool of diesel. Who the hell's dropping all this? I wondered. When we pulled into the yard at the back of the hotel in Tamanrasset at 3am, I found the answer.

Three very battered-looking Volvo trucks and large trailers bearing 'Wake Bros, Hull' logos were parked up there. Then Keith told me that he'd read somewhere that in an attempt to pirate our idea these very vehicles had left England five weeks before; so naturally we thought they must be on their way back, but the next morning at breakfast we met the intrepid truckers and discovered they were in fact still en route to Nigeria and were already complaining about the state of the road.

'Are you kidding?' I laughed. 'This is the good bit – wait until you get to Niger!'

I offered to give them a hand but their guide was obnoxiously certain that he knew what he was doing and thought it was going to be 'a doddle'. I warned him that the area had seen a lot of bad weather since he was last there but they set off while we were still doing our paperwork.

About 90 kilometres up the road, we caught up with the

rearmost of the three trucks, bouncing along uncomfortably in a huge cloud of dust, and soon passed the other two, suffering similarly. 'What a load of dicks!' I said. Then we stopped at the top of a steep incline to have a brew. Soon we heard the terrible racket of their trucks approaching, attempting to negotiate the hostile terrain with little 4x2 tractors and trailers with tyres designed for the autobahns of Europe.

'Would you like a cup of tea?' I shouted to the first guy.

He gratefully accepted my offer and got out of his cab sweating profusely. Twenty minutes later, number two pulled up, and more tea drinking followed. After half an hour, the third truck hadn't appeared so the lead truck went back to look for him. Meanwhile, we set off south as I thought I'd be buggered if I was going to offer them any help, seeing as they'd tried to nick my idea and were making a right pig's ear of it!

When we pulled into Assamaka, the border post at the northern end of Niger, we found they'd sure had some weather up there. Huge dunes surrounded the place and we crawled along in low-ratio gears. The border guards knew me and explained that the only route was via Arlit, and that I should follow their own recent tracks. I didn't hold out much hope for those other trucks coming up behind us. There was only one set of tracks to follow, and 50 kilometres outside Arlit even they disappeared into the side of a large dune. It took nearly an hour to drive around it and find the tracks again. We finally trundled into Agadez about 15 hours behind schedule, but in time for dinner. As I downed a much-needed Bacardi and coke at the bar, a diminutive Englishman with a sunburned face and a northern accent approached me. 'Have you seen three trucks?'

His name was Johnny Butler and he worked for a firm called Quest 4 that ran Sahara safaris, taking punters on desert adventures. His boss was a guy called Ken Slavin, who would become a good friend. He explained that he'd been called in to save Wake Bros. We had dinner together and I told him that it would be a good idea if he could locate them before they hit Niger. For his part, Johnny told me that the track south wasn't too good and gave me directions to follow another route through Tahoua, a road I was unfamiliar with.

It was the time of the 'Harmattan' wind and the desert dust had cut visibility down to about a mile. I was flying along the sandy track at a good 80mph, two-wheeling sideways round the curves; Wake Bros had cocked up and I was happy! It was also the month of Ramadan and up ahead I spotted a guy on a moped zig-zagging slowly all over the track. To make him aware of my presence, I let go with the four huge air horns that sounded like a demented banshee. He shot over to the left side of the track, the wrong side, and I let go with the horns again, three really long blasts this time and he shot over to the right. At last, he'd woken up! I put my foot down and he stayed tight to the right until I was about to pass him when he suddenly swerved right in front of me. As I hit the brake, I struck him, and both he and the moped went underneath the Range Rover. I skidded to a halt in a cloud of dust and ran back.

'He's got to be brown bread,' I said to Keith.

After some discussion, we decided to carry on to the next town and report it there. At length I saw a sign for Tahoua, but there was only a track – not a building in sight. Two hours later, we came into another town, where I pulled up at the gendarmerie and reported the accident. They wanted me to take them back and followed me in a Land Rover, but when we got there the man was gone. They got on their radio and took us to Tahoua which had been invisible in the Harmattan fog. Keith and I were arrested because it transpired that our victim had been one of the Tahoua gendarmes. I had run over one of their friends and I was now in deep shit!

Our passports were confiscated and we were taken to jail, while our victim had now been located, lying in a hospital in a coma. There were communication problems because they only spoke Hausa and French, whereas I knew only Yoruba, which they didn't and they refused to let me near a phone. We discovered that as it was Ramadan the gendarme had been out on his rounds all day in the hot sun with nothing to eat or drink and had probably been so disorientated that he hadn't even heard my horns. The interrogation became even more heated. Finally, they brought in an American interpreter called Mr Love. When he translated my explanation to my captors, they didn't seem very convinced.

Mr Love managed to get us out for a while and took us to the hotel via the post office, where I sent a telegram back to the office saying, 'I'm in jail in Tahoua. Help!' We also sent a telegram to the Canadian Embassy in Naimey. We just had time to grab some food before we were returned to jail and only released a couple of days later thanks to the Canadian Ambassador. I was told to return for my trial, which I didn't. The victim died a couple of days after we left and my sentence was £30,000 fine plus three months in prison.

When I arrived in Nigeria and related this incident to Commander Wally Bucknor, he told me off big time and said I was lucky to be alive. Apparently, if you have an accident in Africa… keep going!

I got back to England and one night in the Speakeasy I met up with Paul and Adrian Gurvitz. Strangely enough, these two had been present during the Air Force bar-room brawl in Dusseldorf and so this was a good opening gambit for them. They invited me to come and play at a rehearsal, and the Baker Gurvitz Army was born. Their manager was Bill Fehilly, an impressive Scot. Large, jovial and bearded, he looked like Santa, loved music and had amassed a fortune by owning every bingo hall north of Manchester.

He wanted to see if he could lend a hand with the various

problems I had concerning the demise of the studio. So Bill, Colin, Ian Farrell and I flew out there together and, in the VIP lounge at Heathrow, Bill produced a huge wad of £20 notes and divided it into four, each a good inch thick. 'Just some expenses money,' he explained. But the one thing I never needed in Nigeria was money – Colin always had an enormous supply.

We took Bill to the polo club and, when he saw the sorry state that the studio had now become, he agreed that to sell was the only way out.

But I felt that at least I still had the trucking venture to continue my ties with the country.

Bill was now very keen for the Baker Gurvitz thing to get off the ground so he and Ian flew back to London. However, they still had these huge wads of sterling on them and Ian got caught with his share. He yelled at Bill to 'run', which he did and safely boarded the plane, but Ian left the next day several hundred pounds lighter!

I also got to know a few of Nigeria's favourite scams. I was driving back from a chick's house in the pouring rain when a very smartly dressed man stopped me to say his car had broken down. I agreed to give him a lift to fetch a vital part and he showed me a good route out of the traffic. When we got to near where he said the garage was, he left two cigarettes and a lighter in the car and asked me to lend him 15 naira for the part. Stupidly, I pulled out a wodge of notes. He went away for a bit, then came back saying he needed another 60 naira. It was 25 minutes before the penny dropped that I would never see him again.

At the polo club, they all fell off their chairs laughing and ordered a bottle of champagne that I had to pay for, for being such a silly sod.

Another good scam happened when I broke down about 150 yards from a restaurant I'd been in. A guy appeared and asked if there was a problem. He said that he was a mechanic and could fix it. He worked out it was the coil, took it out, went away and returned with a new coil box, did something else under the hood and the car started. I gave him 50 naira. When I told John Thornton of the rally team, he laughed and called me a 'silly bastard'. He explained that those guys disconnected the fuel line themselves. I ended up fixing my fuel line about half-a-dozen times after that and would simply sail past the culprits waving at them.

Now Bill wanted me back in England to record an album with the Gurvitz brothers; so he bought me two polo ponies as an incentive. The first Baker Gurvitz album was recorded at The Who's studio near Battersea power station. I provided the tyre squeals for 'Mad Jack' with one of my famous 180-degree skids in the Range Rover outside the studio, scaring the life out of the local residents. I did another great stunt in the studio when I was sitting in a revolving chair on wheels at the far end of the control room. I shoved myself off the wall, across the studio and proceeded down a flight of about ten stairs to the bottom, where I got up unharmed. Adrian Gurvitz missed the great moment and asked me to do it again which was a huge mistake. This time I forgot to pull my elbow in and managed to whack it hard before I landed at the bottom of the stairs.

I pulled stunts like that all the time in those days. Crazy things would enter my head and I'd just do them, like sitting in chairs and going over backwards. This still happens sometimes, but not intentionally nowadays.

In August of 1974, I took the family on holiday to Marbella with Paul Gurvitz and his wife Jane. We hired some horses and went galloping through the Spanish hills. One night we were having a meal in a smart restaurant when I remarked that a woman's place was at home in the kitchen. Liz took exception to this and slashed me across the back with a serrated steak knife, tearing my shirt and drawing blood. Then she stormed out and set off to walk back to the hotel. It wasn't long before she became aware of a man following her with his trousers round his ankles. At the time she was carrying a huge pair of platform shoes, which she brandished at the bloke shouting, 'Fuck off!' A phrase that is well understood in any language!

On our return, the Baker Gurvitz Army set off for a tour of the States backing the Doobie Brothers. I had a few days off in Florida and I went and checked out the Gulfstream Polo Club. It was there that I met Butch Butterworth and the Wigdahl brothers Dave and John, who were very kind in arranging some wild chukkas for me. I'd brought some crates of beer because that was the penalty if you fell off and sure enough they were needed. I also met Tommy Harris and Bill Mulcahy who were to remain good friends.

I was straight and well now and I told Bill to cancel the west coast part of the tour, because it was the drug capital of the world and I wanted no part in it.

Back in Nigeria, the sale of the studio had gone through and Ken Slavin (of Quest 4) took the idea for our trucking venture to the Algerian government. The Algerians had always been friendly and co-operative and not anticipating any problems we had already ordered 14 6 x 6 tractor units from Mack Trucks and 20 heavy-duty trailers from York Trailers. But a letter arrived that said, 'Permission refused'! I was devastated. That was yet another dream gone.

Chapter Twenty-Three
Polo in England: 1975–78

On my first visit to Ham Polo Club, I roared up the drive in my desert Range Rover with its cow catcher on the front. A lady rider shouted, 'Slow down, you blithering idiot!' as I sped past. That was one of the cardinal rules of horsemanship that I learned quickly at Ham: always slow down for horses (try riding something traffic shy and you will understand why)! Polo player Billy Walsh ran the place with a rod of iron and his indomitable spirit ensured that the girl grooms lived in mortal fear of his wrath.

Both Billy and his daughter Peggy spent a lot of time helping me with my riding. A compliment from him was a rarity and he constantly chewed me off, but I was honoured that he spent so much time with me. Peggy taught me how to get the better of my grey horse Pampero, who was always throwing me off. One day, I managed to sit out ten of his violent corkscrew bucks. 'You've got him now!' Peggy laughed.

I was out on my own one day, flying along at a fast gallop past the practice pitch in the park when a nice-looking woman on horseback came up. I tried to be charming to her but, rather than succumbing, she issued me with a speeding ticket instead! Then one of the head girls gave me a telling-off for returning with my horse sweated up – I didn't realise that you had to walk the last part of the ride to cool it off.

One day, a visiting high-goal Argentinean player told me that my horses were too well fed; so I asked Peggy to cut their feed down and she nearly bit my head off. 'If you don't like the way we do it, then take them somewhere else!' she said.

I was mortified and quickly realised that many South Americans underfeed their horses so that they are easier to play. Barbarous!

The atmosphere at Ham was wonderful and, after a few whiskies in the clubhouse, Billy would unbend and became a lovable and witty Irishman. Liz enjoyed the social scene and my life at home improved. I would leave every morning at 7am to go on a controlled ride around Richmond Park with a posse of more than 20 horses. Billy led the 8am ride and Peggy the 9am, with strict instructions that no one must pass the leader. 'Ginger! Control that horse!' was a typical morning's instruction from Billy.

My playing had improved by leaps and bounds by the start of the 1976 season. Liz began doing the hanging baskets at the clubhouse and I formed my own team, the Dragonflies. The original line-up was Chris Tauchert, Derek Copeland, the sculptor Sam Houston and I. We won the Assam Cup in Rutland two years running.

I had a friendly rivalry with music impresario Bryan Morrison, whose team was called Chopendoz. Bryan turned up there one day with Kenny Jones and got him started in polo; he always claimed he started me off as well but that was untrue. This later caused us to have a disagreement in *Hurlingham* magazine, in which I said he'd lost his memory because of too many polo accidents. Unfortunately, just after that he had the accident that led to his recent death. It was very sad.

Nevertheless, both our teams seemed to get into every final that summer. But, due to the hard ground from the heat wave, my favourite horse, the mad grey Pampy, went very lame and I discovered that he had an undisclosed illness and that I'd been sold a 'bum steer'. Billy explained to me that the bone in my horse's foot had disintegrated and that he would have to be put down. This horse had taught me so much and I took him for a last walk with tears running down my face.

I had met Lord Patrick Beresford with Colin Edwards in Nigeria and I bought another two horses from him. Colin came to England on a visit and invited me to play at Guards Polo Club, Smith's Lawn in Windsor Great Park. Everyone was very impressed and I had many invitations to join the club, but I was happy at Ham. I felt very honoured when the great Art Blakey came down to see a match and he thoroughly enjoyed being royally treated in the clubhouse (where a picture of moustachioed comedian Jimmy Edwards, who had been a club member, stared down from the wall).

Towards the end of the 1976 season, the great player Paul Withers was due to visit us for a tournament. I had invited my mum, but I discovered that I had two horses lame. Billy said he couldn't hire me a horse and I expressed my disappointment to Paul, completely unaware that he and Billy were not on good terms. He said that it was outrageous that Billy had been unable to help me and suggested I spend the following season at Cowdray Park Polo Club in West Sussex. I thought it a wonderful proposal and was very excited by the prospect.

I was invited to the end of season Ham Ball. I hadn't owned a tuxedo for years and decided that I would go and have a really flash suit made. On the recommendation of my friend Terry de Havilland, who ran the shoe shop Cobblers to the World and had already made me a beautiful pair of polo boots, I tried the boutique Granny Takes A Trip.

'Tell Byron I sent you,' said Terry.

'Hello, luv!' said Byron in a very camp manner as I walked through the door. I was sure he was gay, though he turned out not to be.

But unwittingly I had walked into a disaster area because, as he carefully measured me for my suit, he asked, 'Fancy a line of smack, luv?' in a curiously off-hand manner.

Although I'd been off it now for over a year, I heard myself saying, 'Yeah, that sounds cool,' and I left that shop flying.

Every fitting that I had for the suit followed the same routine and Byron was extremely generous with the smack. Soon I was a regular visitor and my habit was back. It turned out that Byron was the biggest dealer in London. But the suit was completed and it was very impressive: in dark green, with velvet collar and velvet inlaid into the flared gaucho-style trousers.

The next season at Cowdray Park I turned up on the field with such great English players as Howard and Julian Hipwood and Alan Kent. But Julian came over to me and said, 'No, Ginger, you're playing over there.'

So I went 'over there' and it was just silly chukkas. I didn't enjoy it and was very pissed off. I wanted to play good polo. We did sort it out and thereafter I played in the afternoons with Hector Crotto, Eduardo Moore, Gonzalo Pierez and Alan Kent, where we'd have get-togethers with no hats and no umpire.

The Baker Gurvitz Army had recorded three albums and Bill Fehilly was the best manager anyone could wish for, but I found it hard to get along with Adrian Gurvitz and his habit of getting off with every chick that I fancied. His guitar playing was just too loud, but, when I told Bill I wasn't happy, he was wonderful.

'OK, Ginge, why don't you get you own band together?' he suggested. 'I'm right behind you.'

My admiration for him grew as he never pushed me to stick with such-and-such a contract, as others had tended to do. He also had the Alex Harvey Band and Nazareth under his wing. Sadly, on his way home to Perth after seeing Nazareth play in Blackpool, tragedy struck. He was in a plane with his youngest son and the company's chief accountant when they crashed into the mountains, leaving no survivors. With bitter irony Mountain Management was no more. A young Scotsman named Derek attempted to carry on, but without Bill it was just a charade. This didn't help my habit and I continued to visit Byron.

Studio time had been booked for me to do an album, so I got a band together, but my heart wasn't in it. I missed Bill and I was nearly always stoned. Then I fell in love with one of the singers in my band and she gave me a really hard time. My habit got worse and as a result my album entitled *Eleven Sides of Baker* wasn't very good. Polo was the only thing that was still making me happy.

My friend Ken Slavin from Quest 4 lived on the 2000-acre estate that incorporated the villages of Ashton Wold and Polebrook, which was owned by the world-renowned naturalist Miriam Rothschild, and through this connection I wintered three of my horses up there. I then bought three more horses from Lord Patrick Beresford, which Colin housed down at his place near Windsor Great Park.

Colin had acquired this splendid house in Winkfield Row from an interesting little ruse back in Nigeria. He distributed fuel all over the country and had struck a deal whereby he agreed to deliver 16 large new tractor units plus 16 tanks of gas to Chad. Colin then sold the trucks, said he'd been attacked and got the insurance money. As the CFA was closely affiliated to the French franc, he then went to Paris to launder the cash. With that he bought the Windsor house and a white Rolls-Royce with a personalised number plate, CE 20. But I had a row with him about not feeding the horses properly, as a result of which Nettie took over.

I still missed Bill, my habit continued apace and it was in this condition that I began the 1977 polo season at Cowdray Park.

One day, I got into real trouble with Paul Withers 'cos I'd put myself down for ten chukkas (as by now I had several more horses) and every single one was bad. So I just went off into an empty field and stick-and-balled. I felt very disappointed and believed that the polo had been infinitely better at Ham.

But apparently it was a social plus just to say you had *played* at Cowdray. Paul said that I'd let everybody down so I told him that I'd come here to play polo and not to fuck about and that didn't go down too well. I also got into trouble for driving too fast and scaring the pheasants! Nevertheless, I decided to move down there and Nettie (who was now my groom) and I lived for a while in a cottage with Alan Kent. I kept my horses with him until I found a yard to rent in the village of Lodsworth.

I was in trouble yet again when I took a fancy to a girl groom named Kat. Because of her lowly status, the affair was inappropriate. We all stayed for a while in the Angel hotel in Midhurst which caused a great scandal. One of the polo people told me that I was supposed to be 'an officer and a gentleman' and that it was only the Argies who consorted with the stable hands!

Then Kat had an accident when we were riding out on the South Downs. I had told her to stay well behind me, but she came flying past at a hundred miles an hour on Chrissy, the thoroughbred ex-racehorse mare. The wicked horse headed for a low tree which she knew she would clear but the rider certainly could not. I hurried to catch up and was confronted by this bloody mess on the side of the track. Oh, fuck, I thought. What do I do now? The horse's back foot had smashed Kat's cheek and I took her off to hospital.

Chrissy reappeared looking happy with her ears forward; she was a wonderful pony and played till she was 23.

While out stick-and-balling one day, I met up with Luis

Basualdo. We became friendly and he did my polo a lot of good by getting me to play on the near side all the time. I had also become friendly with Major Ronnie Ferguson whom I liked immensely and Nettie got on well with his daughter Sarah. My polo continued to improve and the Dragonflies gained quite a reputation. I got together with Phil Rhodes and we had 20 horses between us.

With Charlie Graham and Gonzalo 'Gonzo' Pierez on board, we entered a medium-goal tournament. When I asked Gonzo what the plan was, he said, 'Ginger, the plan is to win!'

We got into the finals again opposite Bryan Morrison's Chopendoz, this time with Alan Kent on their side. We lost 10–9 and it was a great experience. But I found I was still getting a lot of hostility from the Cowdray estate manager.

Then I met Miriam Rothschild's adopted son Benny Fisher (who wanted to write my biography) and we went to see her again. She asked me if I would be interested in organising a polo match to coincide with her annual flea symposium. Benny and I toured her estate and found a clearing that seemed to have been used as a polo pitch in earlier times. We decided it would be ideal. We also discovered a huge greenhouse full of marijuana plants. In her capacity as an entomologist, Miriam was carrying out government research to find a pest that would devour cannabis plants. Outside the greenhouse was a sign that read simply, 'We know who you are'. Caterpillars thrived on the dope and lived four times as long as their normal counterparts. Miriam even went on the BBC to explain that the secret to longevity appeared to be connected to a diet of marijuana!

Miriam's match was played against a team from Rutland Polo Club and it was a great success apart from the fact that an Argie recommended by Basualdo didn't show up. We had to arrange a hasty substitute and lost the game. But the atmosphere was relaxed and I began to think about forming my own polo club at Ashton

Wold. Basualdo thought this was a great idea and was very supportive, but what I didn't know was that he had seriously fallen out with Lord Cowdray. Basualdo was Lord Cowdray's son-in-law and was not treating his wife too well. He had already been told that he 'would never play polo in England again'. I was now heading for complete disaster.

But I was still unaware of this as I moved into a cottage on the Polebrook estate early in 1978 and converted two large barns for my horses. Due to the technological advances of farm machinery, many of the labourers' cottages were empty, which suited the purposes of a polo club perfectly. Benny and his half-sister Jane were also staunch allies and, although Miriam herself was keen on the venture, it has to be said that her estate manager was not.

One day when I was out riding on my young horse Project, I met up with what seemed like a hundred people on horseback all congregated outside the Chequered Skipper pub in Ashton Wold. This was the Fitzwilliam Hunt and I approached the master and asked him politely if he minded avoiding my paddock full of horses. He agreed with alacrity and I was then invited to join the hunt, even though, dressed as I was in jeans and an anorak, this was by no means the correct attire. It seemed churlish to refuse, so I joined them, stayed well back and my horse jumped everything.

I was in the middle of a bunch of people all saying it was 'Jolly nice, pip, pip', hurtling along the tarmac roads (which I wasn't keen on, because of the damage it does to the horse's legs) to the sound of the hunting horn; then galloping over the plough. We caught a fox on the estate, which can't have gone down well with Miriam or her sister – they loved foxes. Back on tarmac again, I gradually got over on to the grass verge and hooked up. It was insanity.

Shortly after this, I flew out to the Elvira Polo Club in Argentina, where I met with Basualdo and his friend Luis Oddone in order to try out some horses. The polo was great, but I wasn't impressed with the way they treated their animals. I played up to 20 horses a day and most of them were terrible. I also upset my hosts by saying that Argentina was like Africa because there was the same enormous gulf between the haves and have nots. Despite this, I arranged to fly 30 horses out for the club, to be sold on during the season, with me taking five per cent of the profit and being reimbursed for my outlay. This new project was to be called the Eldorado Polo Club.

Sadly, as I basked in my excitement concerning my new venture, tragedy struck. My great friend Benny Fisher died of a brain haemorrhage in a London taxi at the age of 32. Hot on the heels of this unfortunate event, I received a letter from Paul Wither's wife, Sheldon, written on paper with black edging like an obituary. This concerned an unpaid bill for some horse supplement I had ordered from them. It was a genuine mistake because my friend the vet PJ McMahon had forgotten to bring me the invoice and I had already sent the money two days previously, so we had crossed in the post. It was a very upsetting piece of correspondence though, because in it she stated that people like me gave the game of polo a bad name and that she wished me all the worst for the sum of £29!

Now that Benny was gone, Miriam asked me whether I should think again about the club and I had a feeling then that I should have followed her advice. But Basualdo would have none of it and explained that I was now committed because the horses were ready to be shipped over. Reluctantly, I felt I had no choice but to continue.

On the other hand, Major Ronald Ferguson sent me a much more cheerful note, filled with congratulations and offering me all the help he could. He dropped in to visit me one day en route to a clinic he was giving at Rutland Polo Club and he invited me along. 'Ask me lots of questions, Ginger,' he said and I did. I felt very bad for him in later years when the press tore him apart for visiting ladies of ill-repute. He was a wonderful man who was only human like the rest of us.

Thanks to Major Ferguson, I regained my enthusiasm for polo and set about converting more unused agricultural buildings to house the horses once they arrived. For the grand opening game, Basualdo sent over three five-goal Argentinean players and I invited a player called Phil Rhodes. I also invited Rex Racca, a friend from Africa, who had fallen foul of the Nigerian government, had his 20 horses confiscated and had been deported. Lagos Polo Club secretary Anne Lyle agreed to help me manage the club affairs. Several sponsors were in place and Robert Stigwood donated a beautiful cup to be played for later in the season. The BBC's *Nationwide* filmed the arrival of the horses at Stansted and the subsequent match.

Nettie agreed to come and groom and brought along her boyfriend's 18-year-old sister Sarah, who chatted me up and was very naughty indeed. We soon started an affair, a fact that Anne Lyle duly reported to Liz and everything started to go wrong.

One of my grooms took my Land Rover without permission when I had left specific instructions that it was not to be driven because the brake lights weren't working. When I saw it had gone, I jumped in another car to find the girl. I located her in a nearby country lane and flagged her down; she stopped suddenly and an old man on a moped ploughed into the back of her. I called an ambulance but he later wanted to sue me for £30,000. We had several sponsors for the club, but none of them helped out financially and the bills for the upkeep of 40 horses began to mount up. I was facing financial ruin.

One day when I was coming out of Byron's, I met The Who's manager Kit Lambert in a coffee shop. He said he'd wanted to talk to me for a while because Keith Moon was in a bad way. He thought it would be a good idea if I went to see Moonie and have a chat with him as he felt I was the only person he would listen to.

'Look, Kit,' I said, 'I've got so many problems of my own at the moment that I don't think I could help him.'

Soon afterwards, Moonie was dead. I don't know whether or not I could've helped him, but I felt very guilty that I never complied with Kit's request.

Despite everything, I was still playing a lot of good polo. I entered my team for the Blue Coat Cup, which was then the top eight-goal tournament in Britain and we got through to the last eight teams. We would be playing at Sam Vestey's Cirencester Park in Gloucestershire. Stevie Winwood lived nearby and he let me stable my horses at his place for the week. I honestly thought that if we won the tournament then my club would be on the map, we would attract a good sponsor and my financial worries would be over.

Charlie Lane (Miriam Rothschild's son) came down and he made it clear that we needed to win. I had every confidence because we'd already beaten Los Locos (the team headed by Simon and Claire Tomlinson) in the semi-finals. Prince Charles was playing in the final and we met in the pavilion. 'Oh! You're that famous drummer chappie, aren't you?' was his opening gambit. Was he for real? But I found him to be very pleasant and we ended up talking far longer than protocol demanded. He must have heard about my financial problems because he said, 'I hear that you've put all your money into polo. I do hope that it all works out.' His bodyguards kept trying to extricate him from the conversation, but I was impressed with his sense of humour.

The big game was suddenly under way and we were up against a very strong team that was captained by the great ten-goal Argentine player Eduardo Moore. Patrick Beresford's young son was also on their side and he was playing far above his handicap. It was an exciting game and the scores remained even right up until the last chukka. I executed a beautiful neck shot and was astounded to hear the umpire's whistle blow a foul. 'There was no one near me!' I shouted in disbelief.

Eduardo Moore rode over to me. 'That was no foul, Ginger,' he said kindly. Then he nailed the penalty shot and we lost the game.

At the party that night, Stevie and I played some great music together and the whole place was jumping. Everyone was enjoying it so much that I hardly noticed that Charlie Lane was ignoring me. Nevertheless, we had lost. The next day I got a phone call from Sam Vestey, the owner of Cirencester Park, in which he complained about the state of some horses being played by an Argy on my team. I was upset because I considered him to be a friend and we had stick-and-balled together at Ham.

'But they weren't my horses,' I explained.

'Ginger, they were on your team. There's no excuse,' was his uncompromising reply.

I was crestfallen and shaking as I put the phone down. The writing was on the wall and suddenly I was the bad boy of polo. I cancelled the Stigwood Cup – no way was I going to let Basualdo take it back to Argentina. But he was soon on to me for money for his players.

'What about my money for the horses?' I asked.

'You'll get your money for them at the end of the season,' he answered.

I didn't believe him but I wrote a cheque that I knew would bounce just to get rid of him. This was a huge mistake because now I'd broken the law. Basualdo had also taken several horses for an away match along with tack, buckets and bandages and not returned them. This meant that they were now out of my jurisdiction as his clever lawyer was quick to point out.

Liz was on to me now about my affair with young Sarah and my world was unravelling fast. I went over to see my solicitor Wally

Hauser and he advised me to take back some of the horses from the Argy yard at Polebrook to my own close by, in order to cover what was owed to me.

This seemed to me to be a good idea. I had made some risky friends in Chelsea through my connection with Byron and one of these was the notorious John Bindon, who used to hang out in the World's End pub on the Kings Road. John was indeed a very amusing tough-guy actor, who had carried his role over into real life, and he lived with Vicki Hodge, a relative of my polo-playing acquaintance Johnny Kidd. At this time, I considered Bindon a friend and it was his idea that I report my grey Jensen stolen and pick up the £2,000 insurance money. Then I mentioned to him the trouble that I was having with Basualdo and he came up with a plan whereby he and two of his cronies would come up to Polebrook to ensure the safe return of three of the horses to me. We would then confront Basualdo in London in order to get the money that he owed me. For this, Bindon and friends would be paid £2,000.

We drove to Polebrook, took the three horses and, with Nettie and another groom, rode them along the lanes to a place on the other side of the estate. Stage one had been accomplished easily and the Argies were nowhere to be seen. But, just as Bindon and his buddies were leaving, they reappeared and Bindon's lot got very heavy, scared the living daylights out of them and threw them out of their cottage. I thought this was totally unnecessary and I told them so on the way home. Then on the M1 we got pulled over by the law, which was hairy as they were all armed to the teeth with knives and what have you. But the policeman only told me off for speeding before sending us on our way.

The thugs knew that Basualdo was well connected and refused to carry out stage two of the plan. The Argies might have called Basualdo who had then phoned the police. I dropped them back in Chelsea and went home. At least I've got the horses, I thought.

Then I had a riding accident on a tarmac road and broke my collar bone. This incident was not without its lighter side though, because the medics were really knocked out to have Ginger Baker swearing in their ambulance.

But then Bindon began to demand his money with menaces. I told him that not only had he not finished the job, but that I didn't have the money. 'Go and get it from Eric,' was his reply. This was because Eric had already lent me £9,000 and no way was I going to ask him again. Firstly, Bindon threatened to cut all the horses' throats and so I had to move them to safety. Benny's sister Jane kindly phoned the head of the local police for me. After that, Bindon progressed to threats which involved harming Liz and the kids.

I had managed to get a paying gig in Berlin playing alongside Fela, with Mick Turner as my roadie. This was a strange period for Fela and his 'super radicals' and he had something like 83 people in his entourage, who were staying in East Berlin. Fela refused to play with me but Tony Allen and Henry Kofi accompanied me in a show-stopping drum set (which was recorded). But on my return, of course, Bindon now knew that I had been paid.

As I put the money for Bindon into a brown envelope, Liz said, 'Here, I've got something to go in with that.' And she produced a rune written in red ink that we slipped in between the twenty-pound notes. 'When that bastard gets the money, he'll get more than he bargained for,' she snarled. 'He's going to get severely knifed!'

'Bloody good!' I replied.

I went down to Byron's and had my toot. Bindon was waiting for me outside the World's End. It was only about ten days later that he was involved in a brawl with Johnny Darke at the Ranelagh Yacht Club. Darke died and Bindon fled badly injured to Ireland but returned to face charges and was jailed to await trial. I was visiting Byron often during that time and one of Bindon's buddies in the area threatened me, but later apologised. Bindon was found to be innocent and I saw him after his release outside Byron's, where he started throwing money at me. He just couldn't understand why I wasn't terrified of him and had blown him out.

Meanwhile, Liz had arranged for her friend Norman to overhaul the white Jensen for me and he did a good job on everything except the prop shaft, which he had failed to notice was badly worn. As I sped towards London one day, it just let go and as it was forward-facing it smashed the newly refurbished engine to pieces. The car went into Jensen's but unfortunately I just didn't have enough money to pay for the repairs.

This was a very bad period. I wasn't playing polo any more, I had to gradually sell off the horses and I discovered that that was much harder than buying them, I can tell you.

By now, I had acquired quite a habit again and was meeting a lot of people on the hard-drugs scene. I got into dealing and running messenger trips for Byron. In this capacity, I picked up a large amount of coke for Eric and the rest of his band when they were recording an album in London. I took the stuff along to the studio, but it was very degrading and I didn't feel too good about it. I got my daily toot for which I was grateful, because it made the fact that I'd totally blown it easier to cope with. My polo dream had gone to pieces and I left Polebrook owing money left, right and centre. There was no way I could pay anyone. During the height of these troubles, my old friend Rex Racca called me to his hotel in town and gave me £1,000 in cash, which was incredibly kind of him.

I put my horses into a very smart yard in Chalfont St Giles that belonged to Clive Holmes, a friend of Ann Lyle's. The young England polo player Oliver Ellis took my best horse, assuring me that he would sell it. I couldn't afford the livery bill at Clive's and so I lost another horse to pay what I owed. Then Phil Rhodes recommended a friend of his called Roy Ward, whom I'd previously met (but not liked), when he was manager of the Petworth Park Hotel in Sussex. Phil assured me that he was just the person to get me back up on my feet, so against my better judgement I took him on as manager. Roy found me a place where I could keep my horses cheaply on the premises of an old widower called Arthur Richardson.

This place had a six-acre paddock and some ramshackle old sheds that I spent a week trying to make habitable for the horses. Arthur was a nice old boy and he suggested that I also move into the house along with my new love Sarah and Nettie as groom. This solved the problem of having clandestine meetings while I lived back at home. Of course, Liz went mad about this and the financial situation, and Nettie wasn't too pleased either.

Chapter Twenty-Four
Denham Days

In May 1979, I took Sarah, Nettie and my dog Toerag along to Hurtwood Edge for the party to celebrate Eric's wedding to Patti Boyd. At one point Lonnie Donegan handed me a pill. It was an awful experience and I was really pissed off because it didn't do me any good at all and made me feel really rough. Then later, when the fireworks display came on, Toerag ran away and I was very upset, but Eric promised that he had some people out looking for him and he was found tied up outside a gypsy caravan. I borrowed a car and drove to get him.

In a further reference to silly drugs, I was in the club J Arthurs one night with some acquaintances who were using this stuff that you sniffed; amyl nitrate, they called it. There was a large bottle of it in the centre of the table and somebody mentioned that it was supposed to be a great sex drug. I just struck a match and the whole fucking bottle disappeared in a flash! The guy whose gear it was wasn't very pleased and neither was I because I didn't like it at all and was one hundred per cent against it.

Roy Ward's sister owned a cafe in Warple Way, Acton, and he talked me into building a small studio in the flat above it. With my previous expertise in Africa, I fitted it out and soundproofed it really well. Roy sat happily in the office with all my gold discs on the wall behind him, organising tours of sorts (not that we ever got any money).

I took my new band Energy to Berlin by coach. I was trying to get off yet again at this time but I soon noticed that my roadie Phil's eyes were very pinned. This was because Byron had come along with his girlfriend Mandy and a phial of smack. Byron's wife, a French girl, flew out and brought over some more. So that was that.

The roads in Germany were treacherous with black ice, and the coach, fitted with cheap tyres, had a maximum speed of about 63mph. We had a blow-out on the front and came to a sudden halt. Then Roy and Byron proceeded to have a fight outside the coach. As Roy picked up the tyre iron, Byron wailed, 'Not the iron bar, Roy,' which I found to be highly amusing.

Byron flew home only to return with yet more heroin, and while he was gone I spent the night in a hotel with Mandy. I decided that when the tour ended I had to get straight and stop seeing Byron.

As soon as I returned home to Denham, I popped down to the local farm, where the farmer's son Dennis, turned out to be a big fan of mine. He invited me to a party where he proceeded to lay out a line of smack; he and his mates were all at it. The whole of the young population in that area, most of whom came from very good families, were using and a very big-league dealer lived nearby. Girls often turned up at my place asking me to fix them, and thank God I had stopped fixing myself and was now snorting it, because nearly all of them died of AIDS. Dennis was also heavily involved with a guy that ran a scrapyard and did a roaring trade flying car parts stuffed with hashish and marijuana over to Ireland. The police discovered three cars at Heathrow with no number plates and became convinced that this guy was gun-running for the IRA. The farm was raided, Dennis was arrested and the cops were still sure that they were going to find Pershing missiles or similar. Dennis went to jail, and coincidentally so did Byron for some other unrelated matter.

When Dennis was in prison, I helped his dad Stan by driving their truck to a market in the mornings. I went to see Dennis in jail and passed him smack when I shook hands with him. Then I got a bit of work as a brickie with another guy on the drug scene called Dave Carpenter. He and his brother Tony helped me nick the bricks and cement I used to build my new stables.

Now that I was living with Sarah, problems with Liz began to mount up. I took the younger kids down to my mum's again because I feared for their safety, but Liz got them back. We went through a very acrimonious divorce. One day, I was informed that I had just 25 minutes to get to the High Court from Denham. I threw on a jacket, borrowed Arthur's car and flew up there to meet my lawyer. Liz and I did battle for the kids and my drug use was brought up. In the end, I negotiated a plea bargain whereby she got the kids in return for me getting the divorce. But when the judge finally awarded her the kids I stood up and shouted, 'No! You can't do that!' because I was so furious about it. My lawyer had to physically restrain me. 'Sit down, Mr Baker, or you'll be arrested for contempt of court,' he warned.

All this happened in 1980, when I joined the band Hawkwind. The guitarist Dave Brock came to see me and offered decent money, so I agreed; but musically they were awful. They were more into the look of it on stage and the light show than the music.

I went down to a farm in Wales with them to rehearse and was approached by a chick who I think worked for the *News of the World*, and was interested in doing my biography (again). At first I agreed, but she only wanted tales of sex and drugs, so I blew her out and she threatened to sue me.

I stayed with the band long enough to record the *Levitation* album and got about £600 for it, not the sort of money I was promised at all. I described Harvey Bainbridge as 'the worst bass player in the world' and left shortly afterwards.

In September that year came the sad death of Led Zeppelin drummer John Bonham. It was said that it was the result of his massive drinking at a party, but I have my own theory. We were all hanging out with the Chelsea lot then and John was a dabbler in heroin. Byron had got hold of some extremely strong smack and when I took it I was so stoned that I left my car in Chelsea, walked all the way to Acton and back to Chelsea again until I was able to drive. That same night, Led Zep had the party when John died. I had a habit and could handle the extra-potent gear, but, being only an occasional user, he could not.

There was more trouble when I played the Glastonbury Festival in 1981. I had formed Ginger's Nutters with vocalist and saxophonist Ian Trimmer and guitarist Billy Jenkins. The festival's organiser Michael Eavis had some sort of problem with the curfew so we all had to finish dead on time. We were following Roy Harper (the sheep farmer!), who was playing the sort of music I loathe. He ran way over his time and we were going to have to cut our set down because of him. I kept saying, 'Come on, man, we've got a set to do,' but then he told the audience that I had insulted him! When we finally got on stage, I was hit on the head with a rock. *Bam*! There was blood all over my snare drum, but I finished the number. 'OK,' I said. 'You've got your blood, now sit down and listen.' The crowd warmed to me and it turned out to be a good gig, although I ended up having three stitches. Michael Eavis was very apologetic.

When I got home, I watched a BBC documentary about Winston Churchill and I finally discovered the full facts surrounding my father's death in the disastrous Dodecanese campaign. So the futility of my dad's death was on my mind and then to cap it all I was hit with a massive tax bill written in red ink. This concerned a company called Carsbrook that I had formed with the Robert Stigwood Organisation and, as Stigwood was one of the directors, it had to be paid. The RSO office paid this bill, but that took care of my royalties and for the next six months I had no money at all coming in.

I couldn't believe it when, a week later, another red-ink tax bill arrived, this time demanding £84,684. This should have been disputed within a three-month deadline, but I'd never seen the previous bills because they'd gone to the Harrow house and Liz had thrown them all on the fire. I phoned the guy at the tax office and shouted at him for about five minutes but there was nothing I could do. If it's gone through the court, you owe it and that's it – according to the 'Inland Robbery' in the UK. To pay it would have taken several years and left me totally broke.

I was still having a problem coming off smack and kept on banging into people who were using it all the time. I decided that I had to get out of the country and go somewhere where I didn't know anybody. I'd recently done a tour in Italy where I'd met a DJ who had told me how great Tuscany was. At the same time, another guy tried to get me out to the States. So I discussed it with Sarah and she decided we would go to Italy where we'd be near enough for her parents to visit.

Chapter Twenty-Five

Italy: 1982–88

With the help of the DJ guy, I found a house at Monte Morello, in the beautiful Tuscan hills. I used my royalties to pay a year's rent in advance, then Sarah and I loaded all our possessions and dogs into my 1948 Land Rover and set off to drive to Italy. My two horses arrived by lorry shortly after. I finally came off heroin and started a drum school with another guy. But he began putting adverts out saying that I was playing with his band. This was crap, so I went round to his house and punched him on the nose as soon as he opened the door.

After about a year, we started to have disasters. I spent a lot of time building my stables, but, when the landlady saw they were on the other side of the wall to a shrine, she went mad. Then the sewer cocked up and it was a total mess.

Some friends at the drum school told me about a woman they knew who had been left this 800-year-old, semi-derelict, abandoned house. The deal was that I could live there rent-free in return for doing it up. Sarah was very unenthusiastic about living without basic utilities and returned to England. Before she came back, I had to dig a trench down the side of the mountain for the water pipes and it was a hell of a job. I got a huge tank, and I had just dug a deep pit for it, when the neighbour whose land it was on asked me to move the hole.

Earlier, I had been so broke that I'd asked local builders for work, much to their disbelief. They gave me a job and I did so well that whenever they got a lot of work on they'd come round and ask me to help them. Now they helped me talk the neighbour out of moving the water hole and we worked on both the house and the stables. I decorated the top of my new pumping house with a sculpture and a water tank went in on the third floor. We got a bathroom suite very cheap because it was yellow and no one else wanted it. Neighbours talked me into farming the olive trees which had been neglected for many years. One of them, Giordano, was the top olive farmer in Tuscany and he taught me how to prune and care for the trees. I was often out there for 16 hours a day.

We settled in and I married Sarah in 1983, in the local town of San Rocco di Larciano and felt happy at last. Unfortunately, though, Roy Ward was taking 75 per cent of my royalty cheques and giving me the remaining amount, telling me that that was what I had.

In 1983–84, I formed the Ginger Baker Trio with guitarist John Simms and bassist Ian Macdonald and we did a tour that included Malta, Spain and Germany; but I can't remember anything about it due to the fact that I was drinking so heavily.

In the autumn of 1984, I had a big family reunion. My three children came out along with some of Nettie's male friends. I thought it was all going well but after a while my neighbours hinted that something was wrong. They had noticed that Sarah was getting off with one of these English friends under my very nose. Apparently, my son found out but this guy threatened to bash him if he spilled the beans. When they finally left, Sarah told me that she was pregnant and wanted to go back to England because she didn't want to have the baby in Italy. But then I realised that she'd gone off with this other guy. I was totally destroyed. I had all these dogs and the two horses to look after. I filed for divorce and it went through in such a way that at no time could she ever get any money off me. This was really one of the nastiest things that ever happened to me. If I ever come across this guy in the future, he's a seriously injured bloke!

On New Year's Eve 1984, there was a huge snowstorm – and in this place where it hardly ever snowed. The road was impassable and Giordano came over to inspect my best olive trees, close to the muck heap. He grabbed the bark of one and it came away in his hand. 'That's a dead tree,' he said.

In the end, I only lost 10 per cent of my trees, though another 70 per cent were damaged. Giordano and I got off lightly because we were very close to a hot spring running through the mountain. It kept our trees warmer than those on the plain below which were decimated. It was a chainsaw massacre down there. The Land Rover died as well so I had to get a second-hand Volkswagen.

I was struggling on my own and very despondent, but, although the olive production that year was very low, the price had doubled. It didn't help much, but I persevered and did odd local gigs at Communist party rallies where I'd play a drum solo and get quite good money for it. But at one point I was still so broke I lived on the leftover bread that the baker would bring up at the end of his rounds. A restaurant down the mountain was run by really cool people and the owner gave me a slap-up meal really cheap with a bottle of wine thrown in. I was also able to run up credit for horse feed and that's how I survived.

I got a message that my son Kofi was coming out from England with a friend. I'd always said I'd give him the train fare, but he paid his own way and they got as far as Paris before running out of money and hitch-hiking the rest of the way. They overshot my place, so I went mad and set off to find them in the bloody VW, which exploded. I had to borrow another car (eventually, I replaced the VW with a very cheap 1942 US army Dodge truck that had been converted into a tipper and the local mechanic converted it to run on LPG or petrol). But by the time I got out to where Kofi and his friend were supposed to have been, he'd gone on again so I went home. He was on the other side of Italy by the time Giordano's son and I finally found him. What a joke. Most of the time Kofi and I had nothing to eat except rice. But I valued spending time with him and helping him with his drumming. On 31 January, I wrote to Mum and Pop:

> Kofi is coming along well. He's got what it takes. I keep opening doors and seeing the look of wonder on his face as he understands. I really need to be with him longer; he needs to work hard for a bit. I actually spoke to Liz yesterday, when I'd phoned to speak to Nettie. It was nice to talk and be friendly after all this time. However, she wants Kofi to return quite soon as he has gigs and things to do.

We didn't even have enough to send him back to England, so we did a drum gig in the local cinema to raise the money for his fare.

In 1985, American producer Bill Laswell recruited me to record Public Image Limited's 1986 *Album* in New York, which received great acclaim. I never met or even spoke to John Lydon, it was all arranged for us to go into the studio and just put the tracks down. Tony Williams and I did half each, but, as they released the record without the personnel on it, all the reviews and write-ups could never tell who was who. We had a big laugh about it.

I did quite a few recordings with Bill and for one of these I needed to get a visa in a hurry. They organised it so well that they opened the American Embassy in Florence on a Saturday morning and gave me the visa with the waiver and everything in place.

I did a tour of Scandinavia and Germany with bassist Jonas Helborg and drove my old truck all the way. I also took it to the 1986 Nice Jazz Festival, where I performed with Jack Bruce, banjo player Birelli Lagrene and a brilliant young West Indian sax player called Courtney Pine. I worked with Jack on numerous other occasions and it was always initiated by him. He would call me and apologise for previous problems and we would begin again. Frankly, I did these gigs for the money. It was here that I saw Buddy Rich for the last time. He was on the same gig as us and was eating just two tables away in the hotel. I didn't speak to him and I know I really should have done.

Back in Italy, I began seeing a lot of another neighbour, Natalino. I got very close to his whole family, especially his daughter. I decided that when she was 21 I was going to ask her to marry me. I would do building jobs with him, and his daughter and her friends would keep house for me.

I'd heard stories about Natalino's musician son Enrico using drugs, but, whenever I attempted to tackle him with this, he always denied it. Yet, when he was arrested in Montecatini, they found 24 small packets of heroin in his pocket which he was going to sell. The family got passes to see him in jail, but his sister would only go on different days to her parents. When he was released a couple of weeks later, I knew he'd come straight from the jail, but he was obviously stoned. How did he get the stuff? There was only one answer: the sister. When I tackled her, she burst into tears, saying she loved her brother and was not involved.

When I went to pick up my hay, my friend who ran the place refused to talk to me. I asked him what was wrong and he told me that everyone thought that I was a drug dealer because I was going abroad occasionally to do gigs and these three girls were regularly visiting my house. It was true; the girls would often visit my house on their scooters and, if the police were down the road, they would ask if I could take them home, leaving the scooters behind. If they were in the car with me, they weren't going to get stopped as I had joined the local voluntary ambulance service and knew all the local police quite well.

The local bank had donated an ambulance to the commune of San Rocco di Larciano, co-financed by contributions from all the inhabitants. Once a month, two farmers would spend the night at the ambulance station in the village playing cards late into the night with the local police and staying ready for any emergency calls. We only had very basic training and so would call up the medic and go with the ambulance to the scene of the emergency.

When the girls told me they were regularly going to gay clubs in Livorno, I began to get very suspicious and decided to set a trap. I told one girl that I was very down and could do with a big turn-on. She came back and told me that a club owner in Montecatini wanted to meet me and off I went. Once in the club, two of the girls disappeared into the toilet almost immediately, and this guy, who turned out to be mafia, said he was a fan and invited me into his office to look at his guitar. He laid out two five-inch lines of coke on the table. I did one line straight away and he said he could get hold of any drugs I wanted.

So it was true that these girls were selling coke, smack and whatever to all these clubs and using me as a cover. They called me *lui de su* ('him up there') because I lived on the mountain. I let it be known how pissed off I was and from then on it would have been hard for me to continue living next door to them.

But, as it was, it didn't look like I would be able to stay anyway. The owner offered to sell the house to me, but at about three times as much as the place was worth. This upset me because the house was only worth as much as it was because of all the work I'd done on it.

By then, I had been off smack for six years and I thought I could move on without getting fucked up again. A guy had started writing to me from LA, telling me that the way I looked I had a wonderful career in films and sending me parts. So in 1988 I set off for the US.

Chapter Twenty-Six
California

As I was gearing up for the move to the States, I went very easy and saved my royalties, having got rid of Roy in the meantime. I had been stupid and given him power of attorney which he had abused; so he went, taking all my gold discs with him (which I believe he still has). All of a sudden, the royalties stopped coming through because the company who sent them out had changed office and they were really quite shitty on the phone. I waited in Italy for three months for the next payment, during which time I had a very short-lived affair with a red-haired Italian vet. I daily expected to come under attack from the mafia so I slept with two Molotov cocktails on the bedside table by the window that overlooked the yard. For extra safety, three dead olive trees blocked the driveway every night.

When I was finally able to plan my move, I flew out to LA and Nettie followed on with all the animals. I rented a place at Agua Dulce, about 45 miles from LA, where I built some stables with concrete floors and steel poles with bolts in record time. But now

I'd spent all I had in the world on the horse transport. I had water at my new place, but no fridge and it was hard going. An idiot called Bob put an advert in the local paper, which the *News of the World* spotted. They came out and took photographs for their Sunday magazine. There was a picture of me carrying a water bucket underneath the lurid banner: 'WRECK OF A ROCK STAR'!

I was told that I'd got a part in a film, but when I got there I found out that it was an audition. This was very embarrassing especially when people recognised me. I went to two or three of these – one for Captain Hook – before getting a part in a TV police series called *The Nasty Boys*. It was shot in the desert and I had to meet with these totally insane Hollywood writers at 6am every morning. The plot centred on a bunch of gangsters who were running a drug lab in the desert and the Nasty Boys (four 'top cops' of different ethnicities) were after them. We (the baddies) had to catch them but rather than blow them all away as you would have done if you'd really been in that situation, we put them in the back of a lorry, from which, of course, they quickly escaped. I was supposed to dance up to the truck and go, 'The last one on's a rotten egg,' which I thought was ridiculous. So instead I said, 'The last one on's a nancy boy.' Oh dear, they didn't want that; they didn't want that at all!

Finally, we had a gunfight with the policemen. I had to shoot and reload while the hero dived for his rifle and shot me. Well, I've never seen anyone scream when they get shot – you just fall down. So I did a fantastic fall, over one of those three-legged barbecue stoves; but the director said, 'Great fall, but you've got to go, "*Aaahhh!*"' Hollywood! They wanted the '*Aaahhh!*'

In the last bit, the coppers had to blow up the chief bad guy and the crew strung up a wire across the road to garrotte a motorcyclist. This was quite funny because they cocked it up and nearly killed the biker a few times for real!

They also got a plastic container filled with petrol which was thrown in the back of the lorry to blow it up. Well, that didn't work, did it? The container has to be glass that breaks on impact to ignite. I did point this out to them but they weren't having any of it and the Nasty Boys won the day. That was the most ridiculous thing I have ever done and was the end of my acting career.

I also encountered an English porno director called Jon who wanted to get Nettie into porn films! I went to his house once and there was a glass case with a huge dildo in it that said, 'In an emergency break the glass.' And, of course, the glass was broken. Extraordinary people!

I decided to stick with music, so Jonas and I did a jazz tour which included Bruce Springsteen's club. The audience started shouting their opinion that we should have been playing rock'n'roll rather than cool jazz and our version of Eric's quiet ballad 'Tears in Heaven'. We could hardly hear ourselves play through the din. It was a terrible gig and from that point on I didn't think much of Bruce Springsteen. Another reason for disliking him was that it was his manager who had been responsible for that Cream-bashing article in *Rolling Stone* back in 1968.

I had a blonde hairdresser called Cindy, who was a wannabe star chick with little tits. One day she asked if she could bring her friend Karen over when she came to cut my hair. I suppose the reason I quite liked Karen was because I'd been on my own for so long. I started taking her out a few times and it wasn't very long before she moved in. 'My parents mustn't know about it' was her favourite refrain, so, because I was beginning to earn some kind of money again, I bought her an incredible engagement ring. She decided we'd hold our wedding aboard a big yacht and the guests included my mum, my daughter Leda and drum company boss Bill Ludwig.

I acknowledged my 50th birthday in August 1989 by throwing a party in LA which my manager (whose name I have forgotten) attended. During my speech, I said, 'I'd like to thank the management for the abject poverty,' and he didn't last long. When he bowed out, Karen decided that she would take on the job. What a joke!

I was pleased when Sandra from the Fela days turned up and invited me along to see him play in LA. I did see Fela but I was quite disappointed with his band. It was nothing like his original one, but by then he was already really sick and it was very moving just to see him. I actually gave him a kiss and I've only ever kissed two guys in my life (the other was Eric).

In June 1991, I went over to England to attend Nettie's wedding to Mick Lewis. Later that same year, I was pleased to discover that I was to become a grandfather, because Nettie had had an operation in 1986 and been told that she might not be able to have children. My granddaughter Zara was born in June 1992 and I always think of her as 'the miracle baby'.

The band Masters of Reality came about around the same time as this, via manager Marty Schwartz who I met while playing polo at Will Rodgers's place in LA. Marty told me about some great musicians he was handling, so I got together with Chris Goss, guitar/vocals, Daniel Ray, guitar, and Googe on bass. I was surprised that it was actually enjoyable and we made a record for Delicious Vinyl. It was a good album, but they wanted to market it as heavy metal (which it wasn't). We did a disastrous tour for nothing – or for 'promotional' purposes – in one of those touring buses, which was bloody murder. Hence, the title of the album *Sunrise on the Suffer Bus*. We recorded enough stuff for two CDs, but I soon fell out big time with Marty and the record company.

I was also less than enthused by yet another offer to do my biography. But Karen was all for it and reckoned that I would get a lot of money. 'Writer' Geoffrey Giuliano came down to our place in Santa Inez and I have to say that from the outset he struck me as being a very odd person. He was quite a good salesman, though. He had all these Beatles books that he'd done and he'd also got a deal with St Martin's Press, so I decided I'd give it a go. He went over to England to see Liz and took a lot of stuff from her and then he did the same with my mum. Unfortunately, these personal possessions were never returned and later appeared for sale on the internet.

He attempted to write a book of sorts and I thought it was a load of crap. But he went ahead against my wishes and sent it to the publisher, saying that I'd OK'd it. I went absolutely mad and St Martin's Press attempted to placate me by saying they had another writer in the pipeline. It was incredible: all she did was copy what Giuliano had written. It was still rubbish. Liz phoned me and said she'd seen an early copy of the book and that it was terrible. I had no choice but to stop them from publishing it. At which point St Martin's Press sued me for return of the whole advance. I got hold of a lawyer in New York and agreed to pay back what I'd personally received, but no way was I going to pay Giuliano or his crooked agent. Even after all this, Geoffrey retained some copies and distributed them on the internet. What else could go wrong?

I got a phone call from Jack asking me to do a tour with him and it was for reasonable money. He made it clear to me that I would be working 'for' him and not 'with' him. But Karen was keen for me to do it and, although I did try to explain to her what Jack was like, she clearly didn't believe me, so I accepted the gig.

But, before the tour started, I did a gig in New York with some friends of Bill Laswell's. In the car on the way to the airport I got a pain in my gut, which got steadily worse. I had a row with the flight crew on the plane because they didn't have any pills for it. We booked into the hotel in New York, but during the night Karen woke me and said, 'Man, you're burning!' The sweat was pouring off me and I had an unusually high temperature so she called an ambulance. I was rushed to hospital and operated on for a ruptured appendix (which I had thought was wind!) at four o'clock in the morning. Karen had probably saved my life.

I explained to the medical staff that I had a tour starting and the surgeon completed the procedure without cutting muscle. This was very decent of him and it wasn't long before I was walking around with my drip and smoking my pipe. I went to convalesce at my new in-laws' place in Arlington, Virginia before setting off on the road with Jack.

The rehearsals went quite well, and I thought I had made it very clear that I didn't want him to play too loud because it hurt my ears. But, on the first gig, we got on stage, 1,2,3,4, and the sound... Jack was at full volume! So was the guitar player and I couldn't bring my sticks down because I was in excruciating pain. Then Jack started screaming and shouting at me. Karen saw it for the first time. I said, 'That's it, we're out of here,' and we went back to Arlington.

That afternoon, the police came knocking on the door and informed me that it was imperative that I perform at the next gig. I don't know how Jack managed to get them to do this, but he did! He was begging me to go back and so I finally agreed. At the airport, we boarded a little twin-engine plane and had just taken off when things went very quiet on the left-hand side. 'Uh oh, he's lost an engine,' I said. We had to land immediately on one engine and wait for a back-up plane to come.

Obviously, we arrived at the venue very late, but, although technically it was Jack's gig, the audience were on their feet screaming for me. Then in the middle of a drum solo Jack took the mike and shouted at me! Karen just couldn't believe it, even though I had warned her. Somehow I managed to finish the tour. Jack's guitar player had big bushy hair, so I amused myself by whacking cigarette ends into it with my stick – I was always trying to set him alight on stage.

When we played Israel, the security to get on the El Al plane was something else. I noticed many strange religious types on board in all manner of odd attire. Then, when we got to Jerusalem, I encountered a big problem in getting a hamburger and a milkshake together, because they won't let you do it there. I found this odd.

The promoter and some other young guys were very keen to take me out and show me where a rocket had landed. A bloke my son's age said to me, 'You don't understand: Arabs are not humans, they're animals.'

'What?' I said. 'Well, I've spent a lot of time with them and I think they're OK.'

I did go to the Dome of the Rock and, even though it was surrounded by gun-toting Israeli soldiers, it remained a very holy place. It had a wonderful atmosphere and it was a strange experience, because once inside it I too felt the need to pray.

Jack and I did a TV show there, just the two of us, with me on the snare drum. Jack had decided to do the blues number 'Sitting on Top of the World' and during the rehearsal when he sang, 'She's gone and left me,' I added, 'I'm not surprised.' I kept on taking the piss and all the crew were laughing. Jack went purple and started shouting, 'You've got to pay your dues before you do that to me!' Oh, no, you can't take the piss out of Jack! He threw an incredible number: he was the band leader and I was his drummer. After that, I vowed I'd never go to Israel again.

Back in 1988, I had been at a big Hollywood party when I was approached by a lawyer from Bob Toolapan's company who dealt with musicians and their visas worldwide. He said they were 'really worried' because a change in the immigration laws that year meant my status was tenuous. It turned out that, although I had married Karen, the authorities wouldn't give me a green card and I had to renew my work permit every two years. This involved getting all the paperwork done and then flying to the American Embassy in

London, where they would take as long as possible to process me because it involved a drug bust.

The first time I had to renew it was in 1993 when my mum died and I was staying with my sister in Sidcup. Karen and I got to the embassy in London at 8.45am and there was already a queue right the way around the block. It was freezing cold and it wasn't until 11.30am that we got to within 20 people of the gate. Then an official thug came out and said, 'Go away now,' in a very unpleasant manner. So the next morning we had to get up extra early to catch the first train from Sidcup in order to be right up in the queue. I was interviewed by an Englishwoman who was also very unpleasant and insinuated that I had only married Karen to get a green card. Karen later wrote a letter of complaint to the US government about this treatment. It was appalling.

When I finally got back to LA, I was asked to do a session for Robbie Robertson's *Storyville* album. He takes years to make a record and all I can say is that I've never needed more than two weeks to make an album in my life. We did a really fantastic take and, in a similar vein to a Cream thing I'd done. I had to spend all day in the studio and then they didn't use it. His producer didn't want to hear my hi-hat and put a rubber sheet between the cymbals to deaden them! They asked American jazz-rock drummer Billy Ward to do it and as soon as he heard the tape he said, 'That's Ginger Baker, it's fantastic.'

In 1993, I was invited to attend the Rock'n'Roll Hall of Fame Awards and this heralded a new chapter in my financial life. My Chicago-based lawyer Tom Swift teamed up with Eric's manager Roger Forrester and forged a new deal with the record company. Years before, a guy called Kipper at the Stigwood office had told me that they'd been taking a 25 per cent management cut out of our royalties from the days of Cream. By now, they owed us millions and, although I had written to the record company about this

On Pepe at Cowdray Park.

Above: Pampy, in 1976, who went lame and had to be put down.

Below: With Leda, Kofi and Nettie at Denham in 1981.

Above: Marrying Sarah in Italy in 1983.

Below left: On the day of the wedding in Larciano, Tuscany.

Below right: Just me, my Dodge and a dog called Basil.

Above: Marrying Karen in 1990.

Below: With Mum at the wedding reception.

Above: Nettie's wedding: me, Nettie, Kofi and Jack Russell, 1991.

Below: The case of the exploding tin of cat food – Nick and I discover the reason for the smell in the Grand Am, Colorado, 1997.

Top: Nightmare in Colorado with Nettie, Liz, Leda and Kofi.

Below left: Very pissed off at Kofi's wedding.

Below right: Dueting with Kofi – polo and jazz in Denver.

Above: Charlie Watts presents me with my Achievement Award in December 2008.

Below: Playing at the ceremony in London.

© Courtesy Zildjian

Top left: With my horses in South Africa in 2008.   © *Jay Bulger*

Top right: Lisa, Kudzai and me.   *Courtesy of Norman Collins*

Bottom left: With Kai in 2009.   *Courtesy of Norman Collins*

Bottom right: My granddaughter Zara, Kudzai and Nettie at the Zildjian awards dinner in 2008.
                                             © *Courtesy of Zildjian*

many times, I had unsurprisingly received no reply. I even threatened litigation to no avail. But now Roger and Tom managed to get the royalties backdated for eight years, rather than 25 as it was then, and upped them to a more reasonable standard. It was great to have this rectified at last and in this happier state of mind I prepared for the awards – which turned out to be a nightmare.

The rehearsals were pretty good and very enjoyable. But we had to sit for hours at a table while all these other idiots like Jim Morrison's band picked up their awards. They made long speeches saying, 'I'd like to thank my mother and my uncle who lent me 50 bucks 20 years ago, my kids, my animals and my dog's granddad…' Each had this whole list of people they wanted to thank! Every one of them was doing this and they were all a load of wankers. Despite this, I quite enjoyed sitting with Naomi Campbell, who was with Eric at the time. I really liked her. When it finally came to our turn, my back was aching from sitting on an uncomfortable chair for ages listening to these silly speech makers so I just said, 'Well, everybody's said it all, so… "Thanks, guys",' and that was it. The actual gig wasn't as good as it could've been but it was OK.

As my financial situation had changed quite considerably, I was able to play polo again. I'd had to hire a kit for a TV show sometime before and by complete coincidence the shop was owned by Ken Berry, a polo player I'd met on the Baker Gurvitz Army tour in 1975. He invited me down to Ventura to play some polo and then on to a tournament. I took my green horses that hadn't played for ages and Project had a head-on collision with one of the Domingo brothers! Project became quite famous and I used to play some amazing shots where he would go up on his hind legs and the ball would go underneath.

We did a charity match at Santa Barbara Polo Club where I played pretty well. On the other team was an actor who coincidentally appeared in a soap opera as a polo player. He really had a go at me on the field so I offered him out, but he apologised and became a friend. It was an exciting game with Miguel Torres and some good Argies on the field and I did my best chukka on my new horse, Babe. I was now playing four-chukka polo and I went with the actor to the 40/40 game in the desert, where I met up again with my old friend Bill Mulcahy from the Gulfstream all those years ago. He had a string of the best horses in America at this time and was mounting Memo Gracida and the Heguys.

The actor had his eye on a horse called Charmain and took her home but decided against buying her, so Bill asked me to look after her. She was so good to play that I tendered an offer. Bill wanted $14,000 and I paid him off over 18 months. I'd built four stables at Agua Dulce and had a little Mexican groom who, with bright-red hair and freckles, looked more like Howdy Doody and not a Mexican at all.

I made a friend in Santa Barbara who invited me to his place to play and I drove the 140 miles there in my green truck and red four-horse trailer. It was a helluva caper to drive, but it became a regular thing at weekends. It was at one of these games that I damaged a poor woman who rode into a nearside back shot of mine. The club wouldn't let beginners wear face masks for some reason, and if she'd had one on she would've been OK but as it was I got told off!

As I was spending so much time there, Karen decided that it would be a good idea to move nearer to this club. We found a place where the dogs managed to roll in cow shit all the time and we had to hose them down three times a day.

An acquaintance from Hawaii sent three new horses but they arrived in such a state my English groom Helen wanted to report him. One of them had a Wellington boot for a foot so I gave it away. Another one, Fearless, was a good horse and played well, despite having one leg shorter than the other. So I kept two of them and now I had six. It cost $3,000 per season to play at the club and I had an agreement whereby I would pay $2,000 at the beginning of the season and $1,000 at the end.

After we'd settled in, I went off to play with Bill Laswell in Japan for five weeks. We only played six gigs and, although they were good, I wasn't very pleased about sitting around with nothing to do. When I came back, I discovered that the club had refused to let a friend of mine play my horses when I'd given my permission and that, even though we were only halfway through the season, they now wanted their $1,000.

We decided to move to Colorado.

Chapter Twenty-Seven
Colorado

Karen said that if there was one place other than California that she'd like to live it would be Colorado. As luck would have it, the Hawaii polo team had a game in Denver where I met an estate agent who found me a property with a large barn. To be truthful, I didn't like it that much and I wasn't pleased when Karen went straight back to Colorado and bought the place. But I set to work once more. My first job was to prepare the barn to deal with massive snow build-up in the winter and my nephew Ken came out from England to help me. I actually managed to lay the concrete floors for ten stables in one day!

Hannah (my new groom) and I then set off to collect the horses. We took a different route back that led us through perilously steep mountain passes 10,000 feet up. I thought at one point that the truck wasn't going to make it, but luckily an enormous rig came past and dragged me up in his slipstream. We arrived back at 3am to find that Karen had locked the door and there was no straw in the barns. It was a nightmare, but I finally got it sorted out.

In 1994, I got a phone call from Jack, who asked me to do a session with him and Gary Moore. They readily agreed to my demands for good money and first-class travel and so I went over to a studio in England for a week. It went so well that they asked me to come back and do some more and I flew home to consider it.

But, even though Karen had got me paying taxes of $40,000 a year and I'd bought a property, the usual thing happened. I arrived at the old Colorado airport where they took one look at my passport with all the waivers in it and the red lights went off. I waited around and was ushered in to see a grey-haired old woman who happened to be the chief immigration officer.

'What is the purpose of your visit?' she asked me.

'I'm coming home,' I replied.

'No, you're not.'

'What do you mean?' I asked. 'I live here and I've bought a property.'

'You don't live here,' she said. 'You're not allowed to.'

Well, you can imagine the state I was in, having flown back from London on a no-smoking flight, still in a no-smoking zone and getting really very cross indeed. After about two hours I lost my rag. 'What are you doing?' I raved. 'I'm English and we're your allies!'

They called Karen in. She had come along with a friend to meet me but until then nobody had told them what was going on. 'Does he get violent?' the officer asked nervously.

I was finally allowed into the country and Karen told me that Tommy Harris, who I'd met at the polo club in Florida and who'd become one of my best friends, had just died of cancer.

I continued to do work with Jack and Gary Moore and I was invited to join the band to do a tour with them. I agreed only if it was to be for serious money. They got a deal that would pay the band $50,000 a gig guaranteed and it looked very good on paper, but I found the music to be very contrived. When I played with

Eric, we would often go off into time things together, it always happened simultaneously and was never in the same place, yet Gary Moore solos were always the same.

Anyway, we set off on this ludicrous tour. After the first gig, I was informed that the next gig was off because Gary had blown his ears. He had this tinnitus problem and indeed the bass and guitar were so loud that I was sitting in a little cubicle surrounded by baffle boards. It seemed as though every hotel we booked into became the scene of a big row that Jack and his family got into because they didn't have the view they required and insisted that their rooms were changed. On one occasion, a smart new Mercedes was sent to pick us up but, as it wasn't a limo, they sent it back. It was getting ridiculous. Then the gig in Paris was cancelled because Gary had cut his finger opening a tin! I thought, What the fuck? I mean, if Eric cut his finger opening a tin, he'd put a plaster on it and play the gig! This sort of behaviour turned Gary into the 'Pampered Pompadour of Pop' in my opinion and Jack was Dr Jekyll and Mr Hyde. They were throwing these scenes everywhere we went.

There was a big gig in Berlin planned for August, but I had booked the rest of that month off to prepare for a memorial polo tournament for Tommy Harris. However, the night before it started, Gary's management told me I would have to fly to London to do a rehearsal. I didn't think we needed one. I said there was no way I could do it because I'd already arranged to drive my horses back over the mountains, drop them at my place, then go back with the trailer, pick up my friend Bill Mulcahy's horses and drive them to Boston. So Gary's management said they would organise the transport for Mulcahy's horses and pay the bill.

With this agreement in place, I drove my own horses back and flew out from Denver. I arrived at Gatwick early in the morning after having had no sleep on the plane and a car took me to my hotel, where I had a full English breakfast and crashed out. Next thing I knew the phone was ringing, 'Where are you?' they asked. 'The car's waiting outside and you're late for a rehearsal.' They'd hired the Brixton Academy for an astronomical £11,000 and as soon as I stepped out of the car I could already hear the guitar from outside the building!

The rehearsal was essentially the gig in its entirety, solos and all, including some syncopated prearranged thing. It was note perfect. It could, and indeed it should, have been the gig. But they insisted on rehearsing because every now and again I played something that they didn't like; it always had to be exactly the same. Why they didn't just put tapes on and mime to it like Pink Floyd do, I don't know. So now everyone was happy and the vast amount of equipment that had been unloaded just for the day was reloaded and dispatched to Germany.

The next afternoon, the call came from Gary's manager. 'The gig's off.'

'What?'

'Yeah, Gary's blown his ears on the rehearsal. I just took him to the doctor.'

'Why don't you take him to a psychiatrist?' I replied. That was the end of the conversation. I mean, how insane can you get?

So the gig was off and by now my drums were on the way to Berlin, but they promised to send them home. As I flew back I thought, That's the end of that, never again! Jack had been an absolute prick throughout, trying to be my band leader and acting as though he was above me. They were cancelling gigs right, left and centre because Gary played too loud on the rehearsal and blew his ears. I mean, is this sane?

My drums finally arrived with the bill, which I paid along with the one for Mulcahy's horses and sent the invoices on. But they didn't pay them as promised and never spoke to me again because I had suggested that they take Gary Moore to see a psychiatrist instead of a doctor.

They put an album out with a photograph of me in a leather coat, smoking a fag, standing in front of these angel wings on the cover. I got some reasonable royalties from the sales in Europe but it never sold well in the States. I knew it wouldn't because it was a pretend Cream thing, with Jack trying to write Cream-type numbers. That was the BBM experience, absolutely unbelievable. But I was then asked to do some experimental drum stuff for Andy Summers, who was a nice guy; it came out on a 1995 album called *Synaesthesia*.

Now that I was properly settled in Colorado, I bought a 12th share of the field at Running Brook Polo and joined the club. Unfortunately, this turned out to be another nightmare. On the first day out, they were playing 15-minute chukkas (supposed to be seven) on unfit horses and I wouldn't have it. I wrote an article that appeared in the polo magazine about cowboys and horses. In it, I explained the English definition of a cowboy. I mentioned that in California they kept their horses on sand and tied them up in head collars all day so they couldn't get their heads down. I found I couldn't get on with these polo people at all and one guy in particular really took umbrage at this. I was a two-goal player and had been put in charge of umpiring, because I was so knowledgeable on the subject and had disagreed in print about the ridiculous whip-and-spurs concept.

In one tournament, a girl tried a silly manoeuvre that caused her horse's leg to snap and this one guy who disliked me was all for getting a gun and shooting it there and then. So I got the vet to put it down humanely and he was not at all amused about that. Later in the same match, he tapped the ball to draw me in and then took a huge swing, not at the ball, but at the sole of my boot. He tried the same trick again and this time he deliberately whacked me on the shin. This caused a big row and I threw him off the field. I got home to discover a huge bleeding mark on my shin and wrote a letter to the club committee complaining about him. I discovered that this is how he behaved if he didn't like people, and had once broken somebody's hand! The committee, however, refused to take action and so I resigned from the club (which pissed Karen right off because I'd already paid my subscription).

On one occasion, I was invited to play in a two-chukka celebrity polo match in New York. One of the horses was duff, but I played well and we won the game easily. The writer Hunter S Thompson turned up with his editor Shelby Sadler to write an article about the match, in which he mentioned me. Shelby was yet another person who wanted to do my book, and somehow I ended up with them in a huge black car. Hunter was driving and it was quite alarming. We got totally lost in the car park and couldn't get out of it.

By now, I'd got to know the people at Salisbury Equestrian Centre nearby, where they played practice chukkas. I put on a 15-goal arena game at the local stadium and sold 861 tickets, which isn't bad, because when the US Polo Association did a 27-goal game in Florida they only sold 450. We invited Hunter as the guest of honour. Karen and her brother were supposed to bring him round backstage, but instead they tried to go in the front door which was pretty stupid 'cos he didn't have a ticket. When he did get in, he immediately lit a cigarette in the no-smoking arena and got ejected by the stewards!

When he stayed at the Crown Hotel in Denver, we went to visit him. He'd got a bull whip with which he was terrorising people and a hand mallet and ball that he was whacking around his room, smashing pictures in the process. I was looking out for a suitable polo field so Hunter took us round an old (and, unfortunately, highly radioactive) airbase in his SUV. He had a round tin full of coke in the vehicle into which he continually dipped a straw and sniffed. I was sitting in the back seat with a bucket of ice and a bottle of Chivas Regal, which Hunter kept reaching back for, still driving of course! He once turned up at polo wearing a white plastic mask. He was totally insane, absolutely crazy.

After he had gone, I started the Mile High Polo Club, and with Karen's friend who worked in the Chamber of Commerce at Parker we came up with the idea of putting on polo and jazz. A local council meeting unanimously agreed that I could use their fields to stage the event and this meant that the practice field used by Running Brook was now unavailable to them; divine retribution in the circumstances as we were also playing better polo. I began to pull in big crowds because I knew plenty of good polo players like Mike Daly, Donny Healy and Fred Barratt who would bring all his horses up from Texas and sell them during the tournament. Others who helped make the club happen were Kimo Huddleston, John Eicher, Barry Stout, Santiago Bottaro and Daniel Gonzales.

I'd already got The Ginger Baker Trio together and I recorded 1994's *Going Back Home* in LA, before I left for Denver. It featured guitarist Bill Frisell, bassist Charlie Haden and was arranged by my old friend and music journalist Chip Stern. I was amazed to find that the engineer was none other than Malcolm Cecil, a good friend who used to play bass at Ronnie Scott's in the 1960s. When he and his wife had moved to the States, Liz and I had given their cat a home in Neasden.

We recorded with Malcolm in three days; it made number five on the *Billboard* jazz chart and received a helluva lot of critical acclaim. Chip Stern knew Max Roach and he suggested we do a gig in Verona with Max, his band M'Boom and my old friend and rival Tony Williams. Chip arranged the gig and we rehearsed at the Lincoln centre in Harlem. Max and I sat outside in the sunshine of Harlem; we chatted for ages. I was very impressed with what a nice guy he was and we became great friends. Karen and I also hung out with Tony and his wife Colleen, with whom we had a lot of fun.

The gig in Verona went great but the recording of it wasn't very good and so we planned to record at a studio in New York. It was all arranged when the terrible news came through that Tony Williams had died during a gall bladder operation. So instead of going into the studio, Max and I went to San Francisco with a lot of other musicians and carried Tony's coffin. It was very, very sad.

The title for the follow-up to *Going Back Home* came as a result of a DIY disaster. I was building a porch when a high wind began to blow. I only needed to get a couple more rivets in when Karen got fed up with holding the ladder and went inside. I had one foot on the ladder and was lying on the 45-degree angle of the roof, but as I put the rivet in the ladder went. I slid down the incline and landed flat on the floor unconscious. I was flown to hospital in a helicopter and it turned out I'd broken two ribs and got concussion. Meanwhile, my son Kofi, who was living with me at the time, was in his little flat completely unaware of all this, when he was supposed to be helping me as well! I wasn't very happy with this. So the title of the next album had to be *Falling off the Roof* (1996). Bill Frisell, Charlie Haden and I recorded it in Oregon near Bill's place.

After the release of *Falling off the Roof* I heard that Bill Frissell was doing a gig in Denver so Karen and I went along. Bill was playing with Ron Miles and Artie Moore was on bass. They really impressed me, we got chatting after the gig and we decided to do some music together. Ron brought in pianist Eric Gunnison and we played several gigs at a local jazz club. I asked the guys if they'd come at play at my polo and jazz events to which they agreed with alacrity. So we formed the Denver Jazz Quartet To Octet and played at my events every Thursday night throughout 1996. We used to rehearse at Ron's little house in Denver where he produced the score for *Jesus Loves Me*. It started in 17/8 and time signatures were changing all over it. 'Christ, Ron, you've gotta be kidding!' I said.

Ron smiled, 'Ginger, I wrote this specially for you,' he replied and sure enough, when we played it, it really worked. Ron was a gentle genius and it was an incredible piece of music!

We got a gig for a week at a big jazz club in New York. When we arrived there was a cock-up with the hotel but the guys were really cool about it and four of them stayed in one room for the night. What a difference to what I imagined would have happened with certain rock musicians of my acquaintance.

I'd mentioned quite a few times to Yves Beauvais of Atlantic Records that I'd got a fantastic band together in Denver but he just didn't believe me. The first night at the club was a sensation and the crowd really loved the music so by word of mouth Atlantic Records turned up for Wednesday's gig. The next day a huge bunch of flowers from Atlantic was delivered to my room and they'd got the message.

Max Roach came to a couple of gigs and on one occasion I got taken over by the spirit of Baby Dodds and played the best solo I've ever played. Max was blown away, it was a fantastic night and we went on to have a wonderful week in which Karen and I went for several meals with Max and his girlfriend. At the weekend we did three shows a night because the band was so popular. Yves wanted us to make a record and James Carter was invited to play as a guest. We only had time for one rehearsal at Ron's, with Fred conducting James through the intricate parts. We recorded the album *Coward of the County* in just two days, straight onto two-track. It was the band live and James did an amazing job. Released in 1999, it turned out to be the best jazz record I ever made.

I also caught up with other friends from the music world. Carlos Santana did a gig nearby and he called me up on stage to play with him. Robert Plant also came to see me and I sat in on 'White Room' when Ringo Starr was in town. When the Rolling Stones played, my old friend Charlie Watts dropped by. 'I'd give you some tickets,' he said, 'but I know you wouldn't come!'

After I'd been in Denver a while, I joined the Rattlesnake Fire

Department on a voluntary basis. At that stage, Karen wasn't that interested, but I went for my firefighter one written examination and passed first time with flying colours, which nobody else had ever done before. They were a bunch of idiots! I'd been up and down ladders all my life, but they'd all be going, 'Careful, careful!' Only a couple of the guys were any good and the assistant chief got very pissed off that I did so well. I actually saved a house once when I got there before him. I acted fast because those wooden places really burn and I made sure we got water on it quickly, but when the assistant chief arrived he accused me of being a 'cowboy' for putting it out without waiting for him. Previously they had lost a house when they'd insisted on waiting for that dickhead to arrive.

But the training was great. They would set a test house on fire and measure your heart rate and blood pressure before and after each exercise. My readings were actually lower when I came out, which they found hard to believe. On the third test on one particular training day, I gave my leadership role to another colleague. We were required to go upstairs in the house and search for so-called survivors. By that point, the fire had started to get out of hand and what with the thick smoke and the breathing apparatus we couldn't see anything much. We were also alone up there because – without informing my companion and me – the others had stayed downstairs. Suddenly, there was a hand on my foot and it was one of the top men, also named Baker, who motioned me down. My partner had already retreated and turned his hose to spray instead of full jet, which unfortunately heated it up of course. He was doused with boiling water and had to be taken to hospital. The other Baker and I managed to get the fire under control but then had considerable difficulty finding our way out because of the poor visibility. I was hugely complimented because my pulse was still down. I actually found it quite enjoyable, but as usual the assistant chief did not.

When we attended a false alarm due to a faulty smoke alarm, he pitched up and shouted, 'Baker, get out of that house! Move!' He ended up bringing two fire engines and the whole fire department with hoses and everything, when there was absolutely no need for it. He bollocked me in front of everybody and I went mad. If there had been a real fire somewhere else they wouldn't have been able to get to it.

Our relationship wasn't helped when the chief of the professional fire department asked me to help train some of his young guys because he thought I was so cool under pressure. Our assistant chief was even more annoyed when I was recommended as captain of a new fire station they were proposing to open. He wanted the job. So tensions began to build, but, as it happened, these events coincided with other things that led to my departure from the US.

Chapter Twenty-Eight

Nightmare in Colorado: 1997

Life in Colorado was busy. My son Kofi was getting married and his wedding day was fast approaching, just as Fred Barrett arrived from Texas with six new horses. My English groom Liz, who'd been with me for two-and-a-half years, seemed really pleased with the new animals and didn't even complain that there'd be extra horses in work now. I finally had the string of my dreams; the season at my Mile High Polo Club was due to start in two days' time and we had been assured of a large crowd. Meanwhile, Liz's green-card application was only a month away from being finalised and she was very excited about it.

Earlier on, I had lent a fellow player a mobile arena, which had been erected on his family's land, but, when his contingent decided not to support the Mile High Club, I asked him to return it. He called to say that as he'd put it up on his father's property it belonged to them. We got into a slanging match on the phone and as I hung up I distinctly caught the tone of threat in his voice. By what you might say was a strange coincidence, shortly afterwards a report was made to the authorities that my club was employing an illegal alien – Liz. But for the time being I was unaware of this development.

The first game went ahead in front of a good crowd and we drew 4–4. We played some great jazz afterwards, then I went home to turn the ponies out in their paddocks and eat a meal cooked by Karen. I felt it was a great start to the season.

Karen and I were due to fly out for a gig at the Knitting Factory in New York and I planned to stop off in Maryland on the Sunday and Monday to have my new bionic teeth fitted on to the titanium implants I'd had done just before Christmas. I thought it would be great to have them in time for Kofi's wedding. But the gig was cancelled so I told Karen I wanted to stay put and get to know the new horses. Reluctantly, she cancelled our flights.

A few days later, I noticed a car draw up and park close to the beautiful Redwood and Cedar gates that had taken me four months to construct. Two young guys got out and seemed baffled by how to get in, although my vet and farrier who fixed the tractor and various other visitors had never seemed to have any trouble working it out! In the end, they opted for the side gate and knocked on the door as Liz was taking a break. I answered it and they asked for her by name.

They brandished their United States Department of Justice badges just inches away from Karen's face as she rushed to Liz's aid. But it was too late and one, a very smug Mr Cory Vorhis, produced a piece of paper with my signature on (the one I had signed towards getting her green card) and triumphantly announced to me that in his eyes this proved that I had known she was illegal when I signed it. With that, he clicked a set of cuffs on to Liz's wrists and marched her away to be bundled unceremoniously into their car and driven off. Mr Vorhis clearly enjoyed his job.

I got straight on to an immigration lawyer in Denver, but he explained that, as Liz had entered the country on a visa waiver, she had no right to legal assistance. Surely this can't be happening? For the first time since I'd been in Colorado, I didn't watch the ten o clock news; America had suddenly gone sour. I was deeply pissed off, couldn't sleep, drank endless pots of tea and smoked continuously. Now I had to look after all the animals myself. I fed them the next morning and then went out to water the garden.

A young man carrying a sheet of paper walked down the drive; it was Vorhis again, but I failed to recognise him at first. 'How are you today?' he asked.

'Well, nobody's dead,' I answered.

He continued to speak to me as if I was a class-A tax-dodging criminal, so I refused to sign anything and sent the prick away with a flea in his ear. When I took a closer look at the document that my friend Vorhis had given to me, I realised that the authorities seemed to be under the misapprehension that Mile High was a business employing people, when everyone involved worked for it voluntarily. I wrote to the chief officer at the Department of Justice to explain that the proceeds went to charity (Dreampower Ranch for animals, Project Linus which helped children in hospital and the American Cancer Society).

I went unhappily back to the barn and turned the horses out, but now the tractor was dead so I had to use a wheelbarrow to muck out all 11 stables. The only good news was that my first wife Liz, along with Leda, Nettie (who had separated from Mick) and her boyfriend Nick were arriving that very day and I knew they could be relied upon to help out. Nettie joked that she was on a busman's holiday as she'd been working as a groom back home, but she did a great job helping out at our second game the next day when my Dragonflies team beat Boulder 7–6. The band followed with a great set that ended with Kofi and I doing a drum duet.

The house was full of guests anticipating the wedding, but what should have been a joyous occasion was now marred by a vast black cloud of doom. Liz was having a terrible time in jail and I made up my mind that I wanted to leave America.

The next night, we had a pre-wedding party in town, but because I had to finish off all the work at the ranch I arrived late, the food was terrible and I had to go outside to smoke. To cap it all, I was introduced to another guest, a friend of a friend of Karen's, whom I'd never even seen before. Then yet another friend of Karen's, named Ken, decided to smoke too much dope and freaked out later that night. Karen called me and I found him lying in the hallway. 'He needs help,' she said.

'Help, my arse!' I shouted. 'He shouldn't smoke it if he can't handle it. Go to bed, Ken – you aren't going to die!'

After a while I went up to bed but then out of the darkness I heard Karen's voice say, 'You're not going to understand this, Ginger.'

I switched on the light to be confronted by Ken again. He was now in his underpants, lying on the floor, surrounded by Karen (in her nightie), and two other 'friends', kneeling down and holding his hand! I went mad!

'For Christ's sake, go to bed and start acting like a fucking adult, Ken!'

Sheepishly, he retreated.

Bloody hell! My groom was in jail, everything had gone wrong and here's some bozo who's smoked too much dope being comforted by all these women. Karen was right, I did *not* understand.

I woke up on Kofi's wedding day in a black rage. Nettie said that she and Nick would muck out while Leda and I exercised the horses. Thank God for the English! The sun was high in the sky by the time we'd finished riding our second set and then the Yanks appeared, enjoying a leisurely breakfast on the porch. 'Hey, Ginger, you look like a real cowboy!' shouted the girl I'd never met before.

By the time we got in, they'd all gone off to be tourists – it was a shame that my kids never got to go as well.

Karen had relegated my family to travelling in a white Pontiac Grand Am, which sounded very nice but was full of a terrible and mysterious smell of fish that, with no air conditioning and in the boiling heat, was most unpleasant. After some investigation, Nettie and Nick discovered that a tin of cat food had burst in there three weeks previously, so before they could get ready they had to clean it out with a bucket and some disinfectant. Great holiday they were having, while the Yanks swanned about enjoying a marvellous time. I ended up having a row with Karen. I didn't want the States to have another penny of my money – I was leaving and at least I came from a civilised place!

Now that everyone was dressed up, I had to do all the horses on my own and was exhausted by the time I got to the church in my old truck. Kofi was resplendent in a tuxedo and I thought, God! Can this be my son? His bride Cinnamon looked beautiful and I tried to be happy, but the preacher droned on and on. I fell asleep and had to be nudged awake by Karen. I managed to witness the important bit, they were wed and we headed off towards the reception at Le Peeps Restaurant, a place run by Kofi's new in-laws.

But the journey there was complicated by the fact that Clinton and Blair were in town for the G8 summit and half of Denver was closed off. We set off in three vehicles with Karen and her two girlfriends leading in a 4 x 4 Blazer, me behind her and my family in the Grand Am. Kofi's new father-in-law had told me how to circumnavigate all the road blocks and, as we reached the exit, I flashed my lights at Karen, but she was so busy chatting that she just sailed straight past it. What ensued was total chaos – U-turns and everything, with Karen even driving past the restaurant without stopping! I wanted a divorce!

As I sat outside the place fuming, a silly American woman sidled over. 'Hi, Ginger, how're you doin'?'

'I'm still breathing,' I replied.

Karen and I fell out big time and I stormed off home. I took off my suit and went back to my beautiful horses. Now I knew why I preferred them to people. Then I thought that maybe I should go back to the reception but I was so tired I fell asleep on the floor and when I woke up it was past midnight.

I apologised to Kofi the next morning and he and Cinnamon gave me a piece of wedding cake. The kids helped out with the stables again while Karen and my first wife Liz went off on a Harley ride, up in the mountains, as 'Ginger Baker's wives'.

Soon enough, my family returned to England and somehow polo and jazz continued. Liz's birthday arrived to find her still in jail with a bunch of Mexicans and I didn't have much news to give to her troubled family back home. But I found out that, if I paid her fare back to England, I could get her out. She got deported and was put on the plane in handcuffs dressed in the same mucking-out clothes that she'd been wearing the day she was arrested. A friend of mine said that he'd overheard somebody admitting it was him who'd turned me over to the INS. One phone call had destroyed Liz's life and I'd lost my groom.

Now that's all over with, I thought. But the United States Justice Department have enormous power and an immigration lawyer called Robert Heiserman explained to me that my own immigration status was also under review and that in his opinion I need to get 'lawyered up'. He said that I should never have sent the previous letter explaining the club's charity status (especially without a copy) and that incidentally his fees were $325 an hour!

A couple of days later, I was sitting on the porch in my T-shirt when this bloody Vorhis and his mate turned up again. As my Alsatian dog Fritzi ran up to them barking, they went for their guns. 'You get that fucking gun out, boy, and you're dead!' I shouted.

They warned me that I could be done for threatening Federal Agents. Oh yeah? When they had guns and I had nothing? Instead, they issued me with a subpoena, the existence of which I was not to reveal to anyone, because I was under investigation by the Department of Justice.

To take my mind off things, I decided to see Fred Barrett in Texas for a couple of weeks of enjoyable polo, although, due to a fuck-up by a Mexican groom, I lost my best horse, Remington, to colic. It turned out the groom was an illegal worker and he was arrested and deported. I was under investigation myself and they'd given me an illegal Mexican! I wasn't pleased. I loaded up my remaining nine horses and drove home feeling very despondent. I got back to find snow everywhere and that, following a nine-month investigation, I'd been found guilty. But I was only to be fined $2,000.

By then, I'd got involved with Lewis and Floorwax, a couple of DJs who hosted a very humorous radio show and they knew quite a lot of the local politicians. They got me on their radio show and asked me on air if any of their 'goons' had helped me. 'Well, I don't know,' I replied, 'because the immigration people don't like being hassled.'

The next day, my lawyer was told the investigation was to be reopened because of my appearance on the show. In all, I was under investigation for 11 months, with the result that – as before – I was found guilty and fined $2,000 for knowingly employing an illegal alien.

After all this, I had to undergo an operation on the rotator cup in my shoulder, the result of an accident I'd had two years previously. After the op, I was temporarily unable to move my left arm and I could only work it by rigging up a pulley on the ceiling to hoist up my left arm with the other hand.

I still was doing the horses on my own but now with one arm. One day, I brought two horses out and they got their ropes tangled up, with their heads down. So I leaned over the neck of one of them to pass one of the ropes through and as I did this he threw his head up in the air. I flew up, bashed my face on the stable roof, came down, *whack*! and broke three ribs. I went to the hospital and, as I was dressed like a homeless person, with my beard and hair all over the place, they took one quick x-ray and sent me home.

The next day, I fed the horses and then lay on the floor in agony. While I was in this state, Karen had booked a holiday with her friend Tina and was getting ready to set off. 'Are you going to drive me to the airport?' she asked.

'You're kidding! I can't bloody stand up, let alone drive you to the airport.'

Karen got pissed off at this and drove away. Tina rang to find out where she was and I said, 'I don't know, I'm in pain.'

'Take a painkiller,' she said. And off they went on holiday.

Feeling very unhappy I managed to get a friend of mine to take me back to the hospital, where they gave me a bone scan and discovered the full extent of the damage. They put a moulded plastic cast around my torso that I had to wear for ten weeks. I was totally alone, but I managed to get some guys from the fire department to help me with the horses. I began to feel that Karen had badly let me down. She had already bought two cars with cash and had been talking about getting a Harley Davidson. So, while she was away, I went down to the bank where we had a joint account, removed all the cash and put it into my own account. My lawyer and I decided it would be a smart move to transfer my money to the Bahamas.

By the time I was well enough to fly out and organise this, it was close to the time when I had to renew my visa. So, although all my paperwork was in order, they refused me entry on my return to the States (as usual). Once again, I had to fly to London to get my visa stamped and, as we know, because it was a drug waiver, they took forever to do it. Finally, my dentist in the US got the number of an important person at the American Embassy and told them that I needed to return to continue my titanium-implant treatment for which I had already paid him. The very next day, my visa was stamped. But then my lawyers informed me that, when my visa renewal came up, two years down the line, it would very likely be refused. It turned out that all my records of entry into the States ceased in 1967, because the FBI had got them for some extraordinary reason.

When I got back, the immigration lady in Colorado said she was surprised that they ever let me into the country at all! When I had been living there for ten years! Other reliable sources told me that there had been a change in immigration policy, whereby the country would treat all illegals as badly as they treated the Mexicans to show them they weren't being discriminated against. That would explain the terrible treatment they meted out to my groom, but it didn't help me. Immigration had become my nemesis and it continues so to this day.

By then, it was late in 1998, and it seemed that nobody would be able to influence my case. It became very apparent that I had to leave the States, so I took my uniform and badge back to the fire department. I decided to check out the Dominican Republic as an alternative and found 60 acres of land with no house. I would only have been able to afford to get myself and the horses out there, but there wouldn't be anywhere to live. I tried Ireland and I even thought seriously about returning to Nigeria, but close friends told me that it wasn't anything like it had been in the 1970s and advised me against it.

However, while I had been staying at my sister's, I'd popped down to see my old friend Alan Kent a couple of times and he mentioned South Africa. Before the end of apartheid, I would never have considered it, but Alan invited me to play some polo there. I couldn't make it, but I thought it would be worth at least checking out the country.

Chapter Twenty-Nine

Return to Africa

I was now having a lot of problems with my right arm and I had sustained such severe bone damage in my elbow that the nerve was trapped. I found a specialist who knew that I was a drummer and was confident he could treat it successfully by cutting my arm muscle and transferring the nerve to the other side. When the anaesthetic wore off at home, the pain was unbelievable. I had to put an ice-pack on it every two hours, but Karen (who was by then training to be a medic!) had gone out. She reappeared at 6pm and brought me some sushi. The following day, she went off to fire-department training, complete with packed lunch, leaving me alone yet again. When I tackled her about this behaviour, she said, 'You're a bloody pain in the arse.' I was really annoyed and that's when I decided for sure that I was out of there.

Karen flew with me to Durban in South Africa where we looked at polo places and I was impressed by how English everything looked after my American experience. When I discovered how many rand you could get for your dollar, I bought a house close to the polo club right then and there and flew back to arrange the move.

As my plans for the move to Africa got under way, I attended a record company party in New York to celebrate Max Roach's 75th birthday where I had a great time with Max and Harry Belafonte, who was a great old guy. I also went to see Ahmet Ertegun in his office and he was very nice about the *Coward of the County* album, which was released on the same day that I left the US in 1999. I wasn't able to do any promotion for it, but it did get rave reviews.

The DJQ20 lasted from 1996 to 1999, when I left the USA and my biggest regret was having to leave this band behind, after which Karen held an auction to sell off a load of my stuff, including the award-winning artwork for the *Disraeli Gears* cover, given to me by Martin Sharpe, and she kept all the money. I had to sell my tractor and all the farm equipment back to the guy I'd bought it from so that I had some money to go to South Africa.

A friend called Andrew Wardell had arranged transportation for the horses (which for export reasons had to fly via Kentucky) and he sent Mick, his top man, along to help. It was agreed that we could both be with the horses on take-off and landing and we had to stop en route to refuel at the Cape Verdis Islands. Of course, I rushed out to smoke a cigarette and, on the next leg of the journey, one of the crew called me over and beckoned me to follow him right down to the back of this 747 freighter, where we sat and had a smoke!

In Johannesburg, all the horses had to go into quarantine for a month, so that was how long I had to turn the old shed in my new house into a stable. I spent my first night in the city in a jazz club, where I sat in with the band, before going to stay with a friend while working non-stop to get everything ready.

Karen came out again one last time with all the dogs and one remaining horse. She spent a day with me and I began to feel very ill, although she appeared not to notice. She had become a Mormon and went to visit the nearby temple before I dropped her off at the airport. By the following day, I was so ill that a friend's girlfriend took me to the doctor and I was rushed into the intensive-care unit of the hospital. I spent the next ten days there with the most incredible temperature and had hallucinations of imaginary visitors that consisted of my first mother-in-law Ann and my horse Babe! When I had recovered, I got a lawyer in place ready to counter Karen's request for a financial settlement when it arrived with the divorce papers.

Once I was settled in KwaZulu-Natal, I had a member of a prominent local family handling my horses for me. I wasn't very keen on this situation because, whenever he came round and spoke to the staff in Zulu, they would soon have very sullen faces indeed. He was always saying things like, 'You've got to join with your white brothers,' which I found disturbing. Then his father came to visit me. He sat down gravely and explained that, in 'this place', terrible things happened to white people who lived on their own. 'They will break into your house,' he said. 'They'll beat you up and they'll cut your heart out and put it on the table in front of you while you're still alive!'

Do you think you're talking to a five-year-old kid or something? I thought. He was trying to sell me this great fear so that I would pay protection money to his private army. I did so just to keep him happy, but things started happening.

Bruce, a black employee of mine, got a lovely Lurcher-type dog. One day, as I was driving out to Jo'Burg to pick up my own dogs, I saw Bruce's dog, blown to bits and covered in blood on my drive. Those new 'friends' of mine came out with a lame excuse that there was a little bit of my drive that was on a neighbour's property and the dog had trespassed on to that. 'We do things differently in this country,' they explained.

'If you kill one of my dogs, mate,' I replied, 'you're going to end up minus your bollocks.'

They did a lot of things which I found to be highly objectionable. The private army caught a black guy they suspected of stealing a motorbike. 'Why don't you go and bash him?' they said to me. 'Let's see how tough you are.' How can it be tough to go and punch someone who is surrounded by captors? Apparently, this was the Saturday-night thrill in apartheid days, to go out and get drunk, then beat up some black people for fun, knowing full well that there would be no repercussions.

When I went to a party at the polo club, the father of a famous player leaned over to me and said, 'Ah, you've come here to get away from the coons, have you?'

I was practically speechless! When I told somebody else that I found their racist remarks unacceptable, they never spoke to me again. At one of my own parties, I made a speech in which I explained that I didn't come from the same country, that Nelson Mandela was a hero in London and that Ian Smith and FW de Klerk were considered by us to be nasty people. Absolute silence greeted these remarks until a woman piped up, 'I didn't like that speech at all.'

I had to find a responsible head groom to run the stables. A very nice lady came to check me out and ended up interviewing me. She was making sure I would be a good enough employer for her 21-year-old son Kai. Luckily, she approved and I took him on. In the meantime, my 60th birthday arrived. I held a party at the Karkloof Club and we arranged for several drummers of all races to help us celebrate. The evening was hosted by South African Breweries, who had sponsored polo at the club for years. It was very successful, but once again the members of this large and influential family caused some unpleasantness. One of them got on someone's drum kit and as this is the height of bad manners I threw him off. I think it was the first time that black Africans had actually been in the bar there and only because they were guest musicians, but it was turning out to be a hugely successful evening. Kai's mum was happily dancing with a black guy when one of these brothers leaned over to the white brewery representative and said, 'That's my nigger there.' With that one comment, he lost the sponsorship deal. The next week, the family had a tournament and they thought I was going to take my drums there and do it again for the club, but no way.

I was very impressed with Kai. He worked well, was doing great with the staff and was absolutely reliable. He'd been with me a month when one of the notorious family went to the States to marry an American. Without asking my permission, this guy had got Kai to house-sit for him. But I was due at an away tournament at Kopstaad the next day, the horses had gone on ahead and I'd made plans to go from Howick with a friend. 'Don't worry,' Kai said. 'I'll be there at 5.30am to take you down and bring the car back.'

When he didn't turn up, I knew at once that something was amiss, because he was ordinarily so reliable. I phoned the hospitals as I became increasingly worried. Finally, one of this unpleasant family reported that Kai had been mugged. The car he'd been in had been stolen and wrecked, but he was OK and at the house of one of their associates. It wasn't by any means the real story, but by that time we were late and went off to our tournament.

Once there, I kept getting phone calls from this guy's private army saying that now they wanted to arrest my employee Bruce for stealing my *bakkie* (open-backed vehicle) as it had also gone missing! I just kept telling them to hang fire until I got back to sort it out. When I got back, I saw Bruce who told me what had really happened. Kai had gone off to house-sit, but yet another brother decided to invite him to go to the club, where several of them drank until closing time. Then they went to find a late pub in another town. At about 1.30am,

Kai thought, Jesus, I need to get back to pick Ginger up in the morning. And they let him drive. Kai lost control of the vehicle and had a really bad accident. As all the injuries were on his face, he went back to report it and said he'd been mugged.

Kai's mum called me and she was furious; she said that if he'd been mugged why hadn't they called the police and ambulance right away? They'd taken him back to their house and off to the doctor at 9am where he put 37 stitches in Kai's head and said that he had a fractured skull and a broken cheekbone; he was basically busted to fuck and should be in hospital. The reason was that the car that Kai had been driving belonged to the family and wasn't insured, so they just took Kai back to my place. Luckily, Kai's mum was on the case, rushed over and took him to hospital, where they had to pin his face back together. He could have died.

It also emerged that Bruce had taken my car and gone with all the boys to town to do some shopping and one of these 'brothers' had seen him. When Bruce got back, he put the car away in the hay barn, locked it, shut the barn doors and went to visit a relation. The car wasn't visible, so they jumped to the conclusion that he had stolen it. They kept insisting that I press charges against him because they knew 'these people', but I refused.

Then I met the chief halfway up my drive and I really laid into him about letting Kai drive the car. I said that in England he would've been prosecuted for it and so would everyone with him. He started trying to come the hard man with me, 'cos he was the king of the area, you see. I just said, 'You fuck off!' His face went purple, his eyes popped out and his jaw fell open because nobody had said that to him in his life. And with that I threw him off my property.

Kai began to recover, although the bad guys still insisted on pressing charges against him for taking their car without permission. His mother was understandably furious about this and so was I. Then tragedy struck. I did a gig in Durban and had got tickets for Kai and his mum, but they didn't turn up, which I felt was odd. When I got home I discovered that she had been killed in a car crash and yet even then those guys wanted to press charges. I went with Kai to court and offered to swear an affidavit for him, but his mother had got him a good lawyer and the family lost the case. Justice was done.

As I'd upset them, their next step was to try to get me banned from the polo club, even though most of the other players didn't agree with this. So I decided to go and play at another which was about 20 kilometres away. I entered my team, Dragonflies, into the big classic Karkloof tournament and we pissed it, it wasn't even difficult. In the final, we were 4–3 down by the last chukka and won 7–4 with four straight goals and wiped the floor with them.

After damaging myself in yet another horse-riding accident, I kept losing the feeling in my arms. I asked the doctor if I'd had a heart attack, but he said, 'No, it's your neck.' The specialist I saw offered to do a fusion and, even though I didn't quite understand what it would entail, I went off to hospital for it. I woke up in the recovery room after a procedure in which they'd taken a lump of bone from my hip, cut my throat and sewn the bone into my spine at the back of my neck. This opened it up for the nerves so my arms could work.

There were two fat nurses in the recovery room with me and one was attempting to shove my dick into a bottle. 'For Christ's sake, what are you doing?' I asked, adding that I could manage on my own.

'No, you can't.'

'Yes, I can!' My hip in particular was agony but to their dismay I got out of bed.

They told me off for swearing at them but I was discharged wearing a huge neck brace and went home.

It wasn't long before I realised that the only person left on my property was the maid. I'd bought the place with a small settlement of sitting tenants already on the land. Later, I was told that anything that got stolen always ended up there and I thought, Why didn't you tell me that before? But I was always good to them and one Christmas I bought them each a bicycle and helped them to improve their accommodation. But when they realised I was ill in hospital they all fucked off. This had also happened to me one Christmas, when they left the horses out in the rain and I had to get them all in myself.

I'd been building an arena to put on polo and jazz events again. When I'd put this idea forward at the other place, they kept asking how much they were going to earn out of it and I said, 'No! If you do it for charity, it's them that get the money, not you!' I mean, if you're well off enough to play polo, you can give something to charity. But I soon got a nasty letter from neighbours calling it an eyesore. And they complained about me exercising the horses out on the road because of the hoof marks! One day, 30 of them gathered on the other side of the river that ran through my property, firing their guns and trying to scare me. I had had enough and called my friends Selby and Angus, who brought their horsebox. We loaded everything up and they put me up in an old house at their place, which was bloody cold. They got me a maid who immediately stole my gold chain and then turned up to work wearing it.

Selby and Angus went back to collect my truck, but the staff refused to let it go. There was a big row, which meant we had to pay them R24,000 to get rid of them.

I didn't feel comfortable in the new place at all. Apart from the cold and being on my own, there were no facilities and Selby and Angus weren't used to someone who exercised horses and dogs on a daily basis. They put a load of sheep into a paddock nearby and of course the dogs had a field day chasing them, so they said they thought I should have the dogs put down!

Still, the polo was quite good but they charged me a lot of money. I put on a great match that included friends I'd known in Nigeria and an Argie I flew over. The game was covered on the East Coast radio and we made a lot of money for charity, or so I thought, until I discovered that the club took the money and nothing went to charity at all. I was not happy about this and decided I had to leave.

Chapter Thirty

The Western Cape

A friend who had filmed the tournament had just moved down to Tulbagh in the Western Cape and he told me that he'd spotted a big old barn on some vacant property nearby. I contacted an estate agent, traded my Land Rover for one with a back on, put the dogs in, loaded the trailer up and set off on the 17-hour drive south. Once again, I began the mammoth task of getting the barns habitable for the horses when they arrived and I had builders working till ten at night.

I employed a girl who claimed to be an experienced horsewoman, but thanks to her I lost two horses from colic due to bug-infested hay that she had fed them. I had to burn over 200 bales of hay. Everyone I employed appeared to be deeply clueless and one bloke I fired refused to leave and went to the CCMA (employment tribunal), so I had to get my lawyer on to it.

I still hadn't sold the old place in Kwazulu-Natal and I had to borrow money from the bank in order to finance the new property. I was put under certain time constraints and was getting all sorts of hassles. But in the nick of time a very good royalty payment came through. It turned out that either Eric or Jack had discovered that a royalty had been going to Eric by mistake and this had now been rectified. I was so happy at the timing of this good fortune that I sent Eric a fax saying, 'Bless your cotton socks.'

Now I had the money to fulfil the dream of having my own private polo club. I mentioned this to the lawyer who had helped me with my previous labour-relations problems and he introduced me to a charming friend who offered to put in a polo pitch for me. I had already got some other people to tender, but this guy promised me he could do it cheaper. So all these monster machines arrived and I thought, Wow, this is really cool.

At last I began to feel optimistic and while all the equipment was on the field I decided to give myself a birthday helicopter trip to see Alan Kent and the England team playing at Plettenberg Bay. We flew off over the mountains at about 6,000 feet – it was fantastic until, halfway there, this huge black cloud appeared in front of us and it began to rain. By the time we got to the coast, there was a raging storm going on.

'I've got to put it down somewhere,' said the pilot, so we landed on this little bit of sandy beach. I jumped out, busting for a piss, while they got on the radio. Then the pilot and co-pilot went off on foot. I was back in the helicopter talking to Alan Kent on the phone when I began to realise that the piece of beach I was on was getting smaller, because the tide was coming in! If they don't get back soon I'm going to be under water, I thought. By the time they did come back, the sea was only about three feet from the helicopter. They took off in a hurry, flew over the cliff and landed again outside a big hotel.

From there I got a taxi to the game, which had been rained off. But I did meet up with Alan and his family, who put me up in the house he was staying at. The next morning, I boarded the helicopter for the return flight but there was a huge cloud on the other side of the mountains at Ceres and it hung over the whole of the Tulbagh Valley. I suggested that the pilot fly through the pass, but he wasn't keen and so he landed at the vet's place in Ceres and he gave me a lift home. What a trip!

I returned to find the whole polo-field scheme was becoming a similar fiasco. The builder had taken off the top soil by the river and I'd left him to it as he assured me that he knew what he was doing. He'd left a huge slope at the end where I'd requested a bank. Apart from that, it all looked quite good, but when he said he wanted to put a grader over it I expressed concern because it would bring stones to the surface. He reassured me that it would only be a shallow job and, still as charming as when we first met, presented me with the finished field and I wrote him out a large cheque.

The next day I went and dragged the field with the Land Rover and when I'd finished there were stones everywhere – big ones, little ones, some as-big-as-your-head ones! It was clearly a complete disaster and yet the guy kept telling me that it would all be OK when the grass grew, so for whatever silly reason I seeded the field. But I couldn't even stick-and-ball on it. Then I tried getting a whole gang of people to go over it picking up stones, but to no avail whatsoever. It was no use to man or beast and I was deeply disappointed. For six months, I gave up completely and did the house up instead, before at length deciding to sue. We got plenty of evidence together with a top Cape Town barrister. I also got three firms to come along and testify to what needed doing to turn it into a polo field. One of these firms had an appealing plan for levelling and compacting the field and putting more top soil on, so I went ahead with them.

Thirty-One
Cream Reunion

In 2004, I received an email asking if I'd be interested in doing a Cream reunion. I readily agreed because Stevie Winwood was going to be involved. Then all of a sudden he wasn't and, as I felt that Jack was already starting to cause problems, I emailed back to say, 'No way. I'm sorry, I just can't do it.' But then Eric wrote me a letter asking me to take part; we spoke on the phone and he convinced me that it was a good idea. And I'm glad he did.

We had three weeks of rehearsals at Bray Studios in Berkshire. The first time we played 'Spoonful', Jack didn't seem to know the arrangement. As usual, he insisted he was right and I felt he still had the old attitude that drummers aren't musicians and should just shut up and play. Well, we played the old tape of 'Spoonful' and of course I was right, because I'd done the original arrangement. This happened a couple of times and Eric got very annoyed and then it was nearly the end of it all before it had even begun until Jack apologised.

Once we heard the tapes, though, it all got very friendly

because we realised just how brilliant it was. We didn't need the last week of rehearsals as it all came together so quickly. The Albert Hall sold out all four shows in an hour or two and I don't think anybody's done that before! I made a fuck-up during the first show on 'Born Under a Bad Sign', when I finished ahead of Jack, but he laughed about it and was OK. You know, I'm an old man and I made a mistake. The gigs were an absolute joy. It was fantastic, like 1966 all over again, and I thoroughly enjoyed every minute of it – we all did.

Next we took the reunion to the States and, as in London, sold out three nights at New York's Madison Square Garden. It was all looking wonderful and everything was really cool. Eric and I were staying in the Four Seasons Hotel with his professional crew, while Jack stayed elsewhere with his own personal assistant.

We got on stage to do the first gig and it was immediately different to the Albert Hall, where Jack had spent most of the time sitting on a chair. Suddenly, he was jumping about all over the stage like Bruce Springsteen (whose picture, incidentally, I had had removed from the theatre). He was louder than he had been previously and shouted into the microphone all the time, behaving as though he was the band's leader. We played 'We're Going Wrong', a track that someone once remarked was made by my drumming, and all of a sudden Jack turned round and in front of the whole audience shouted, 'No, man, you're playing too loud!'

It was like the Jack of old: he used to do it with Graham Bond, he did it with Cream and, if London had brought back the glory days of 1966, New York transported us back to the bad old days of 1968. I felt I was being humiliated in front of 20,000 people and it wasn't a pleasant experience. Jack got louder and louder as the gig went on and it got very painful. As we came off, he said, 'I wish you wouldn't do that when I'm trying to play.'

'I'm not talking to you, Jack,' I replied, as I continued past him into the dressing room. The next day was like the final tour of 1968, just going through the motions.

Atlantic's Ahmet Ertegun had a party on the Tuesday night and he wanted us all together, so Jack sat next to me with Ahmet and Nettie sat on my other side.

Jack said, 'I'm sorry about the other night, but it wasn't my fault.'

Well, if it wasn't his fault, why was he apologising? He always did the same – did a big number on me on stage in front of a large crowd and apologised afterwards as if that made it OK. Well, it wasn't OK, especially on the Cream reunion.

Just as on the Gary Moore tour, Jack and his wife complained about everything. The atmosphere was terrible and the magic went. I had a long chat to Eric and apologised to him because, when these things had happened before with Cream, my reaction pissed him off. It was all caught on film and the tapes at Madison Square Garden have never been used – for that very reason, I imagine.

The final straw came on the last day, when we did a photo shoot for *Vanity Fair*. Eric turned up wearing a polo neck jumper and jeans and I had my Armani jacket and shirt on, but we had to wait an hour for Jack to appear, which worried Eric as he had a plane to catch. When he finally arrived, he was dressed in this incredible puce-coloured rock'n'roll superstar suit. It was ludicrous! We posed for what must have looked like the most incongruous pictures of all time. There and then we decided that was the end of it, and the position remains unchanged.

Epilogue

I returned to my place in Tulbagh with a healthy bank balance and got the polo field done properly, although it still went way over budget. A huge lake was created with the 20,000 cubic metres of top soil we'd taken off the polo field. Then the environmental department declared the whole thing illegal and a Cape conservation group said they'd had various letters of complaint from the neighbours.

I wanted to build new stables to house more horses, but I couldn't get permission because the conservation people said they wanted an 'environmental impact study'. For a stables? There had already been an old building on the site. I wrote to the governor of the Western Province who sent a nice reply and they sorted it out.

Then the lake was declared illegal. According to the conservationists, I'd built a dam, which was what they called the exercise track around it. I'd used the water for irrigation and directed all the drainage into it, which stopped the staff cottages from flooding. These problems were resolved, although I still get letters of complaint. Yet another problem involved me taking water from the river and a complainant cited a legal document dated 1948. Luckily, the guy from the department of water pointed out that any agreements and documents dated before 1994 were null and void. Similar issues continue to come up with amazing regularity!

Despite it all, I continue to stage regular polo and jazz events which have proved to be increasingly popular. It's my dream realised at last, although the logistics of running such an enterprise are very stressful. Fortunately, Kai, my head groom from my days in Kwazulu-Natal, came back to work for me early in 2008 and his help and enthusiasm has been invaluable.

At the end of 2007, I was contacted by yet another individual keen on doing my autobiography, but my lawyer checked him out and he didn't appear to have been entirely truthful about his credentials. Then I remembered that Nettie had spent many years studying hard for her BA and MA in English literature, as well as being a published journalist, so at last work started on what you have been reading.

The following December, I returned to London for the Zildjan drum awards. I have used Zildjan my entire career and I still have some of the cymbals I chose on my first visit to the factory in Boston in 1967, when I met Avedis Zildjan. It was great to hear from his granddaughters, Craigie and Debbie, who contacted me about the company's 385th anniversary (they've been going since 1623).

We had a wonderful dinner at the Groucho Club the night before the awards and again it was great to catch up with valued friends. Jack was there and we got on OK. I had agreed to play with him at the gig at the Shepherds Bush Empire, where he turned up in his puce rock'n'roll star suit, which I found quite amusing. I enjoyed playing with the other musicians: trumpeter Gerard Presencer played very well, the horn players wailed wonderfully – especially Courtney Pine – and I was impressed by drummer Steve White.

Charlie Watts has always been a real musician in my opinion and a wonderful guy as well. As we go back such a long way, it was fantastic to have him come along and present the award to me; so a big thank you to all concerned.

The next day, I had lunch with Eric. We are still close friends and I continue to admire both him and Steve Winwood musically; my hopes for the future in that direction would be to one day work with both of them again.

The only thing that I got more than a little pissed off about during this visit was Bob Henrit and Geoff Nicholls's article 'British Rock'n'Roll' in the programme for the Zildjan Awards. Eric Delany, Jack Parnell (who in my opinion was never a great), Ronnie Verrell (a good drummer, but just that) and Kenny Clare were cited as the best of the early drummers; but amazingly there was no mention of Phil Seamen (who played with Jack Parnell's band!). I found this infuriating, because Phil was the greatest drummer ever to come out of the UK. The article came to the conclusion that John Bonham was the epitome of a rock drummer (marrying the styles of Mitch Mitchell, Keith Moon and I). Absolute rubbish! I did tackle Bob Henrit at the show and asked him if he had ever attempted to play the drums! Incidentally, John Bonham once made a statement that there were only two drummers in British rock'n'roll; himself and Ginger Baker. My reaction to this was: 'You cheeky little bastard!'

Acknowledgements

With thanks to: Liz, Leda and Kofi Baker. John Blake. Peter Brkusic. Jay Bulger. Norman Collins. John Gale. Kai Hansen. Jackie Herbert. Kudzai. John and Pat Wallis. Kieron Maughan. Liz Mansell. Russell Newmark. Cecil Offley. John and Maxine Simms. All at Zildjan.